Grandma's
Miracle
FOOD FIXES

Dedicated to our grandmas, with thanks for their timeless and loving advice.

Publisher's Note

This book is intended for general information only. It does not constitute medical, legal, or financial advice or practice. The editors of FC&A have taken careful measures to ensure the accuracy and usefulness of the information in this book. While every attempt has been made to assure accuracy, errors may occur. Some websites, addresses, and telephone numbers may have changed since printing. We cannot guarantee the safety or effectiveness of any advice or treatments mentioned. Readers are urged to consult with their professional financial advisors, lawyers, and health care professionals before making any changes.

Any health information in this book is for information only and is not intended to be a medical guide for self-treatment. It does not constitute medical advice and should not be construed as such or used in place of your doctor's medical advice. Readers are urged to consult with their health care professionals before undertaking therapies suggested by the information in this book, keeping in mind that errors in the text may occur as in all publications and that new findings may supersede older information.

The publisher and editors disclaim all liability (including any injuries, damages, or losses) resulting from the use of the information in this book.

God is our refuge and strength, an ever-present help in trouble. Therefore we will not fear, though the earth give way and the mountains fall into the heart of the sea.

Psalm 46:1–2

FC&A Medical Publishing®
103 Clover Green
Peachtree City, GA 30269

Produced by the staff of FC&A
ISBN 978-1-935574-47-7

Table of Contents

Indigestion:
Natural remedies that put out the fire 155

Inflammatory bowel disease:
Diet plans that conquer the pain 169

Joint pain: Foods that fight the ache 179

Tummy troubles: 11 ways to quell the queasies ... 285

Ulcers: Quick fixes to end the suffering 297

Urinary problems: Dodge the dangers with superfoods 307

Blood sugar control

Nutritional solutions that defeat diabetes

How to eat carbs and not blow up your blood sugar

You can have your mac 'n cheese and eat it, too, even with diabetes. All you may need to do is drink this before a meal to keep your blood sugar on an even keel. Vinegar – the sour drink with sweet results for those who battle diabetes.

A shot of vinegar curbs the rise in blood sugar by keeping your body from absorbing the carbs in high-carbohydrate foods, studies show. Researchers have used between one and four tablespoons of vinegar to study its effects on animals and people. They think it may be the acetic acid in vinegar that blocks enzymes from digesting starch.

This superstar liquid also blocks hunger pangs and may help you eat less throughout the day, boosting weight control and helping you manage your diabetes.

"Vinegar appears to have effects similar to some of the most popular medications for diabetes," says Dr. Carol Johnston, a leading nutrition researcher from Arizona State University. "There are also studies suggesting that if people with prediabetes take these medications, they might reduce their chances of getting diabetes."

Vinegar may serve as a cheap, but effective, alternative to medication. Dr. Johnston's latest research suggests one tablespoon at mealtime twice a day lowers blood glucose levels in people at risk of type 2 diabetes better than metformin or rosiglitazone, two popular prescriptions. But drinking it straight could harm your teeth and esophagus. It's best to add the vinegar to a big glass of water and sip it with your meal, Johnston says.

Don't think of vinegar as a cure-all. If you have type 2 diabetes or are at risk for developing it, talk to your doctor and discuss vinegar as an option.

COOK IT

Turn vinegar into a tasty treat

Does the idea of drinking vinegar make you sour? Make homemade flavored vinegar — it's a perky way to add vinegar to your food and your diet. Here's how.

Rinse a cup or two of your favorite berry. Blueberries, blackberries, raspberries, and strawberries all work great. Place in a sanitized jar. Use the same amount of white wine vinegar or apple cider vinegar as berries. For instance, if you're using one cup of berries then use one cup of vinegar.

Heat the vinegar, but don't let it boil. Pour the vinegar over the berries. For extra zing, add thyme or mint leaves. Cover and allow to sit in a cool, dark place for at least three weeks.

Strain the vinegar until it comes out clear. Pour over garden salads or mixed fruit for a zesty flavor, especially with high-carb sides like white bread or baked potatoes.

All-natural drink tackles nerve damage and more

A delightful beverage may shield you from some of the pain of type 2 diabetes. This magic elixir is chamomile tea, made from a mild herb used in folk medicine for thousands of years.

Chamomile lowers blood glucose levels when taken with meals, shows an animal study published in the *Journal of Agricultural and Food Chemistry*. Researchers say the mild-tasting tea blocks two enzymes that trigger vision loss, nerve damage, and kidney damage.

Chamomile keeps one of those enzymes – aldose reductase – from turning glucose into another sugar called sorbitol. This sugar does not move around in cells as freely as glucose, so it ends up getting stored in nerve and eye tissue. The outcome? Serious damage leading to neuropathy and blindness.

Scientists believe it's the phytochemicals in chamomile, including quercetin and esculetin, that do all the hard work. They even tackle inflammation, skin diseases, wounds, gout, and ulcers, and can suppress the growth of human cancer cells. Not bad for a pretty little plant.

Drink a cup with each meal to add chamomile tea to your diet. You may feel better, see more clearly, and enjoy some of the traditional benefits of this age-old herb – peaceful sleep and stress relief.

And don't be surprised if chamomile takes center stage in medications down the road. Researchers say their discoveries may lead to new chamomile-based drugs for type 2 diabetes.

3 smarter ways to eat sweet

Sugar – just the mere mention of the word makes your mouth water. But if you battle type 2 diabetes, sugar can wreak havoc on your blood glucose and your weight. Try these sweet options instead.

Maple syrup is bursting with healthy compounds. There's something wholesome about warm maple syrup. And rightly so. Scientists have found 54 healthful compounds in this liquid sweetener.

These compounds have antioxidant and anti-inflammatory properties that help battle diabetes. Scientists say it's the phenolics, the beneficial antioxidant compounds, in maple syrup. These antioxidants block two enzymes that break down carbohydrates, which helps people with diabetes better manage the disease.

Scientists aren't saying you should fill up on the delicious sweetener. But if you're going to pour something over your pancakes, reach for pure maple syrup and not processed products loaded with high fructose corn syrup.

Consider honey's pros and cons. You've probably heard conflicting reports about honey and diabetes. Research shows honey can help people with diabetes lose weight, lower bad cholesterol, and raise good cholesterol. But it also raises your A1C level, which affects your blood sugar average over several months.

The bottom line? It's OK to sweeten dishes or even substitute sugar with honey, but do so carefully. Check with your doctor if you have questions.

Agavin: a sweetener with health benefits. A new sugar substitute could have you kicking up your heels. Researchers with the American Chemical Society say agavins, derived from the agave plant used to make tequila, maintained blood sugar levels and helped with weight loss in animals. Agavins also increase insulin and help you feel fuller after meals.

But don't get too excited because agavins aren't on the market yet. Don't confuse them with agave nectar or syrup. These sweeteners are broken down from fructans into individual fructoses, so they're more like high fructose corn syrup. Agavins are long-chain fructans that act more like fiber and can't be digested, which is why they don't spike blood sugar. Good news if this sweetener ends up on grocery store shelves in the future.

Yummy desserts that help your blood sugar

Baked peaches with chocolate drizzle. Chocolate peach mousse. Fresh peaches with mocha sauce. If your mind says yes but your blood sugar says no, listen to this good news. You can put these foods together for a delicious end to your dinner.

Chocolate is rich in diabetes-fighting flavanols. Charles Schulz once said, "All you need is love. But a little chocolate now and then doesn't hurt." Nutrition experts believe the Peanuts comic strip creator was definitely on to something.

People who ate chocolate from once a day to several times a month lowered their risk of getting diabetes, says a recent study published in *Clinical Nutrition*. Experts say the risk was lowest in people who ate two to six 1-ounce servings a week. The study did not say which chocolate was best – dark, milk, or white. But past studies have found dark chocolate to have the highest amount of flavanols, rich phytochemicals that help regulate your blood sugar metabolism.

Peaches battle risk factors like obesity. You could say peaches are "peachy-keen" for your health. Research shows the phytochemicals in peaches battle obesity and the diabetes risk associated with obesity.

The powerful compounds called phenols wage war on obesity, diabetes, inflammation, and bad cholesterol, experts say.

And it's not just peaches. Try other stone fruits like plums, nectarines, and apricots for savory treats with the same benefits. One study found that replacing fruit juice with whole peaches, plums, or apricots reduced the risk of type 2 diabetes an average of 11 percent.

Enjoy a cuppa joe and lower your risk. Pair your evening goodie with a rich cup of coffee. Research shows that drinking three to four cups a day lowers your risk of type 2 diabetes by up to 25 percent. If you're not a big coffee drinker, try adding another cup and a half per day, and you'll lower your diabetes risk by 11 percent in just four years.

Coffee is high in polyphenols and antioxidants, which scientists think may steady blood sugar levels and improve insulin sensitivity. Drinking caffeinated coffee also revs up your metabolism, which increases energy and helps burns calories.

But it may not be just caffeinated coffee that fights diabetes. French women who drank a cup of regular or decaf daily at lunch cut their diabetes risk by 33 percent, a Brazilian study shows. So if you prefer, you can enjoy a steaming cup of decaf to finish off your meal.

The healthiest bread you've never tried

Whole-wheat bread may be the most popular bread in America, but it's not the healthiest. Give rye a try and you'll discover the white bread that's actually healthier than wheat.

Bread baked with flour made from the inner, white part of the rye kernel will give you better insulin and blood sugar levels, suggests a study out of Lund University in Sweden. Scientists aren't sure how it works, but they do see better results with white rye compared to wheat bread.

The natural fiber in this rich, hearty grain also helps keep you "regular" and makes you feel fuller longer. The more satisfied you feel, the more likely you are to not overeat. And when you have diabetes, weight control lowers your risk for complications.

But not all rye is created equal, say researchers. Rye flour sold in stores is usually a mix of different types of ryes. Your best bet is to buy flour labeled "whole-grain rye" and make your own bread. Or, if you like oatmeal, make rye porridge from whole rye berries or kernels. This comforting food will fill you up while helping to control your blood sugar.

"This gives you all the benefits of rye," says Liza Rosén, the study's lead researcher. "The bran includes many healthful fibers, vitamins, minerals, and antioxidants. This also helps give a feeling of satiety and helps lower blood sugar responses over the long term."

COOK IT

Cozy up with a warm bowl of rye

Cooking rye is easier than you think. Start by rinsing and cleaning the rye berries. If you want to make porridge, add one part rye berries to two-and-a-half parts boiling water, and toss in a pinch of salt. After the water boils again, cook and simmer for one to two hours. Once it's cooked, add honey or maple syrup to sweeten it for a delicious breakfast.

To make rye porridge into a savory side dish, cook your berries in chicken broth. Then add sautéed mushrooms and onions. Stir and serve with baked chicken or broiled salmon as an alternative to rice.

Recipe makeovers take rice off your no-no list

People eat a whopping 456 million tons of rice a year, making it the number one food staple in the world. But if you have prediabetes or type 2 diabetes, rice can shoot your blood sugar levels sky high. Here's how to enjoy rice while lowering your risk.

Brown rice keeps blood sugar stable. White rice is simply brown rice that's been polished. Polishing removes the bran layer, which lowers the amount of fiber. It also raises the starch content. And typically, a food that's high in starch will raise blood sugar levels.

Several studies suggest white rice raises the risk for type 2 diabetes. Thankfully, you have an alternative – brown rice, which has been shown to lower your risk. Scientists think one reason may be that the bran layer in brown rice blocks digestive enzymes from releasing the inner starch, which helps keep blood sugar levels stable.

Shorter cooking time means less starch. You wouldn't think the amount of time it takes to cook rice would affect your blood sugar, but it does. Studies show that steaming rice or boiling it for a short amount of time is better for blood sugar levels than longer cooking times.

Researchers think it's because cooking rice for a longer period of time makes the grain swell and split, producing more starch, which triggers higher blood sugar levels when eaten.

Combine rice with foods that blunt sugar hikes. If you're like most people, you eat rice as a side dish in a bigger meal. Choose the right foods or condiments to accompany the rice, and you're more likely to keep your blood sugar stable.

- Beans served with rice lowers blood glucose levels, shows a study. In fact, the addition of any legumes like peas and lentils works just as well. Researchers think the soluble fiber in legumes helps slow the emptying of your stomach, making it less likely your blood sugar will spike.

- Add vinegar to your rice meal and you've got a winning combination. But you don't have to pour vinegar directly into your rice. Just eating a pickle on the side blunts blood sugar hikes.

■ Two grains are better than one, suggests a study. When you mix rice with barley, your blood glucose remains steady. Scientists think it's because barley is brimming with soluble fiber.

COOK IT

Tricks to make brown rice tasty

Does the thought of eating brown rice make you cringe? For some people, the taste leaves a lot to be desired. Here's how you can make brown rice a delicious dish.

Follow the cooking instructions for your package of brown rice. But cook your rice in chicken broth instead of water for added flavor. Then drizzle it with two teaspoons of vinegar or citrus juice for extra zing.

And don't think of rice as just a side to a main course. Add it to soups or salads as a hearty, healthy ingredient.

Microbe magic: secret to stable blood sugar

One way to ditch diabetes is to get your fill of tiny microbes that live in your gut and pump up your health. These powerful bugs, called probiotics, hang out in your belly by the billions, helping you digest food, fight off infections, and maintain a healthy digestive tract. Studies show probiotics also lower inflammation throughout your body and raise your sensitivity to insulin, which helps keep blood sugar stable.

Two probiotics in particular, *lactobacilli* and *bifidobacteria*, seem to work best at preventing and treating the disease, research shows. One study found that animals with low levels of those probiotics were more likely to develop type 1 diabetes. Researchers believe probiotics tackle diabetes risk factors by doing what they do best – keeping your gut healthy.

Yogurt is a well-known source of probiotics, with millions of live, active cultures in every container. But you can also try kefir, sauerkraut, and Japanese miso soup for other great-tasting sources.

Probiotics and people have something in common – they need food to survive and thrive. That's where prebiotics kick in. Prebiotics are carbohydrates and fibers that can't be digested or fermented. They deliver food and fuel for the billions of probiotics in your body. But prebiotics do more than that, studies show. They also help lower inflammation, fight bad bacteria, boost your immune system, and promote healthy blood sugar levels.

Prebiotics are easy to add to your diet. Look for prebiotic-rich foods like barley, oatmeal, legumes, asparagus, pistachios, bananas, and Jerusalem artichokes.

2 high-fat foods you should be eating

Yup'ik Eskimos in Alaska eat salmon and sardines for lunch and dinner, and maybe even breakfast. And this could be helping them battle diabetes. Researchers found a lower occurrence of diabetes among this group of people, even among those who were overweight or obese. Scientists believe omega-3 fatty acids have something to do with it.

Load up on protective fatty fish. Fish like salmon, mackerel, herring, lake trout, sardines, and albacore tuna are all high in omega-3 fatty acids. These healthy fats seem to protect Yup'ik Eskimos from the harmful effects of obesity-related diseases like diabetes and heart disease.

If you don't love the taste of fish, fish oil supplements work just as well. Scientists from Harvard School of Public Health looked at information from 14 clinical trials involving people who took fish oil supplements. They found that the supplements raised levels of adiponectin, a hormone that helps maintain blood glucose levels, keeps inflammation at bay, and lowers the risk of heart disease.

"Results from our study suggest that higher intake of fish oil may moderately increase blood level of adiponectin," says Dr. Jason Wu, the study's lead author. "And these results support potential benefits of fish oil consumption on glucose control and fat cell metabolism."

Flaxseed boasts significant amounts of omega-3. These itty bitty seeds about the size of sesame seeds pack a powerful dose of omega-3 fatty acids. And they may also protect against diabetes.

Foods prepared with flaxseed are less likely to spike blood sugar levels when eaten, several studies show. These observations led scientists in India to study the effects of flaxseed on type 2 diabetes. They found that the powerful seeds lowered fasting blood glucose as well as glucose levels over longer periods of time. They also lowered bad cholesterol and raised good cholesterol levels.

You can find whole, crushed, or ground flaxseed in your local supermarket or drugstore.

Experts suggest you buy your flaxseeds whole then crush or grind them for the best health benefits. Otherwise, the seeds will pass through your intestines without digesting them. Store them in an airtight container for several months. Sprinkle over your cereal or yogurt, or bake into breads and muffins.

One-two punch slashes diabetes risk

Your doctor says you have prediabetes, or you find out you have a gene that puts you at high risk for the disease. That means you're well on your way to getting type 2 diabetes. Two powerful nutrients may be just what you need to cut your chances of developing this disease.

Vitamin D helps lower blood sugar. Scientists have found a link between people with low levels of vitamin D and prediabetes, a blood sugar level that's not quite high enough to be called diabetes. Researchers in India found people at risk for diabetes who had higher levels of vitamin D in their blood also had lower fasting blood glucose. And the more vitamin D participants took, the lower the risk of the disease progressing to full-blown diabetes.

Scientists think vitamin D reverses high blood sugar to normal levels by improving insulin resistance and inflammation.

You can get vitamin D from milk, salmon, halibut, fortified juices and cereals, and daily exposure to sunshine. As you age, it's harder for your body to get enough D from food and sunshine alone, so talk to your doctor to see if you need supplements.

Beta carotene protects people at high risk. A study found a strong connection between the amount of beta carotene in the blood and the progression to diabetes in people whose genes show a high risk for the disease. It seems the more beta carotene in your blood, the lower your risk, say researchers at Stanford University.

Scientists say beta carotene may interact with one of the genes that affects diabetes risk in a preventive way, but they're not sure. More research is underway.

In the meantime, if you have prediabetes or are at risk for diabetes, add leafy greens like kale and spinach, greens like collards and turnips, and carrots to your diet. They're loaded with beta carotene and good for your blood sugar.

Go nuts over these good-for-you dishes

Sink your teeth into these delicious dishes topped with almonds, pecans, walnuts, or pistachios. These wholesome treats maintain blood sugar levels thanks to their protein and fiber content and healthy nutrients, say experts. Pair them with other savory foods that battle diabetes, and you've got several mouthwatering combos.

Baked crusted fish or chicken

Finely chop pecans or pistachios, and add flour in a shallow dish. Pour egg whites into a separate dish. Dip trout, salmon, or chicken in egg whites, then coat with flour and nut mixture. Bake per instructions for fish or chicken.

Sautéed veggies with nuts

Finely chop almonds, pecans, or pistachios. Chop veggies like bell peppers and onions, Brussels sprouts, kale or spinach. Heat olive oil over medium heat in a skillet. Sauté vegetables for a few minutes, then stir in nuts and sauté until heated through.

Crunchy grain pilaf

Chop walnuts or pecans. Toast over medium heat for four to five minutes until lightly brown. Add to a pot of brown rice, quinoa, or barley.

Look to plants to curb diabetes dangers

It's best to manage diabetes by making smart food choices. But sometimes a supplement can help. Check out these three supplements, and discover alternate ways to deal with diabetes.

Alpha-lipoic acid boosts blood flow. An antioxidant found in spinach, broccoli, and potatoes, alpha-lipoic acid (ALA) may be an answer to prayer for people who suffer excruciating nerve pain associated with diabetes.

ALA seems to work by boosting blood flow in nerves, acting as an anti-inflammatory, and keeping blood clots at bay, suggests a study published in the *European Journal of Endocrinology.*

Berberine may be as effective as drugs. This powerful, bright yellow compound has been used medicinally in China for thousands of years. It's found in plants such as barberry, goldenseal, and tree turmeric. And it shows promise as a treatment option for type 2 diabetes, suggest two studies.

Berberine supplements lowered blood glucose levels as well as metformin, a popular diabetic drug, in newly diagnosed patients, say researchers out of China. Supplements also lowered blood glucose levels when combined with insulin therapy in people who were not managing their diabetes well.

Glucomannan slows sugar absorption. This soluble fiber found in konjac root lowers fasting blood glucose, bad LDL cholesterol, and body weight, according to research published in the *American Journal of Clinical Nutrition.* Experts think one way glucomannan works for diabetes is by slowing the absorption of sugar during digestion, which helps sugar levels remain stable.

Bone health

Easy ways to eat & stay strong

Do this every day for rock hard bones

Sit down for a moment in your favorite chair, and enjoy a steaming mug of tea. Believe it or not, a simple daily habit like this may help strengthen your bones and save you from the ravages of osteoporosis.

Your body constantly gets rid of old bone and replaces it with new bone. If your bone-building cells, called osteoblasts, fail to keep up with bone-removing cells – osteoclasts – your bones will develop tiny holes like Swiss cheese. Experts call this low bone density.

Weak, fragile bones become more likely as the years pass. But long-term tea drinkers have better bone density and bone strength than non-tea drinkers, say studies from Britain and China. You just need to sip the right teas – those with powerful polyphenols – to reap the benefits.

Green tea battles brittle bones. Both green and black teas come from the evergreen shrub *Camellia sinensis*. But green tea has more of the polyphenol compounds called catechins.

Catechins may help reduce the number of bone-erasing osteoclasts in your body. With fewer bone removers at work, your bones have a better shot at staying strong. Catechins may also help expand your population of bone-building osteoblasts, so you replace more of the bone that's lost. That's why green tea is such a shining star when it comes to bone health.

Black tea fights bone loss. When *Camellia sinensis* leaves are fermented into black tea, their catechins turn into healthy compounds called theaflavins. Like catechins, theaflavins may limit the number of bone-removing cells so you lose less bone. If you're an older woman, you may want to take note. Postmenopausal women, in particular, have shown a positive association between tea drinking and higher bone density.

Does your tea come up short?

Tea is shown to fight diseases of aging, from bone loss to cancer. But five out of 10 tea drinkers today choose the one kind of tea that offers practically no protection. If you're one of them, you may not know what you've been missing.

Tea's protective powers come from its natural polyphenols, like catechins and theaflavins. But bottled teas may contain far fewer polyphenols than tea from a tea bag, a study found. One bottled brand had so few polyphenols that you'd need to drink 20 bottles to equal the amount of polyphenols found in one cup of brewed tea. What's more, bottled teas are packed with sugar and calories.

To save your money and your health, switch to a better and cheaper variety of tea — green or black tea that you brew yourself. If you prefer cold tea, just add ice after brewing.

---

2 ways to amp up tea's taste and nutrition. You can easily make black or green tea better tasting and more nutritious.

■ Add lemon to your tea to help your body use more of the brew's nutrients. If you can't squeeze a fresh lemon every day, juice several lemons, freeze the juice in an ice cube tray, and drop a cube into your steaming mug as needed.

■ Not fond of the taste of unsweetened green or black tea? Keep it from getting bitter by using water that's less hot or steeping the bag for a shorter time. Keep in mind you shouldn't use boiling water for green tea. Try flavored green or black teas for bone protection that's always delicious.

Fight bone loss without calcium pills

You know you need extra calcium for your bones so you faithfully pop a calcium supplement every day – just like your doctor recommends. But some studies say those pills alone may not save you from a fracture. If you want strong bones, you need other key skeleton-saving nutrients that pills may leave out. That's why your best bet is to get calcium from a variety of foods that supply all the nutrients your bones need.

Calcium is so crucial to nerves, muscles, and glands that your body steals it from your bones if you don't have enough to go around. All adults need 1,000 milligrams (mg) of calcium a day, but women over age 50 and men over age 70 need 1,200 mg.

To help make sure you get enough, eat a few servings of low-fat dairy products like cheese, yogurt, and skim milk each day. Also, enjoy other good sources of like almonds, turnip greens, kale, canned fish with bones, broccoli, and fortified orange juice. While you're at it, make sure you get enough of these critical bone-building nutrients, too.

Protein helps your body make collagen. Delicious foods like mozzarella cheese and Greek yogurt aren't just good sources of calcium. They're also high in protein, a nutrient you can't get from calcium pills. That's important because your body makes less bone if it doesn't get enough protein.

But eat enough protein, and your bone cells produce more insulin-like growth factor 1 (IGF-1). This compound not only helps your body create more bone-making cells but also more collagen, a basic building block of new bone. Using this protein, your bone-making cells lay the framework for more new bone to help replace what you've lost.

A 1-ounce slice of part-skim mozzarella delivers 15 percent of the bone-helping protein you need plus 20 percent of the daily value for calcium. Other good sources of both calcium and protein include canned crab, canned clams, canned shrimp, and most dairy products.

PREPARE IT

How to grate soft cheese with incredible ease

You love mozzarella on pizza, salads, and even sandwiches, but the preshredded version is pricey and melts poorly, while the block cheese is too soft to grate or shred. Fortunately, you can fix this and save money.

Just tuck a block of mozzarella in the freezer for one hour. Once the cold works its magic, you can shred it in the food processor or grate it by hand without a hitch. To make hand grating even easier, brush the grater holes with a tiny amount of olive oil.

Phosphorus: calcium's bone-building buddy. White beans can be a money saver if you use them to replace the meat in your pasta dish. Thanks to their calcium and phosphorus, these beans can also be a bone saver.

New bone starts with collagen protein, but the outer 65 percent of bone is made of rock-hard hydroxyapatite, an insoluble salt your body generates from calcium and phosphorus. Your body must always keep enough of these two minerals available to make more new bone.

Thinking of replacing your regular milk with almond milk, rice milk, or soy milk? These naturally have less calcium and vitamin D than regular milk. Even brands that are fortified may still come up short. So before you buy, check the label to see how your new milk compares to your old favorite.

Getting enough phosphorus from foods isn't hard. Look for it in pumpkin, squash, and sunflower seeds; Brazil nuts; Romano cheese; salmon and shellfish; and pork and lean beef.

Lose vitamin D and you'll lose bone. A shortage of vitamin D can actually increase the amount of bone you lose. But taking in enough vitamin D helps you absorb more calcium from food and retain it longer, so you keep making new bone to offset your losses.

Canned pink salmon is a great source of vitamin D, and it's less expensive than salmon filets. Try it on a sandwich, mixed with chopped celery, pickle relish, and a splash of lemon juice, or stir in mayonnaise, mustard, or nonfat plain yogurt. Other good sources of vitamin D include rainbow trout, canned light tuna, and fortified dry milk.

How to choose a better calcium supplement

Like most Americans, Mary tries to eat foods high in calcium every day, and – also like most Americans – she has yet to reach her recommended amount. If you're in the same boat, you may need to ask your doctor about taking a calcium supplement to fill in the gap. Use these guidelines and your doctor's advice to help choose the best calcium pill for you.

Pick a pill you can digest easily. Calcium supplements come in several forms, and each has its own advantages.

Calcium carbonate is the least expensive, but you must always take it with food to absorb it well.

Calcium citrate is easier for your body to absorb than calcium carbonate, so you can take it without food. Calcium citrate may also be right for you if:

- you regularly take medicines for frequent heartburn or GERD. These may include histamine-2 (H2) blockers such as cimetidine (Tagamet), famotidine (Pepcid), and ranitidine (Zantac) or proton pump inhibitors like esomeprazole (Nexium), lansoprazole (Prevacid), and omeprazole (Prilosec).

- other calcium supplements you've taken have caused constipation or bloating.

- you have a condition, such as inflammatory bowel disease, that keeps you from absorbing nutrients.

- you have low stomach acid, which is common in people over age 50.

Other forms of calcium, like calcium gluconate and calcium lactate, are expensive and aren't usually used to prevent fractures.

Look for a brand that's been tested. Find your ideal brand and product with these tips.

- Check for the U.S. Pharmacopeia or Consumer Lab seal to find a supplement that has passed independent quality testing.

- Beware of calcium supplements made from bone meal, oyster shell, or dolomite since some may contain dangerous lead.

- Check the supplemental facts label for "elemental calcium," the amount your body actually obtains from the supplement. Keep in mind your body absorbs more calcium if you take 500 milligrams or less at a time.

- Check whether your supplement comes with added vitamin D to help absorb more calcium.

- You may not need as much calcium from supplements if you already take antacids containing calcium carbonate.

If you're at high risk for heart disease, stroke, or kidney stones, or if you have a heart condition, stroke history, or kidney problems, ask your doctor if you can take calcium supplements safely.

Dairy haters guide to getting enough calcium

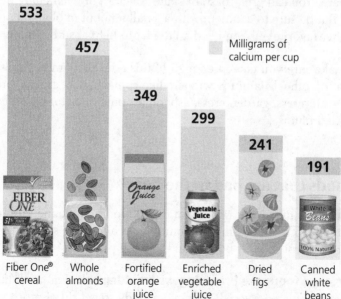

Milligrams of calcium per cup

Fiber One® cereal	Whole almonds	Fortified orange juice	Enriched vegetable juice	Dried figs	Canned white beans
533	457	349	299	241	191

Brand new veggie is all-star for better bones

Coming soon to a supermarket near you – a new vegetable called kale sprouts or Kalettes. They look like deep green flower buds nestled in frilled, leafy "petals" laced with violet. But this isn't just another pretty garnish. This vegetable also delivers a special vitamin your bones depend on.

Vitamin K is one of the key vitamins that helps defend against osteoporosis and fractures, and Kalettes are America's newest source. You need vitamin K to make osteocalcin, which helps create stronger bone. Research shows that people who get enough vitamin K have less risk of dangerous hip fractures than those who don't.

According to Kalettes experts, you need less than one-and-a-half cups of these sprouts to get your full day's supply of vitamin K. And you'll enjoy eating them. Their flavor is described as richly nutty with a hint of sweetness. People who have tried this cross between Brussels sprouts and kale say it has a better taste and texture than either of its parents and doesn't require as much work to prepare. You can grill, roast, or sauté Kalettes, or even enjoy them raw. But be sure to eat them with a small amount of olive oil or another favorite oil. You need a little fat to help absorb vitamin K.

To make sure you take in enough of this critical vitamin, chow down on other vitamin-K winners like spinach, beet greens, broccoli, watercress, garden cress, asparagus, pine nuts, turnip greens, or dried plums.

5 foods that are bad to the bone

Your bones may be at risk if you overdo too many bone-sapping foods. Keep the following calcium thieves and bone stealers under control so your body won't pay the price.

Processed foods are brimming with hidden salt. Eat just a little too much salt, and you'll signal your body to get rid of more calcium. The National Osteoporosis Foundation recommends eating no more than 2,400 milligrams of salt per day – roughly about one teaspoon. Limit the amount of processed and canned foods you eat, and read labels to determine how much salt you're taking in. Experiment with spices, lemon juice, pepper, vinegar, and other seasonings to help you use your saltshaker less often.

Soda raises your fracture risk. A recent study analyzing the diets of more than 73,000 postmenopausal women found those who drank soda were more likely to experience a hip fracture. It did not matter whether the soda was diet, regular, caffeinated, or decaffeinated. Each additional serving of soda per day raised fracture risk by an extra 14 percent.

Caffeine addict? Your bones may suffer. One cup of caffeinated coffee or two cups of caffeinated tea is no big deal, but drinking more can trim the amount of calcium your body absorbs from food and slightly boost the amount you lose. Consider switching to decaf after two or three cups.

Over-imbibing leads to bone loss. Drinking more than three alcoholic beverages a day can lower your body's calcium supply, and heavy drinking can lead to bone loss. Keep to two drinks or less a day, and your bones – and the rest of your body – will thank you.

Spinach blocks your body from absorbing calcium. Popeye may have downed his can of spinach in seconds, but you may want a more leisurely approach. Spinach is a top source of oxalates or oxalic acid, a compound that affects how much calcium your body absorbs. In fact, if you drink milk with your dinner, that side of spinach will keep you from absorbing calcium from the milk. Spinach and rhubarb have the highest oxalate content, while sweet potatoes and beans contain somewhat less.

Meanwhile, beans and wheat bran contain other calcium-blocking compounds called phytates or phytic acid. These may also reduce the calcium you absorb from food – just not as much as oxalate does.

That doesn't mean you should be afraid to eat oxalate-rich foods or foods with phytates. Skipping them means you'll miss out on other nutrients your bones need. While some experts claim oxalates block a lot of calcium, others say oxalates and phytates have little effect on your calcium levels as long as you eat a wide variety of foods. So don't go overboard, but continue enjoying these foods as a regular part of a nutritious diet.

Strontium: bone-building wonder or health risk?

Strontium is an amazing metal that may draw extra calcium into your bones. A formula containing strontium has been prescribed as an osteoporosis drug in Europe for several years. So why hasn't your doctor mentioned it?

The European osteoporosis drug, strontium ranelate, was recently linked to a higher risk of heart attacks, skin rashes, health dangers related to blood clots, and other problems. Alarmed by these risks, European authorities changed the rules for prescribing the drug. Today strontium ranelate can only be prescribed to people with severe osteoporosis or those who can't use other treatments.

The U.S. Food and Drug Administration has not approved strontium ranelate. But strontium is available in dietary supplements like strontium citrate, strontium chloride, and strontium carbonate. No one knows whether these supplements can fight bone loss as effectively as the prescription drug, or whether they have the same risks and dangers. So don't try strontium supplements without getting your doctor's permission.

3 powerful reasons to 'go bananas' for your bones

A banana is more than just a great way to beat the mid-afternoon slump. This sweet snack also delivers three bone builders that may surprise you.

Carbs boost calcium absorption. Bananas contain special carbohydrates called inulin and fructooligosaccharides (FOS). Most studies suggest these nondigestible carbs help your body absorb more calcium from food. To make sure you get plenty of FOS and inulin, also eat more garlic, onions, Jerusalem artichokes, chicory, wheat bran, and asparagus.

Silicon helps create bone. "Beer helps increase bone density," headlines around the world declared. But it wasn't the alcohol that helped bones. It was the trace mineral silicon, which you can also get from bananas. Experts aren't sure how silicon works, but they know it plays a key role in making new bone. That may be why getting enough silicon has been linked with better bone density in both men and premenopausal women.

Bananas can help you take in more of this mineral, but your body can only absorb part of the silicon they offer. To really beef up your silicon tally, spruce up your menu with more wholegrain cereals, pastas, and breads, and make green beans a regular part of your menu.

> Try these tricks to speed up using bananas in recipes. For easy mashing, use a potato ricer or stick blender, or put the fruit in a large, resealable bag, and mash with a rolling pin.

Potassium fights bone loss. Bananas are famous for their potassium, and new research from the University of Surrey suggests this mineral can be good for bones. Researchers found that people who took potassium citrate or potassium bicarbonate supplements lost less bone and less calcium.

Fortunately, these potassium compounds are plentiful in fruits and vegetables. So fill your diet with potassium-rich foods like bananas, raisins, dried apricots, orange juice, baked potatoes, avocados, and pistachios, and you'll be well on your way to stronger bones.

'All-natural' products that may thin your bones

Your instant breakfast drink or drugstore remedy may be slowly thinning your bones, especially if you use it daily. Why? Some products contain far more vitamin A than anyone expects, and too much vitamin A can sap the strength from your bones.

What's the right amount of vitamin A? Remember Goldilocks from *Goldilocks and the Three Bears*? She wouldn't accept too little or too much of anything. That's a good approach for vitamin A, too. Your body needs this vitamin to maintain healthy bones, so women should get no less than the recommended daily amount of 700 micrograms (mcg) or 3,000 International Units (IU). Men need at least 900 mcg or 2,330 IU.

Too much vitamin A may raise your risk of bone loss and hip fractures. Experts suspect that vitamin A overload makes bone-removing cells multiply and interferes with bone-protecting vitamin D, so you lose bone faster. Fortunately, you can keep vitamin A at safe levels just by learning the difference between harmless vitamin A – beta carotene – and the kind of vitamin A that can wreak havoc on your body.

Preformed vitamin A can be toxic. In plants, vitamin A is in the form of carotenoids, like beta carotene, that turn into vitamin A in your body. Plant foods rich in carotenoids are good for your bones. This form of vitamin A has never been linked to fragile bones, so you don't have to worry about eating too many carrots, sweet potatoes, or pumpkin.

The vitamin A to watch out for is preformed vitamin A. It comes from animal products like liver, and because it's fat-soluble, it stays in your body a long time and can build up to toxic levels if you get too much. The scary thing is that preformed vitamin A also shows up in supplements, multivitamins, and fortified foods like breakfast drinks, energy bars, and chewing gum.

Be sure to check labels for ingredients like retinol, retinyl acetate, or retinyl palmitate to see if you're getting more vitamin A than you need. Don't take in more than 1,500 mcg or 5,000 IU of preformed vitamin A a day.

Eat like a jetsetter to battle bone disease

Eating native dishes is part of the fun of traveling internationally. Pick the right ones and you can help strengthen your thinning bones as well. Here's how to reap the benefits of foreign fare without even packing your bags.

Go Greek to fight fractures. Want a balmy Greek-style dish that can also give you a little skeletal support? Mix up a salad with olive oil, lemon juice, salmon, artichoke hearts, roasted red peppers, and romaine lettuce. Add extra flavor with either capers or sliced black olives, and top it all off with shredded mozzarella cheese and a sprinkling of flaxseeds.

All these ingredients are good for you, but the olive oil, flaxseed, and salmon are the most important to your bones. Eating extra olive oil may raise levels of bone-strengthening osteocalcin in your body. It may also help you make new bone to replace what you're losing, a Spanish study reports. What's more, higher blood levels of omega-3 from eating foods like salmon and flaxseed have been linked to a lower risk of hip fracture.

South African rice boasts bone-building turmeric. Try a rice dish that's right at home in the mountains and beaches of sunny South Africa. Cook one cup of rice, along with raisins or diced dried plums. Include a little oil or butter, honey or brown sugar, and a teaspoon or two of turmeric. Research suggests that curcumin, a powerful compound in turmeric, may help prevent bone loss.

By replacing the raisins with dried plums, you'll help your bones even more. A Florida State University study suggests eating dried plums can help improve bone density and reduce bone loss.

Mexican stir-fry: surprising source of vitamin C. Mexican restaurants often use stir-fried bell peppers and tomatoes in their dishes. You may be surprised to learn those tomatoes and peppers are good sources of vitamin C. Your body needs that vitamin to build the framework for new bone.

So grab your frying pan and toss in some diced tomatoes and chopped peppers with a little oil, lemon juice, garlic or onion powder, and salt and pepper to taste. Combine with chopped or shredded, cooked chicken. Mix in some corn and black beans for variety, and you'll soon be enjoying a healthy, bone-building meal.

Brainpower

Healthy treats for an ageless mind

Fast food: a fast track to dementia

Living on fast food and junk food for just one week could harm your brain and your memory. A month of this junk may raise your risk of Alzheimer's disease (AD).

Just look at what happened to animals that ate a steady diet of junk food such as cake, biscuits, sugary drinks, and lots of fat. Researchers found they developed inflammation in part of the brain related to memory, resulting in memory problems within a week.

"What is so surprising about this research is the speed with which the deterioration occurred," says Margaret Morris, professor in the School of Medical Sciences at the University of New South Wales.

The animals ate some of the same foods featured on your favorite fast-food menu. So the next time you're in the mood for a burger and fries, think about what a typical fast-food meal does to your brain.

Cheeseburger and fries: fat-filled demons. That cheeseburger and small fry pack a lot of fat. A typical cheeseburger boasts a whopping 14 grams of saturated fat, while a small fry adds another 1.6 grams. Not all of it goes straight to your hips. Some of it winds up wreaking havoc in your brain.

- Women who ate the most saturated fat on a regular basis had the worst memory and cognition and saw bigger declines in both over time. Their brains seemed to age six years in just four years.

■ Saturated fat may also contribute to Alzheimer's disease. Eating foods rich in saturated fat every day for a month led to the buildup of amyloid-beta in people's brains, a sticky protein believed to cause Alzheimer's. A chemical called apolipoprotein E moves amyloid-beta out of the brain, but saturated fat and sugar block this from happening.

Dangerous trans fat lurks in fast-food apple pie. Before you order that pie for dessert, think about this. A single slice is loaded with 4.7 grams of trans fat, a type that's even more dangerous than saturated fat. "While trans fats increase the shelf life of foods, they reduce the shelf life of people," warns Beatrice Golomb, professor of medicine at the University of California-San Diego.

Golomb headed a study that linked trans fat to worse memory in young and middle-aged men. Other research showed that elderly men and women who ate the most trans fat scored worst on tests of memory, attention, thinking, and overall cognition. In addition, their brains shrank more than seniors who ate less trans fat.

> Trans fat is so bad for you that the Food and Drug Administration has banned it in foods.

Try to avoid margarine, a major source of trans fat, and check the Nutrition Facts panel on prepackaged foods such as frozen pizza and baked and fried goods.

Soda packs a load of sugar. You think you're being smart by choosing a small soda instead of a 32-ounce giant. But a 16-ounce soda contains an amazing 10.5 teaspoons of sugar, most of it in the form of fructose. That's bad news for your brain. High blood sugar leads to inflammation in your hippocampus, the area of your brain that processes and makes memories. Not surprisingly, rats that drank sugar water for six weeks experienced brain changes that hampered their memory and learning.

"What you eat affects how you think," says Fernando Gomez-Pinilla, professor of neurosurgery at the University of California-Los Angeles School of Medicine. In one study, older adults who ate the most sugar were 1.5 times more likely to develop mild cognitive impairment (MCI) within one year, compared to seniors who ate the least sugar. MCI is a forerunner to Alzheimer's disease.

"While nutrition affects the brain at every age, it is critical as we get older and may be important in preventing cognitive decline," Margaret Morris explains. That means seniors who eat poorly may have more trouble thinking clearly and remembering. Feed your brain right. Make sure you eat foods that will keep your mind sharp into your 80s and beyond.

Sugar makes you stupid — smarten up with fish

Overindulge in birthday cake yesterday? Serve yourself a big piece of salmon for dinner tonight. The healthy fats in some fish may offset the damage that sugar does to your brain.

Despite what you've heard, sugar isn't all bad. "Sugar fuels the brain, so moderate intake is good," explains Rosebud Roberts, an epidemiologist at the Mayo Clinic. "However, high levels of sugar may actually prevent the brain from using it – similar to what we see with type 2 diabetes."

High fructose corn syrup: the baddest of the bad guys. Foods made with a sugar called high-fructose corn syrup (HFCS) seem to be especially bad for your brain. HFCS harms your brain cells and interferes with their ability to communicate with each other. This cheap liquid is six times sweeter than sugar, and manufacturers love to add it to processed foods like soft drinks, applesauce, and condiments.

Start reading labels, and you'll see HFCS everywhere. That's bad news, says Fernando Gomez-Pinilla, professor of neurosurgery at the University of California-Los Angeles School of Medicine. "Eating a high-fructose diet over the long term alters your brain's ability to learn and remember information."

Healthy fats come to the rescue. Here's where fish come in. Some fish are chock-full of healthy fats called omega-3 fatty acids. One type, called DHA, protects the connections between your brain cells. Cells "talk" to each other by sending electrical impulses across these connections, called synapses. "DHA is essential for brain cells' ability to transmit signals to one another. This is the mechanism that makes learning and memory possible," says Gomez-Pinilla.

Not having enough omega-3, particularly DHA, could lead to thinking and memory problems. Sugar makes those problems worse, researchers found. They tested this theory on two groups of animals – one fed food with added sugar and the other fed food with added sugar plus omega-3.

The animals ate this way for six weeks, then were put into mazes. The group that ate only sugar ran the maze more slowly, had trouble thinking clearly, and struggled to remember how to escape the maze. But those that also ate omega-3 navigated the maze just fine. The DHA in the omega-3 fatty acids seemed to protect their brains from sugar-related harm.

Fish: a fountain of youth for your brain. If you want a younger brain, keep eating fish. It may protect you from dementia and mental decline, too. In one study, elderly men who ate as little as one serving a week of fatty fish, like herring or mackerel, experienced fewer mental problems as they aged. New research in women may explain why. You lose brain cells as you age, which causes your brain to shrink. But women who had the most omega-3 in their systems had larger brains and less shrinkage, especially in the area that deals with memory. It was as if their brains were two years younger than their peers' brains.

What's more, a study of more than 14,000 people in seven different countries confirms that fish may protect you from dementia. People who ate the most fish were the least likely to develop dementia. Omega-3 may play a particular role in preventing Alzheimer's disease (AD). It protects brain cells from amyloid-beta – a toxic protein that causes AD – and helps remove it from the brain. People who eat the most omega-3 have the least amyloid-beta and a lower risk of AD.

COOK IT

How to boost the fats in your fish

Bake or broil your fish for the most brain benefits, says James Becker, professor of psychiatry at the University of Pittsburgh School of Medicine. "Our study shows that people who ate a diet that included baked or broiled, but not fried, fish have larger brain volumes in regions associated with memory and cognition." Why? "Baked or broiled fish contains higher levels of omega-3s than fried fish, because these fatty acids are destroyed in the high heat of frying," explains Cyrus Raji, who led the study.

Baking a fillet can be tricky. You want to cook the thickest section all the way through without overcooking the thin areas. Here are two ways to do it.

- Slice into the thickest portion every half-inch or so to help it bake faster.

- Cover the thinnest areas with aluminum foil to slow their cooking. Leave the thick areas uncovered.

Fish only help if you eat them. Your body can't make all the DHA it needs, so it's up to you to get plenty in your diet. Don't let your brain deteriorate when you can so easily power it up. Give it the nutrients it needs for a better memory.

The U.S. Dietary Guidelines recommend adults eat at least 8 ounces of seafood each week. Three out of four people don't. If you're one of the smart ones who do, make sure you pick the right kinds of fish. Not all seafood seems to protect your brain.

- Women who ate dark-meat fish such as tuna, salmon, mackerel, sardines, herring, trout, or swordfish at least once a week had stronger verbal memory.

- Eating shellfish or light-meat fish such as halibut, haddock, or cod had no benefit. Experts say shellfish and light-meat fish may not pack enough DHA and EPA to help your brain. Plus they are often fried, which harms what little DHA they do contain.

Check the fish chart below for a quick comparison of the amount of omega-3 fats in a 3-ounce serving of fish. Aim to eat enough each week to get at least 1,750 milligrams (mg) of omega-3.

Choose fish high in omega-3

Atlantic salmon	Atlantic herring	Bluefin tuna	Canned sardines	Rainbow trout
1,921	1,885	1,414	1,258	1,051

Canned white tuna	Pacific halibut	Flounder	Pacific cod	Haddock
808	569	479	241	225

Omega-3 content (in milligrams) in 3 ounces of cooked fish

Fish aren't the only sources of omega-3 fatty acids. Walnuts and flaxseed oil contain them, too, in smaller amounts. So the next time you splurge on sweets – say, after sampling every dessert at the Thanksgiving table – bake a nice, fat fish fillet the following night. Your brain will thank you.

COOK IT

Make a memory-boosting meal in 10 minutes

Take two foods rich in carotenoids, add a little olive oil, and what do you get? A meal that will make your mind happy.

Cut a butternut squash in half lengthwise and scoop out the seeds. Peel it and cut it into one-inch cubes. Heat two tablespoons of olive oil in a large, nonstick skillet over medium heat. Add two cloves of finely sliced garlic, and sauté until soft but not brown. Add the cubed squash and stir to coat it with oil.

Coarsely chop one bunch of kale leaves. Once the squash is golden, but not soft, add the kale along with another tablespoon of olive oil. Stir again to coat with oil, then cover and cook for five minutes. Remove the lid, stir, and continue cooking until kale and squash are tender. Season to taste with salt and pepper, or garnish with walnuts and dried cranberries.

Colorful foods sharpen your mind for years to come

Carrots, spinach, tangerines, split pea soup. Filling up on fresh, colorful produce during middle age pays off big when you're older. If you want to keep your mental edge and memory in your 60s and 70s, experts recommend you eat lots of orange and green vegetables, fruits, and soups in your 40s and 50s.

What's so special about these foods? They're natural sources of plant compounds called carotenoids, the pigments that make fruits and vegetables orange, yellow, and red. They also seem to protect your brain.

▨ Your brain is fatty – it contains high concentrations of delicate fat molecules that it needs to function. These fats are easily damaged by compounds known as free radicals, which may harm the DNA in brain cells, too.

▨ Your brain needs some free radicals to help its cells communicate with one another, but not too many. It's a fine balance. Carotenoids may be key in maintaining that balance, by neutralizing extra free radicals before they do harm.

Researchers looked at nearly 3,000 people between the ages of 45 and 60, studying their eating habits and measuring the amounts of carotenoids in their blood. Around 13 years later they tested their memory and thinking skills. Those who ate the most orange and green produce in midlife, as well as soups and oils made from them, had stronger mental function and memories as seniors.

Carotenoids and where to get them

Beta carotene	Alpha carotene	Lutein	Beta cryptoxanthin
sweet potato	pumpkin	kale	butternut squash
pumpkin	carrots	spinach	hubbard squash
spinach	butternut squash	Swiss chard	Japanese persimmon
kale	hubbard squash	mustard greens	papaya
carrots	split pea soup	turnip greens	tangerines
turnip greens	minestrone soup	collard greens	sweet red peppers
mustard greens	plantains	garden cress	orange juice
butternut squash	vegetable soup	summer squash	hot chili peppers
collard greens	hot chili peppers	green peas	cooked carrots
hubbard squash	vegetable juice	split pea soup	oranges
Swiss chard	cocktail	beet greens	yellow corn
hot chili peppers	collard greens	pumpkin	dried plums

The carotenoids that stood out from the pack and were more strongly linked to long-term brain function were beta carotene, alpha carotene, lutein, and beta cryptoxanthin. Try to work them into your weekly meals. The sooner you start, the better for your brain.

Check the chart on the previous page for good food sources of these nutrients. They're listed from the highest to the lowest amounts. Notice that some foods are rich in several free-radical-fighting carotenoids. Think of butternut squash, carrots, collard greens, hubbard squash, pumpkin, and hot chili peppers as over-achievers. Those are the foods you want to pile on your plate.

Foods vs. supplements: which one wins the memory matchup?

Eat this food! No, take a supplement! Wrong, the food version is better for you! This just in – supplements are good again! Do you have whiplash from fast-changing nutritional news? You're not alone. The truth is, sometimes you're better off getting a nutrient from food. Other times, a supplement really is the best source. End the uncertainty with this simple guide.

Fish oil supplements provide brain-boosting DHA. Fish and fish oil are top-notch sources of DHA, a type of fat that guards your brain against dementia, memory loss, and age-related mental decline. Fish have a better track record of preventing dementia and mental decline than fish oil supplements do.

On the other hand, if you already struggle with mild memory loss or mental decline, then supplements may help, especially if you don't eat much fish. Seniors with mild memory loss who rarely ate fish improved their memory after taking 900 milligrams of DHA daily for six months. Unfortunately, DHA supplements don't seem to slow mental decline in people with Alzheimer's disease (AD).

B12 supplements help if you're deficient. Don't bother taking B vitamins to prevent Alzheimer's or normal, age-related forgetfulness. Experts used to think they would protect your brain by lowering your levels of homocysteine, an amino acid associated with inflammation. A review of studies involving 22,000 people showed that taking extra B12 and folic acid did, indeed, lower homocysteine levels but had no impact on their memory or mental function.

"It would have been very nice to have found something different," says Robert Clarke of Oxford University, who led the review. Unfortunately, "B vitamins don't reduce cognitive decline as we age," and "taking folic acid and vitamin B12 is sadly not going to prevent Alzheimer's disease."

Taking B12 can aid your brain if you are deficient in it, though. A B12 shortage is sometimes the culprit in four of the most common signs of aging – poor memory, balance problems, tiredness, and loss of appetite. As many as 15 percent of all Americans don't get enough B12. Some people lose the ability to absorb this vitamin from food as they get older. When that happens, you need B12 injections to beat it. Oral supplements won't help. Your doctor can diagnose this deficiency with a simple blood test and prescribe shots if you need them.

Vitamin E pills fight Alzheimer's. Supplements may help people with Alzheimer's disease take care of themselves longer. People with AD who took 2,000 International Units (IU) of vitamin E daily, in addition to their normal AD drugs, were able to perform normal activities like shopping and making their own meals for six months longer than those not on vitamin E. Large doses like this can increase your risk of bleeding, so only take them under a doctor's supervision.

Vitamin E supplements may not protect you from developing dementia in the first place, but foods rich in vitamin E might. People who got the most vitamin E in their diets were 25 percent less likely to develop dementia. Sunflower seeds, almonds, and fortified cereals are all excellent sources.

Don't waste money on vitamin C pills. Some studies suggest that vitamin C supplements lower your risk of Alzheimer's disease, while others say food sources offer the best protection. In one study, taking large doses of vitamin C for nine years, along with vitamin E and beta carotene, did not slow mental decline in women with heart disease. But another study showed the amount of vitamin C in your bloodstream could be related to your dementia risk. People with the lowest levels of vitamin C and beta carotene were more likely to develop dementia.

For now, get your vitamin C from foods such as oranges, sweet peppers, and strawberries, and save the money you would have spent on supplements. As an added bonus, foods that are top sources of C, like citrus, also contain flavonoids that may protect your brain.

Boost concentration with a stick of gum

Popping a stick of gum can boost your concentration and maybe fend off dementia. People in one study remembered more random numbers if they chewed gum during the test — especially at the end of the 30-minute test, when their brains were getting tired.

Scientists say chewing in general, not just gum, may improve blood flow to your brain. Being able to chew hard foods like apples predicts your future mental abilities and risk of dementia, regardless of whether you wear dentures or have your natural teeth. What matters is being able to chew.

Cocoa: a fountain of youth for your brain

Indulge in a daily cup of hot cocoa, and you won't just feel younger – you'll be younger, too. Cocoa is chock-full of flavanols, phytonutrients proven to slow premature brain aging, fight Alzheimer's disease and cognitive impairment, and keep your mind young.

Flavorful flavanols, found in cocoa, tea, red grapes, apples, and red wine, may battle brain aging by:

- improving blood flow to your brain.

- preventing the Alzheimer's protein amyloid-beta from blocking the connections between brain cells.

- improving brain cells' insulin sensitivity, so that they use sugar, their main fuel, more effectively.

- directly boosting the part of your brain responsible for memory.

Your ability to think depends on how much blood reaches your brain. "As different areas of the brain need more energy to complete their tasks, they also need greater blood flow," explains Farzaneh Sorond of Harvard Medical School. "This relationship ... may play an important role in diseases such as Alzheimer's."

Sorond's research found that drinking two cups of hot cocoa each day improved blood flow in people whose brains weren't getting enough beforehand, boosting their memories at the same time.

Even more exciting is that the least processed form of cocoa may help fend off Alzheimer's disease. Flavanol-rich lavado seems to protect your synapses, the connections between brain cells that enable them to "talk" to each other.

In Alzheimer's, amyloid-beta protein forms sticky clumps that clog your synapses. The clumps also trigger your immune system to attack – except instead of killing germs, it damages your brain cells. Lavado cocoa may prevent amyloid-beta from clumping together, keeping your brain in tip-top shape.

That cup of hot chocolate may also help if you're experiencing mild cognitive impairment (MCI), a condition marked by memory loss that can eventually lead to Alzheimer's disease. But only if you make it with flavanol-rich cocoa. Elderly people with MCI who drank high- or medium-flavanol cocoa had better memories, improved insulin resistance, and lower blood pressure after two months. Those drinking cocoa low in flavanols didn't.

Clearly, not all cocoa powder is made equal. Here's how to tell the difference.

- Lavado, sometimes called "unfermented cocoa," contains the most flavanols because it undergoes the least processing. The cacao beans are simply washed, dried, then ground. Look for it in health food stores or on the Internet.

- Natural, or "non-alkalized," cocoa powder is made by fermenting the beans for several days, which destroys some of their flavanols. The cocoa powder sold in supermarkets is often natural cocoa.

- Dutch cocoa is the worst for your brain. Not only are the beans fermented, but they're also treated with an alkali solution to make the cocoa less acidic. All this processing removes up to 90 percent of its flavanols. Check ingredient lists for words like "alkalized," "European style," or "Dutched."

Lavado cocoa can be hard to find in stores, so natural cocoa may be a reasonable compromise. Although Dutch-processed cocoa has a milder flavor, it's not the best choice if you want to bolster your brain.

COOK IT

Homemade hot cocoa —
10 minutes to chocolate heaven

Read the ingredients in popular, premade mixes, and you'll likely see corn syrup, hydrogenated oils, Dutch cocoa, artificial flavors, and preservatives. With a list like that, your hot chocolate may not do much for your memory. Ditch prepackaged hot chocolate mixes, and make your own healthy hot cocoa in under 10 minutes.

Heat 6 ounces of milk, and stir in two rounded teaspoons of unsweetened, natural cocoa powder, one teaspoon of your favorite sweetener, and 1/4 teaspoon of vanilla extract. Stir until dissolved. Add a dash of cinnamon on top, then serve. For a Mexican twist, put in a pinch of cayenne pepper. Mix up a big batch of dry ingredients and store for later.

Sip your way to smarter old age

Keeping your brain sharper as you age may be as simple as eating foods rich in catechins, like green tea. Other teas tout health benefits, too, but none come close to this Japanese beverage.

Green tea packs a powerful punch. Green and black teas come from the same plant. The difference lies in how those leaves are processed after picking. Green tea leaves are lightly steamed but nothing else. Black tea leaves are fermented, and that destroys some of their catechins – antioxidants with powerful health benefits. Since green tea is less processed, it packs about four times as many catechins as black tea. All those antioxidants give green tea some potent powers. Research suggests it:

- improves the connections between different areas of your brain and boosts your working memory.

- lowers your risk of brain impairment. Folks over age 70 who drank two or more cups daily were 54 percent less likely to suffer mental impairment than people who rarely drank green tea. Black and oolong teas had no effect.

- helps you live independently longer. Seniors who drank three to four cups of green tea daily were 25 percent less likely to have trouble with everyday activities like bathing or dressing. Five to six cups a day provided even more protection.

- reduces your risk of depression, heart-related health problems, osteoporosis, and death from stroke or pneumonia.

Green tea's accomplishments are pretty impressive, but you can make it even healthier by following this advice.

Brew loose-leaf tea for more antioxidants. One teaspoon of loose-leaf green tea contains more epigallocatechin gallate (EGCG), the main catechin in green tea, than one prepackaged tea bag. But tea bags are cheaper, so if cost is a concern, they still offer great bang for your buck.

Tea leaves, especially from China, can contain large amounts of lead. Fortunately, filtering them through paper or cloth keeps the lead from leaching into your tea. Always steep loose-leaf tea in a fine cloth or paper filter. Or drink decaf. The decaffeinating process seems to remove lead.

Don't steep green tea for more than three minutes. Steeping it longer makes it bitter and does not increase its antioxidants.

Add lemon for better absorption. Up to 80 percent of tea catechins get destroyed in your digestive tract. That leaves only 20 percent to be absorbed into your bloodstream. Adding citrus juice, especially lemon, protects these catechins as they pass through your digestive system, making more of them available for absorption.

Drink decaf — it's just as beneficial. Tests by an independent lab confirm that decaffeinated green teas contain at least as much EGCG as the regular kind.

Don't bother with bottled teas. Bottled green teas don't contain nearly as many antioxidants as a fresh-brewed cup, and they cost a lot more. The healthy compounds are what make green tea bitter and astringent. Manufacturers want their beverages to taste sweet and smooth, so they add less tea. A lot less. You'd need to drink 20 bottles of some brands to get the same amount of antioxidants in a single cup of home-brewed green tea.

Indulging in a few cups of tea is much safer than taking green tea supplements, which have caused liver damage in some people. But regular green tea does contain caffeine, although less than coffee. Even decaf tea contains tiny amounts of caffeine. Avoid it if you are caffeine-sensitive or take monoamine oxidase inhibitors (MAOIs) for depression.

Coffee lovers rejoice: your favorite pick-me-up is a boon for your brain

Ahh — that first steaming mug of morning coffee. Just what you need to wake you up and get your day started on the right note. If you think it gives your brain a boost, you're right. Science has proven coffee can help keep your brain sharp and may even fend off dementia.

"The powers of a man's mind are directly proportional to the quantity of coffee he drank," declared 18th-century Scottish politician Sir James MacKintosh. He had no idea how right he was. Memory loss and slower thinking are the sidekicks of normal aging, but coffee may curb both. The compounds in this beverage, including caffeine, temporarily improve thinking skills and short-term memory.

But the best part is that coffee helps your brain long-term, too. Research suggests if you drink moderate amounts of caffeinated coffee in middle age you can protect yourself against mental decline and dementia later on.

In one study, people over age 65 cut their risk of Alzheimer's disease by 30 percent just by drinking coffee almost daily. Picking up the habit earlier yielded even bigger benefits. Those who drank three to five cups a day in middle age were 65 percent less likely to develop Alzheimer's or other dementias later in life.

How you brew coffee determines which compounds wind up in your cup. Drip-brewing through a coffee filter may offer the most protection. Coffee that doesn't pass through a filter, such as French-pressed and boiled, contains substances that raise your "bad" LDL cholesterol and triglycerides, which increases your risk of dementia.

Coffee may even keep people with less severe memory problems – known as mild cognitive impairment (MCI) – from developing full-blown dementia. People with MCI who had higher amounts of caffeine in their blood, equal to having one or two cups of coffee a few hours earlier, were less likely to develop full dementia over the next several years. Only those with low levels of caffeine went on to get dementia.

Want three more good reasons to drink it every day? This delicious pick-me-up also seems to protect against diabetes, ward off Parkinson's disease, and prevent liver damage. But keep in mind, too much coffee can be a bad thing. It protects best in moderation. For example:

- drinking two to three cups a day may lower your risk of Alzheimer's more than drinking just one cup, but indulging in four or more cups daily may raise your chances of dying if you're under age 55.

■ chlorogenic acid, the main antioxidant in coffee, positively impacts your blood pressure, inflammation, and insulin levels, all of which lowers your risk of mental decline and dementia. But getting too much chlorogenic acid can raise your homocysteine levels, increasing that risk.

■ caffeine may help reduce amyloid-beta buildup in your brain, a potential cause of Alzheimer's disease. It can also disrupt your sleep and that, in turn, is linked to developing dementia. So try to avoid it in the evening.

PREPARE IT

Homemade lattes the easy way

You don't need a fancy machine to make luscious Italian lattes, cappuccinos, and café au laits. You need only your regular coffee maker and a microwave. For café au lait, make a batch of regular-strength coffee. For a latte or cappuccino, brew the coffee strong.

Next, create a thick froth with your milk. Fill a mason jar half way with milk. Screw the lid on tightly, and shake it hard for at least 30 seconds until it forms a nice froth on top. Remove the lid and heat the jar in the microwave for 30 seconds. This thickens the foam.

Now add the hot milk to your coffee. Hold back the foam with a spoon as you pour, then top off your creation with a few spoonfuls of thick foam.

Time for an oil change! One more reason to love olive oil

People living in Mediterranean countries eat lots of good food, drink lots of good wine, but have low rates of Alzheimer's disease and mental decline. A single ingredient – olive oil – could be the reason.

Olive oil is a Biblical superstar for good reason. Mediterranean people eat an average of five to 10 teaspoons of extra virgin olive oil every day, and science is now proving its healing powers. Extra virgin olive oil contains phytonutrients such as oleocanthal that other oils don't. Oleocanthal is a powerful anti-inflammatory similar to ibuprofen. Now research suggests it can protect your brain from the mental decline brought on by degenerative diseases.

In Alzheimer's disease, proteins in your brain collapse into twisted tangles, clogging the area around brain cells and blocking nutrients from reaching them. Eventually, the cells starve and die. Oleocanthal prevents these proteins from forming tangles and helps remove excess protein so it doesn't build up.

Get the most benefits from your oil. How you buy and store your olive oil affects how many healthy compounds, including oleocanthal, you get from it.

- Shop for extra virgin, not "light" olive oil for the most healthful compounds. Oleocanthal is what gives extra virgin its strong, peppery taste.

- Store the bottle in a dark cabinet, away from light, with the lid on tightly. Light and oxygen will slowly destroy oleocanthal.

- Don't buy it in bulk. Olive oil can lose one-third of its oleocanthal in the first 10 months.

■ Keep it away from heat. Don't store it in the cabinet above your stove, for instance. Heat makes the oil break down faster. Fortunately, research shows that oleocanthol is fairly stable during cooking if the olive oil has a lot of it.

Use olive oil instead of butter. Olive oil isn't just for salads. You can use it in place of butter or margarine in almost any dish. Plus, it's rich in monounsaturated fats (MUFAs), healthy fats that seem to guard your brain. By substituting olive oil for butter, you'll cut saturated fat and eat more MUFA, doubling your brain benefits.

Older women who ate the most saturated fat suffered from worse memory and mental function than women who ate the least, and they were 65 percent more likely to get worse over time. On the other hand, women who ate the most MUFA had better mental function and memory. They were about half as likely to experience mental decline or memory loss over the next four years, compared to women who ate the least MUFA.

> You can replace butter with olive oil in most baked goods, with the exception of frosting and other uncooked confections. Liquid shortenings like olive oil may make frostings runny and uncooked goods taste funny.

Top ways to substitute with olive oil. What mattered in this study was not how much fat these women ate each day but what kind. One tablespoon of butter packs 7.2 grams (g) of saturated fat and only 2.9 g of MUFA. That makes olive oil, with its 2 g of saturated fat and 10 g of MUFA, the clear choice for cooking and even baking. Follow these tips for successful substitutions.

■ Don't slather your bread with butter. Dip it into a shallow bowl of olive oil mixed with herbs.

■ Drizzle olive oil over pasta in place of a heavy cream sauce. Amp up the flavor with sliced olives and tomato sauce.

- Make mashed potatoes with olive oil in place of milk, cream, and butter.

- In baking, substitute 2 1/4 teaspoons of olive oil for 1 tablespoon of butter or margarine; or 3 tablespoons of olive oil for 1/4 cup of butter or margarine.

Milk does your brain good

Want to win a Nobel Prize? Drink more milk. Countries that drink lots of milk, such as Sweden, Switzerland, and Finland, lay claim to the most Nobel laureates. Countries where people drink the least, like China, have the fewest winners. While the link seems silly, it could hold some truth. Milk is rich in vitamin D, which may help boost your brain power.

Vitamin D helps knock out dementia. People with the least vitamin D in their bloodstream are more likely to develop mental impairment and twice as likely to get Alzheimer's disease (AD) or another form of dementia. Experts say your blood should have at least 50 nanomoles per Liter (nmol/L) of vitamin D. Compared to seniors who had healthy amounts, those who were:

- moderately vitamin-D deficient (between 25 and 49 nmol/L) were 53 percent more likely to develop dementia and 69 percent more likely to get Alzheimer's.

- severely deficient (less than 25 nmol/L) were 125 percent more likely to get dementia and 122 percent more likely to develop AD.

These results shocked even the researchers. "We expected to find an association between low vitamin D levels and the risk of dementia and Alzheimer's disease," says David Llewellyn with the University of Exeter Medical School. "But the results were surprising – we actually found that the association was twice as strong as we anticipated."

Curcumin and vitamin D: a one-two punch for your brain. Brain cells have special docks for receiving vitamin D. When these docks "open" to accept a shipment, it slows the production of amyloid-beta protein. That's a good thing, because having too much amyloid-beta is toxic to your brain and may lead to Alzheimer's disease. By getting plenty of vitamin D, you help ensure your body doesn't crank out too much of it.

Curcumin, the compound that gives turmeric its yellow color, may work hand-in-hand with vitamin D to fight dementia. Together, they stimulate your immune system to clear excess amyloid-beta out of your brain. Turmeric is one of the main ingredients in curry powder, so you could fight Alzheimer's by having a glass of milk in the morning and curry chicken for dinner.

Sunlight or food — which helps more? Getting 15 minutes of summer sunshine will help boost your vitamin D levels, experts say, but your body doesn't convert sunlight to vitamin D as efficiently as you get older. That makes foods and supplements good options. Milk, along with oily fish like salmon and halibut, are best bets for vitamin D.

Only people who have low levels of vitamin D will benefit their brain by taking a supplement. You won't gain extra protection if you already have healthy amounts of it in your system. Ask your doctor to measure your blood levels of vitamin D. Experts say people who are frail and have some mental impairment may benefit from taking 1,000 International Units (IU) of vitamin D daily, but check with your doctor first.

Add pepper to curry for added potency. You can buy curcumin supplements, but experts say turmeric spice contains additional compounds that can benefit your brain. The body doesn't absorb curcumin very well when you eat it, but black pepper can help. Piperine, a compound in black pepper, makes curcumin 2,000 percent more available for your body to absorb. So when you cook curry dishes, spice them up with a little black pepper.

Cancer

Superfoods that pack a punch

Cheap and healthy: 10 superfoods you should buy now

So exactly why should you eat all your broccoli? Or beans? Or spinach? Health experts agree people who eat the most fruits and vegetables have less risk of cancer. In addition to cancer-fighting nutrients like fiber, vitamins, minerals, and water, almost every fruit and vegetable is brimming with phytochemicals, natural plant compounds loaded with amazing super powers.

Phytochemicals, also called phytonutrients, give fruits and vegetables their smells, flavors, and colors like the orange in oranges and the red in strawberries. Scientists have discovered thousands of them, and some experts believe there could be thousands more. Plants use these compounds to protect themselves from fungi, viruses, bacteria, and cell damage. And they're not the only living things to benefit from these powerhouses.

Build your immune system into a powerful wall of defense against illnesses and infections. When you take a bite of an apricot or graze on cherries, these natural nutrients act like construction workers. Here's what they can do:

- protect your cells from damage and lower your chances of getting certain cancers.

■ pump up enzymes that lower estrogen's effects, which reduces your risk of breast cancer.

■ protect against harmful bacteria.

■ keep destructive microorganisms from attaching to your cell walls.

■ defend your bones against osteoporosis.

■ safeguard your arteries from plaque buildup.

■ block the things you eat, drink, and breathe from becoming cancerous.

■ maintain healthy hormone levels.

■ hinder DNA damage and help with DNA repair.

The 10 healthiest, inexpensive foods you can buy. You don't have to break the bank to eat foods filled with phytochemicals. You can pick up plenty of produce at around 50 cents a cup and easily get your fill. And any foods chock-full of these super compounds are bound to serve up lots of nutrients like vitamins, minerals, and fiber. Just keep a few tips in mind to get the best bang for your buck – and your body.

■ Buy produce in season, then switch over to canned fruits and vegetables out of season. Look for the words "low sodium," "no salt added," "no added sugar," or "packed in its own juice" on the label.

■ Fill up your freezer with frozen fruits and veggies. Use year-round in soups, casseroles, and smoothies.

■ Buy small amounts of produce more often. That way, you'll enjoy them before they go bad.

■ On the other hand, buy in bulk if you use lots of apples, carrots, or any other fruits or vegetables regularly. Your savings could be significant.

■ Don't spend extra on packages of precut, prewashed fruits and vegetables. Save your money and cut them up yourself.

Not every food high in phytochemicals is a bargain. Berries, for instance, are phytochemical super foods that can easily blow your budget. Instead, aim to put the following 10 foods in your shopping cart.

Foods	Phytochemicals	How they keep you healthy
Carrots, peaches, leafy greens, sweet potatoes, watermelon	Carotenoids	Prevent or slow cell damage, block cancer cell growth, pump up your immune system
Beans, pears, squash, apples	Flavonoids	Defend against cancer, trigger abnormal cells to self-destruct
Garlic	Allium compounds	Slow down or stop tumor growth

The sweet n' crunchy, go-anywhere, cancer-fighting snack

Instead of eating a candy bar in the afternoon, why not try a sweet, delicious treat with cancer-fighting nutrients? A handful or two of trail mix could be the perfect snack to recharge your energy and protect you from cancer. The trick is to use smart, multitalented ingredients.

Almonds stop polyps before they start. Include these crunchy tidbits in your trail mix for a good source of magnesium. This common mineral helps prevent colon polyps, which can become cancerous. The more magnesium you get from foods, the lower your risk of polyps and colon cancer, suggests a British study.

Almonds have more magnesium than other nuts. But if you're not a fan of almonds, eating peanuts, cashews, pistachios, pumpkin seeds, or sunflower seeds can still boost your magnesium levels.

10 organic foods worth the expense

Many foods are exposed to pesticides during the growing stages. Some experts and environmental groups are concerned about the possible ways pesticides from foods may affect your health over the long haul.

Although U.S. Department of Agriculture (USDA) tests show levels of pesticides in food are safe, a Government Accountability Office study found gaps in the USDA's testing program. For example, the USDA doesn't test for all pesticides.

Organic foods have less pesticide residue, but they're also more expensive. You can play it safe without breaking the bank. The Environmental Working Group issues an annual report listing the supermarket foods most tainted by pesticides. Buying organic versions of these foods means each extra dollar you spend reduces your exposure to pesticides. Here are the 10 most-tainted foods in your supermarket, starting with the worst offender.

- Apples
- Celery
- Peaches
- Spinach
- Nectarines
- Sweet bell peppers
- Strawberries
- Cucumbers
- Grapes
- Cherry tomatoes

Trail mix can't provide all the magnesium you need, so include other magnesium-rich foods like roasted turkey breast, oats, and pinto or navy beans.

Walnuts protect your prostate. Walnuts aren't just a great topping for salads and ice cream. Eating walnuts or walnut oil may slow prostate cancer growth and help lower your cholesterol, a recent animal study found. But keep in mind the animals in the study ate the equivalent of more than 2 1/2 ounces of walnuts a day – that's nearly 500 calories. So include walnuts in your trail mix, but don't go hog wild. Substitute chopped or ground walnuts for part of a high-fat ingredient in another dish – like the cheese in a salad or meat in a pasta sauce.

Delicious dates pack powerful antioxidants. These fabulous fruits are rich in cancer-fighting antioxidants like ferulic acid, sinapic acid, p-coumaric acid, and flavonoids. They also deliver an anti-tumor compound called beta D-glucan. Add chopped, dried dates to your trail mix for all these benefits, plus a chewy sweetness that's too good to resist.

> To keep dates from sticking together, dust them with cinnamon before stirring them into your trail mix.

Sunflower seeds are rich in anti-cancer mineral. Songbirds have good reason to devour those sunflower seeds in your neighbor's bird feeder. Not only are sunflower seeds rich in vitamin E and fiber, they're also a good source of selenium. Research results on selenium and cancer have been mixed, but many studies seem to agree that too little selenium can increase your cancer risk. In fact, low selenium is a problem in parts of Europe. A recent study of more than 500,000 Europeans found that women with higher selenium intakes had lower odds of getting colon cancer than women who got less.

To boost your selenium, stir sunflower seeds into your trail mix. If you need more selenium, enjoy foods like canned light tuna, roasted turkey breast, canned sardines, and pulled pork in barbecue sauce.

A trail mix recipe you can easily make yourself. To make a week's worth of trail mix, measure 3/4 cup peanuts, almonds, cashews, or pistachios. Combine with 1/4 cup walnuts, 1/3 cup sunflower seeds, and 1/3 cup dates. For the best cancer prevention, choose nuts, seeds, and dates that have no salt or sugar added, and eat no more than a handful or two of trail mix a day.

The one food you should never eat for breakfast

Several popular brands of pancake syrup contain a compound that may raise your cancer risk, say researchers from *Consumer Reports*.

Artificial caramel color helps pancake syrup and other foods appear more appetizing, but some coloring contains the potential cancer-causing chemical, 4-methylimidazole (4-Mel). Research suggests lifelong 4-Mel intakes of 29 micrograms (mcg) a day — about the amount in one 12-oz. can of several popular soft drinks — result in one additional case of cancer in every 100,000 people. Further tests found even higher amounts in some brands of pancake syrup — based on one-quarter cup serving size.

Many health experts suggest switching from regular pancake syrup to real maple syrup, trading caramel-colored soft drinks for clear sodas, and limiting or avoiding foods that list "caramel color" or "artificial color" as an ingredient.

2 red superfruits will keep you in the pink

Everyone loves the gorgeous red leaves on red maples, sweetgum trees, and black tupelos in autumn. But don't forget the edible autumn reds like sweet apples and tangy cranberries. These fabulous autumn favorites are packed with cancer-fighting compounds you don't want to miss.

A fruit with more than a dozen cancer-fighting nutrients.
Johnny Appleseed probably had no idea he was planting cancer preventers all across the nation. Yet scientists from Cornell University isolated 13 powerful compounds, called triterpenoids, from apple peels. The Cornell scientists also pitted every triterpenoid against several kinds of cancer cells. All the triterpenoids helped keep cancer cells from multiplying. That could be a good reason to stop peeling your apples before you eat them.

Unfortunately, apple peels can have high pesticide residue, so buy organic apples whenever possible. When you can't buy organic, scrub the apple with a clean vegetable brush under running water to remove some of the pesticide residue.

And if you want to eat the apples tested in the study, choose Red Delicious.

Don't wait until Thanksgiving to eat this super fruit.
Several centuries ago, Native Americans used cranberries as both medicine and food. Today's research suggests that was a smart move. Cranberries give you anti-cancer compounds like these:

- **Quercetin.** This phytonutrient slashed the growth of four kinds of cancer cells in laboratory studies – and you can get it from both cranberries and apples.

- **Proanthocyanidins.** These antioxidant compounds can kill ovarian cancer cells.

■ **Resveratrol.** Animal research suggests this helps inhibit cancer, and it may even help prevent cells from becoming cancerous.

Other anti-cancer cranberry compounds include salicylic acid, ursolic acid, catechins, vitamin C, plus the anthocyanins that give cranberries their color.

Some people like the dried, sweetened cranberries in trail mix, while others prefer cranberry juice cocktail or cranberry sauce. You'll get more anthocyanins, quercetin, and vitamin C from whole cranberries than from cranberry juice cocktail. So mix dried cranberries into oatmeal, cereal, trail mix, muffin mix, rice pilaf, and even chicken salad.

Red meat and cancer: food combos to nix the risk

Don't go looking for Domino Sugar or Dixie Crystals in your next steak. You won't find it. But researchers from the University of California at San Diego (UCSD) have discovered red meat contains large amounts of a naturally occurring sugar that may cause cancer.

A natural sugar that could mean big trouble. The sugar is called N-glycolylneuraminic acid (Neu5Gc). After testing various foods, the researchers discovered that red meat like beef, pork, and lamb were particularly rich sources of this sugar. But that's not all the researchers found. In their animal studies, Neu5Gc triggered widespread inflammation and tumors began forming.

Neu5Gc doesn't naturally occur in your body. And even though your immune system recognizes Neu5Gc as a foreign substance, your tissues still absorb it. That's why the UCSD researchers say frequently eating red meat like beef, pork, and lamb may raise your risk of widespread inflammation – and that could lead to cancer.

Previous research suggests red meat promotes cancer in other ways, too. Eating an additional 3 ounces of red meat or processed meat every day raises your colon cancer risk by 25 percent and rectal cancer risk by 31 percent. Fortunately, this doesn't mean you should avoid red meat.

The smartest way to eat red meat. The federal government's proposed 2015 Dietary Guidelines don't recommend eliminating red meat from your diet. But studies suggest you do need to eat it sparingly to prevent colon cancer, rectal cancer, and other serious health problems. New research even suggests you eat red meat with certain foods to slash your cancer risk even more.

Resistant starches cut the dangers. Potatoes have gotten a bad rap. Did you know they contain more potassium than a banana, 35 percent of your daily vitamin C, and a cancer-fighting compound called resistant starch?

Your stomach and small intestine don't digest resistant starch. Instead, microbes in your colon ferment this starch to produce short-chain fatty acids like butyrate. This might help kill precancerous cells and reduce the inflammation that can raise your risk of cancer.

Even better, resistant starch may reduce one of the cancer-promoting compounds caused by eating red meat, a new study from Australia's Flinders University finds. So how do you know which foods have this powerful starch?

"Good examples of natural sources of resistant starch include bananas that are still slightly green, cooked and cooled potatoes [such as potato salad], whole grains, beans, chickpeas, and lentils," says Karen J. Humphreys, Ph.D., the lead researcher of the Flinders University study.

Of course, you probably don't want to eat green bananas with red meat, but try tossing some beans or sliced, boiled potatoes with a little of your favorite vinaigrette. This simple side not only tastes delicious, but it may also help you avoid colon cancer.

Essential mineral makes processed meats safer

Your hostess made her famous ham casserole. Uh oh. You're not eating processed meats anymore because you've heard they can cause cancer. So what do you do? If her dish has cheese in it, you're in luck. A small European study found that eating calcium-rich food with processed meat may help protect against colon cancer.

After giving up beef and pork for a week, study participants began eating four slices of ham daily. Some also took two 500 milligram (mg) calcium carbonate supplements every day.

Everyone was tested regularly to check their levels of a compound that warns of oncoming colon cancer in animals. After four days, those not taking calcium supplements had higher levels, but people who took the supplements didn't.

So check your hostess's menu for calcium-rich foods, such as cheese, yogurt, or white beans in the casserole, almonds in the side salad, or a small scoop of ice cream for dessert.

Killer tomatoes attack cancer cells and more

Visit the Great Smoky Mountains, and you'll find plenty of mountain-grown produce in their farmers markets – but the hottest item, by far, is tomatoes from nearby Grainger County. Locals can't get enough of them.

Tomatoes can help destroy the body chemicals behind heart disease, cancer, and even aging. They even seem to prevent eight different kinds of cancer. So break out the salsa, and read all about how tomatoes can save you from an early grave.

Prevent kidney cancer with sliced tomatoes. Women who ate the equivalent of four tomatoes a day had 45 percent less risk of kidney cancer, an Ohio study found. So what's so special about tomatoes?

Just as your car produces exhaust from fuel combustion, your body produces molecules called free radicals. Too many free radicals can lead to life-threatening cancer and heart disease, as well as memory and thinking problems, but tomatoes fight back with their powerful antioxidants. Like a hero who jumps in to put out a fire, antioxidants neutralize free radicals, making them harmless.

But if regular antioxidants are like heroes, the tomato antioxidant, lycopene, is a superhero. It has 10 times more antioxidant power than vitamin E and twice as much as beta carotene. That may be why women who eat the most tomatoes have the least risk of kidney cancer.

Slash skin and prostate cancer with tomato juice. Raw tomatoes aren't your only option. Tomato-based foods may be even better. For example, in a study where men consumed products like tomato juice and tomato sauce, those who ate 10 servings every week lowered their prostate cancer risk by nearly one-fifth.

Meanwhile, in a British study, women who ate five tablespoons of tomato paste a day had 33 percent more protection from sunburn, which increases your risk of skin cancer. This doesn't mean you can give up sunscreen, but the combination might provide even more protection against skin cancer and wrinkles than sunscreen alone.

Shut out five more cancers with tomato purée. Studies from around the globe suggest chowing down on tomato-based foods, like red pasta sauce, tomato juice or soup, and tomato purée, may lower your risk of breast cancer, colon cancer, and cancers of the liver and stomach. Eating these foods may even help lower the risk of lung cancer in smokers.

Lower your stroke danger with sun-dried tomatoes. The level of lycopene in your bloodstream rises and falls with the amount of lycopene you get from foods, and that may help you avoid a stroke. A University of Eastern Finland study found that men who had the highest blood levels of lycopene had 55 percent less risk of a stroke than men with the lowest blood levels.

You can boost your lycopene level by enjoying delicious foods like tomato soup, sun-dried tomatoes, salsa, and vegetable juice cocktails like V8 juice.

Keep heart disease away with pizza sauce. Heart disease kills thousands of people every year, but you don't have to be one of them. People who eat the most foods rich in lycopene have the least risk of heart disease, a 10-year study found. Cooked tomato products deliver more lycopene than raw, so why not make a home version of Hawaiian pizza? Spread pizza sauce on whole-grain pita bread. Add small pineapple chunks and top with low-fat cheese.

> You just made tomato sauce from fresh tomatoes, but it's too tart or too acidic. Just add a large pinch of sugar or a tiny pinch of baking soda, stir well, and taste the difference.

Breakfast drinks that give you an edge against cancer

You already eat whole-grains and fruit for breakfast, but don't stop there. Choose the right breakfast drinks to boost your energy and cut your risk of cancer even more.

Green tea fights two of the deadliest cancers. Green tea may help lower a woman's risk of ovarian cancer. In one study, drinking two or more cups of green tea every day lowered the participants' risk of ovarian cancer by 46 percent compared to the women who did not drink green tea regularly. Studies show it may help prevent endometrial cancer, too.

A Chinese study found that men who drink three cups of green tea regularly have up to a 76 percent reduced risk of prostate cancer. With numbers like that, why wait? Start brewing your green tea today.

Experts suggest the polyphenols in green tea are its key cancer fighters – particularly one called epigallocatechin gallate (EGCG). EGCG also helps prevent cancer by fighting inflammation, neutralizing cancer-causing free radicals, and triggering the death of cells that could become cancerous. And a new lab study even suggests EGCG may squelch an enzyme pancreatic cancer cells need to thrive.

But remember – if you make your tea like the people in the Chinese study, you probably brew in a mug or cup. To drink a second cup, you'd probably just add fresh water to your original tea bag. You'll get plenty of EGCG from the first two cups, but very little from a third cup. Use a fresh tea bag after every other cup.

Black tea with lemon: powerful enough to foil a terrifying cancer. Want to avoid ovarian cancer, but can't stand green tea? A study of thousands of women suggests two cups of black tea daily may reduce your risk by more than 30 percent. Adding lemon juice may make your black tea even healthier.

Scare off five kinds of cancer with coffee. That black coffee could be your white knight, thanks to the many kinds of cancer it fights. Researchers aren't sure why coffee makes a difference, but coffee's chlorogenic acid may help prevent a key process that promotes cancer, and its cafestol and kahweol may keep cancer from growing. Scientists suspect coffee may also limit your body's exposure to cancer-causing substances by speeding waste through your colon. But does coffee really prevent cancer? See for yourself.

- Researchers at the University of Southern California investigated the link between coffee and colon cancer. They found that people who drink about two cups of coffee a day have almost one-third less risk of colon cancer than people who don't drink coffee.

- Coffee drinkers have 40 percent less risk of liver cancer than those who don't drink coffee, suggests the results of several studies published in the American Gastroenterological Association journal.

- People who downed four or more cups of caffeinated coffee daily lowered their risk of melanoma by 20 percent compared to people who avoided coffee, according to a recent study published in the *Journal of the National Cancer Institute*.

Two ongoing studies suggest coffee may also help lower the odds of developing endometrial cancer. And a Norwegian study of men ages 20 to 69 found the more boiled coffee the men drank, the lower their risk of prostate cancer.

Boost antioxidants with juice. If you don't have time for your favorite hot beverage, pour a small glass of juice.

A recent study found that women with the highest intakes of flavanones from foods like oranges and orange juice had less risk of ovarian cancer than women with the lowest intakes. Even commercial orange juice may help boost your body's cancer-fighting antioxidants.

And remember, cranberries and grapes are packed with tumor-fighters so their juices are a great way to start the morning, too.

For best results, experts recommend you consume more solid fruits than juice, and make sure your drink is 100-percent juice with no added sugars.

Good news for people who can't drink milk

Avoiding dairy products may not be all bad. According to a recent Swedish study, it could help you escape some of the most dangerous kinds of cancer.

"We found that people with lactose intolerance, who typically consume low amounts of milk and other dairy products, have a reduced risk of lung, breast, and ovarian cancers," says Jianguang Ji, associate professor at Lund University." By contrast, the risks in their siblings and parents were the same as in the general population. This suggests that the lower cancer risk in people with lactose intolerance may be due to their diet."

The researchers say this study doesn't mean milk raises your odds of these cancers. Instead, they suspect people who avoid dairy products reap benefits from substituting nondairy foods that have cancer-blocking nutrients and fewer calories.

3 juicy fruits that lower your chances for cancer

Sweet, juicy fruits are plentiful in the summer, but three, in particular, can help protect you from life-threatening cancer.

Watermelon: two cancer fighters in one sweet package. Don't be fooled by its sweet taste. Watermelon is the biggest, cheapest fruit you're not eating but should be. It's low in calories, high in nutrients, and has at least one cancer fighter you might not know about. Here's the proof.

Devour a cup of juicy watermelon chunks, and you're only consuming 40 calories. Yet you're getting vitamins A and C, potassium, choline, vitamin B6, and promising anti-cancer compounds like lycopene and cucurbitacin-E.

You already know lycopene in tomatoes may lower your odds of cancer, but did you know you absorb even more lycopene from raw watermelon than from raw tomatoes? Just make sure your melon is fully red and ripe so you reap all the lycopene the melon has to offer.

Scientists believe lycopene doesn't work alone. The watermelon compound cucurbitacin-E may also help squelch cancer, thanks to its anti-inflammatory and antioxidant powers.

Black raspberries unleash anti-tumor defenses. Eating black raspberries every day may lower your colon cancer risk. As cancer begins in the colon, it turns off tumor-fighting genes. But a recent study found that eating black raspberries may help turn these genes back on. Unfortunately, black raspberries are only available part of the year, and research suggests you may need to eat them longer for the best results.

Fortunately, scientists devised a way to preserve the cancer-fighting nutrients – freeze dry the berries, grind them into a powder, and use the powder to make candy. But don't be fooled. This candy may be packed with enough cancer-fighting compounds to equal nearly a cup of fresh berries. Scientists hope to have the candy in stores soon. Meanwhile, watch for black raspberries in your favorite produce section.

Peach polyphenols sabotage cancer. Compounds in peaches may kill cancer cells without harming normal cells, scientists say. And new animal research suggests eating peaches may help keep cancer from spreading. Just two or three peaches a day may be enough to make a real difference.

BUY IT

How to pick the perfect watermelon

Is thumping really the best way to pick a watermelon? Many experts say no and offer these suggestions instead.

- Look for melons with little or no surface sheen. Melons start out shiny and smooth, and grow more dull and rough-skinned as they ripen.

- Find the field spot, the cream-colored area where the melon rested on the ground as it grew. Unripe melons have a white field spot or no field spot. Overripe melons may have a bright yellow field spot. A cream-colored or pale yellow field spot usually means the melon is ripe.

- Choose a melon that's heavy for its size. This is one time you want extra water weight. The juicier the melon, the more it weighs — and the better your chances of getting the sweetest melon at perfect ripeness.

The secret way Italians stay healthy and live longer

Eat like an Italian and you may stay cancer-free for life. Why? Because coastal Italians love to eat tasty fish and plenty of olive oil.

"Fish – high in omega-3 – is a staple food in the Italian diet, and this fish is rarely salt-preserved or fried," says James DiNicolantonio, a researcher at St. Luke's Mid America Heart Institute. "The staple oil used in cooking and as a salad dressing in Italy is olive oil, which is quite low in omega-6."

Together, these foods may help prevent a whole host of cancers.

The right way to eat fish to stay cancer-free. "In Italian studies, subjects who consumed fish at least twice weekly as compared to those who ate fish less than once a week, were found to be at a significantly lower risk for a number of cancers, including ovarian, endometrial, pharyngeal, esophageal, gastric, colonic, rectal, and pancreatic," says Dr. DiNicolantonio.

His research review suggests that people who eat fish at least twice a week have less risk of cancer – just don't fry it. And while you're at it, limit processed, packaged, and fast foods that contain corn oil, cottonseed oil, safflower oil, or soybean oil. They are high in omega-6 fats.

Omega-6 fatty acids promote high levels of compounds that encourage cancer to develop, but foods rich in omega-3 fats help limit these compounds. For examples of fish rich in omega-3 fats, see *Choose fish high in omega-3* in the *Brainpower: healthy treats for an ageless mind* chapter.

Are you getting enough vitamin D to prevent cancer? For even more powerful cancer protection, choose fish rich in both omega-3 fats and vitamin D. Fish like salmon and rainbow trout may be two of the most promising foods in cancer prevention, thanks to their high vitamin D content. New research reveals you need vitamin D to trigger cancer-fighting defenses in your cells.

When vitamin D levels are high enough, your body suppresses a protein that encourages cancer cells to multiply. Vitamin D may even help prevent cells from becoming cancerous.

Recent research suggests that people who get enough vitamin D have less risk of esophageal cancer, leukemia, colon cancer, pancreatic cancer, and head and neck cancers than people who don't.

Other studies show too little vitamin D increases your risk of breast cancer and prostate cancer. Yet many people fall short of the amount of vitamin D they need.

Fortunately, raising vitamin D levels to correct deficiencies can lower your cancer risk, and fish rich in vitamin D can help. Besides salmon and rainbow trout, good sources of vitamin D include canned sardines, herring, and Pacific mackerel.

Olive oil ingredient makes cancer cells self-destruct. The olive oil compound, oleocanthal, kills cancer cells in less than an hour, a laboratory study found. But healthy cells treated with oleocanthal don't die. This may explain why people who include high amounts of olive oil in their diets are less likely to get breast and colon cancer. You probably have some olive oil in your kitchen right now. Why not mix a spoonful with some spices and vinegar and pour it over a garden salad topped with slices of grilled salmon?

Simple food swaps will boost good fats

🚫 INSTEAD OF THIS	👍 EAT THIS
Tilapia	Rainbow trout
Fast food chicken nuggets	Canned salmon
Fried fish	Baked fish
Bottled salad dressing	Homemade dressing with flaxseed oil
Sunflower seeds	Flaxseeds

Replace foods high in omega-6 fats with foods high in omega-3 fats.

The truth about red wine and cancer

Can red wine fight cancer like it does heart disease? Some studies suggest it may make a difference in a few cancers, but the rest of the story may surprise you.

How red wine lowers your cancer risk. Men who drank eight glasses of red wine every week reduced their risk of aggressive prostate cancer by 61 percent, researchers reported. But the good news didn't end there. For each additional glass consumed every week, men reduced their risk of developing prostate cancer by another 6 percent.

People who drink red wine also have a lower risk of head and neck cancers than people who drink other alcoholic beverages – and now researchers think they know why.

Alcohol breaks down into a cancer-causing compound that damages your cells. Accumulate enough damage, and you're more likely to get cancer. But University of Colorado research suggests resveratrol from red wine helps kill damaged cells before they can cause cancer.

The flip side — just how dangerous is alcohol? Red wine lovers need to be careful because alcohol raises the risk of liver, colon, and breast cancers, and possibly pancreatic cancer. What's more, women who consume just one drink a day may have a higher risk of at least four kinds of cancer – breast, liver, rectal, and upper digestive tract. But this doesn't mean you can't drink red wine at all.

Instead of aiming for eight glasses of red wine each week, follow these guidelines from cancer experts.

■ Limit alcohol to no more than two drinks daily if you're a man and one drink if you're a woman. One drink is 12 ounces of beer, 5 ounces of wine, or 1 1/2 ounces of hard liquor.

■ Avoid alcohol completely if you have uncontrolled high blood pressure, liver disease, high triglyceride levels, a high risk of breast cancer, or past problems with alcohol.

■ Ask your doctor or pharmacist if you should limit or avoid alcohol when taking any of your prescription or nonprescription medications.

Too much of a good thing?
2 supplements tied to prostate cancer

It seemed like a good idea at the time. Take selenium and vitamin E supplements to help prevent prostate cancer. After all, early studies showed these two supplements, especially when taken together, lowered prostate cancer risk.

So a National Cancer Institute trial tested whether 200-micrograms (mcg) of selenium and 400 international units (IU) or 180 milligrams (mg) of synthetic vitamin E could cut prostate cancer risk. The results were startling. In men with low selenium, taking extra selenium made no difference, but taking vitamin E increased their prostate cancer odds.

On the other hand, men with high selenium levels saw no effects from taking vitamin E, yet selenium supplements raised their risk of a more aggressive prostate cancer by 91 percent. The study concluded men over age 55 should avoid getting more than the recommended daily amount of selenium (55 mcg) and vitamin E (33 IU or 15 mg) from supplements.

---

5 great reasons you should fuel up on fiber today

Your future could be brighter – just by making a simple change in the way you eat. New research suggests fiber doesn't just fight colon cancer and help keep you regular. Eating more fiber can help prevent at least five kinds of cancer. Here are a few things you probably didn't know.

Fend off deadly cancer of the esophagus with popcorn? Want a good reason to choose fiber-packed, air-popped popcorn instead of baked potato chips? According to Irish research, people who eat the most fiber have less risk of esophageal cancer. Experts suspect fiber's power to help control weight and improve gastro-esophageal reflux (GERD) may help keep you cancer-free.

Scary link between refined grains and kidney cancer. People who eat the most refined grains raise their risk of kidney cancer with every bite. Refined grains include foods like low-fiber white bread and baked goods. Fortunately, people who consume the most fiber may reduce their risk of kidney cancer by 15 to 20 percent. Whole grains; legumes like peas, beans, lentils, and peanuts; and cruciferous veggies like cabbage and broccoli may be particularly good protectors.

Experts suggest fiber may safeguard your kidneys by reducing the amount of toxins kidneys must process and helping prevent obesity. Fermentation of fiber in your gut also generates compounds that promote anti-inflammatory and anticancer activities throughout your body.

Shut out prostate cancer with a peanut butter sandwich. Aim for 38 grams of fiber a day if you're a man. A European study of more than 3,000 men showed that those who ate more fiber had less danger of prostate cancer over the next 12 years – especially if they ate lots of insoluble fiber and legumes. For something quick and delicious, try natural peanut butter on whole-grain toast.

Cut stomach cancer risk with just 10 extra grams of fiber every day. This small change in your diet may lower your odds of stomach cancer by 44 percent, Chinese researchers report. If you add more fiber, increase your daily amount gradually over time, or you may experience gas and bloating.

Learn to love fruits, veggies, and whole-grains to evade breast cancer. A British review of research found that women who eat the most fiber have less risk of breast cancer than women who eat the least. Researchers suspect fiber may help block breast cancer by controlling estrogen and blood sugar levels. For best results, women should aim for 25 grams of fiber every day.

Vegetarians: one food triples your defense against colon cancer

Going vegetarian is a smart move if you want to reduce your colon cancer risk. But add a little fish to the mix, and you may lower your risk by a whopping 43 percent. Think you could do even better by becoming a strict vegetarian? Think again.

A seven-year study of more than 77,000 vegetarians compared how well different kinds of vegetarian diets prevented colon cancer. Vegans, the strictest vegetarians in the study, avoid eggs, dairy, and all meat including fish. But compared with meat eaters, their risk of colon cancer was only 16 percent lower. Vegetarians who ate fish a few times each month had 43 percent less risk than meat eaters.

So if you're a vegetarian, consider eating seafood occasionally. You may nearly triple your protection against colon cancer.

Cancer alert! Six everyday foods you should never eat

Your favorite foods might be increasing your cancer risk. If you want to stay healthy, ditching these foods can help.

Canned tomatoes: see what's gotten into them. Add some canned tomatoes to your favorite recipe, and you may end up eating part of the can. The lining of some canned goods contains a chemical called bisphenol A (BPA), a compound that may raise your risk of breast or prostate cancer. BPA can seep into the food inside the can. Even worse, tomatoes and other acidic foods can leach more BPA from their cans than other canned goods, and that may boost BPA levels in your body. To avoid this problem, look for tomatoes packaged in jars or aseptic cartons.

Microwave popcorn: beware the bag. The lining of some microwave popcorn bags contains a chemical called perfluorooctanoic acid (PFOA). High heat, like in your microwave, can draw the chemical into your popcorn. Since PFOA has been linked to cancer, ditch the microwave popcorn, and microwave one-fourth cup of regular popcorn in a brown paper lunch bag instead. When the popping sounds from your microwave are a few seconds apart, after about two minutes, turn off your microwave. Let the bag cool for several minutes before adding seasonings.

Sugary beverages: what the labels don't tell you. The more sugar you get from drinks, the more trouble you may be in. Research shows that men who drink the most sugar-sweetened beverages (SSBs) have a higher risk of prostate cancer. And women who drink the most SSBs have 78 percent more risk of endometrial cancer than women who avoid them.

Good examples of these drinks include uncarbonated fruit drinks like fruit punch and lemonade and any carbonated drinks with added sugars like Coke, Pepsi, and 7Up. Research suggests you may be safer if you avoid SSBs, so start experimenting with new and different unsweetened beverages. You may be surprised at all the good stuff you've been missing.

Hot dogs: save them for the ballpark. Want to cut your risk of colon cancer by 36 percent? Start saving hot dogs and other processed meats for special occasions instead of eating them every day. Processed meats include corned beef, bacon, deli meats, sausage, and even pepperoni. Experts aren't sure if the nitrites and nitrates in processed meats raise your cancer risk or if preservation by smoking or salt is to blame.

SUBSTITUTE IT

A bacon substitute that actually tastes good

You're craving bacon. Before you give in and buy it, take some advice from the American Institute for Cancer Research. Give spicy vegetarian bacon or sausage a try. If you don't like one brand, try another. You can also find delicious meatless sausage and bacon recipes on the Web.

Pickles: stop a rapidly rising risk. Everyone loves the salty taste of pickles, but you can have too much of a good thing. Animal research suggests a high-salt diet may make your stomach cancer risk skyrocket if you're already infected with *H. pylori* bacteria – and you can be infected without knowing it. Around 50 percent of the world's population is infected with this bug, but 90 percent of those people have no symptoms.

Even if you're not infected, eating large amounts of salt, salted foods, and pickled foods may still raise your risk of stomach and throat cancer. Meats preserved using smoke or salt – such as smoked ham – can also boost your body's levels of cancer-causing compounds. So limit salt, salted foods, smoked foods, and pickled foods, and experiment with alternate seasonings such as herbs, spices, and lemon juice.

French fries: when good potatoes go bad. "Do you want fries with that?" Saying no will save you money, and it might save your life.

Cooking potatoes at temperatures above 250 degrees can create acrylamides, compounds that may raise your risk of cancer. French fries and potato chips are notorious sources of these compounds.

Boiling or steaming potatoes doesn't create acrylamides, but frying, roasting, and baking does. When you cook potatoes at home, cook them to a golden yellow, not a dark brown. And if you must fry potatoes, soak them in cold water for 20 minutes first, then blot dry.

Move over tomatoes! Another veggie cuts prostate cancer risk

Eating three carrots gives you enough energy to walk three miles, the World Carrot Museum reports. Now Chinese scientists say these sweet vegetables may also protect you against prostate cancer.

Does Bugs Bunny know something we don't? Scientists from Zhejiang University performed a special research review of studies from around the world. They found that men who eat carrots at least three times a week slash their prostate cancer risk by nearly 20 percent. The Chinese scientists can't pinpoint yet which carrot nutrients help prevent cancer, so your best bet is to eat carrots instead of taking supplements.

Other studies show carrots may help lower your odds of developing lung cancer and colon cancer.

Beta carotene vs. carrots?
Whole foods win against cancer (again)

Pop a beta carotene supplement, and you may miss out on the other cancer fighters hiding in the carrot. For example, scientists say the carrot nutrient falcarinol may have cancer-fighting properties, but you probably won't get falcarinol from beta carotene supplements. But falcarinol is not the only reason to choose carrots over supplements.

- A study of more than 29,000 smokers found that men who took beta carotene supplements had a higher rate of lung cancer than men who didn't.

- Experts suggest the health benefits you get from foods may not come from a single nutrient like beta carotene. Instead, beta carotene may need help from other nutrients in carrots before it can have positive effects on your health.

- You might not be as low on beta carotene as you think. Thanks to research done by the USDA, today's carrots give you 75 percent more beta carotene than carrots from 25 years ago.

How to get 24-"carrot" protection with a few carrots a week.
To eat like the men in the Chinese studies, aim for at least three
servings of carrots weekly. The U.S. Department of Agriculture
says a serving of carrots equals one medium or a half cup of
chopped. But eating more carrots may be easier than you think –
eat them raw, cooked, or even juiced. Try these clever ideas.

- Add cooked carrot coins or grated carrots to prepared
  pasta sauce, soups, stir-fries, and stews.

- Mix 3/4 cup of shredded carrots into a pound of ground
  beef when making burgers.

- Include grated or shredded carrots in muffins and cakes.
  To grate them faster than ever, use a cheese grater.

- Enjoy raw carrots in salads, wraps, and smoothies.

- Add carrots to sweeten homemade vegetable juices that
  would otherwise taste too bitter or bland.

Colds & flu

End your misery with everyday foods

3 savory soups that knock out colds

Chicken soup is good for the soul – and a cold. Just make sure you use the thighs for the most cold-clobbering benefit. They're loaded with zinc, a natural antibiotic that helps fight infections.

Zinc works by interacting with a protein in cells that fight infection. This action then blocks inflammation and boosts your immune system. That's why some experts believe zinc lozenges may help you fight off a virus at the first signs of a cold.

You can get zinc from other foods besides chicken thighs. Try these flavorful soups and stews to bounce back quickly from a cold or flu.

Fight infections with oysters. They may look slimy raw, but tossed into a pot with shallots, chopped up celery, heavy cream, and your favorite herbs and spices, and you've got a delicious delicacy brimming with cold-fighting minerals. Oysters contain more zinc than any other food in the world, a whopping 74 milligrams per serving. That's over 10 times more than the other foods high in zinc like beef and crab.

Power up your immune system with beef. Beef is another great zinc source, especially chuck roast. Cut up a shoulder roast into 2-inch chunks, and toss them into a Dutch oven with olive oil, carrots, onions, potatoes, and beef stock. Add shiitake mushrooms for an extra perk. These smoky-flavored mushrooms pump up sluggish immune systems.

Grab a crab to chase away colds. It's like inviting royalty over. The Alaska king crab delivers a hearty dose of zinc and makes for a majestic bowl of chowder. Mix crab meat in a pot with potatoes, creamed corn, and onions, with salt and pepper to taste.

Feeling crummy?
Breathe easier with probiotics

What if you could have an army of billions fighting your next upper respiratory infection (URI)? You can — with probiotics, shows a study published in the *British Journal of Nutrition*.

The bacteria *Lactobacillus rhamnosus* (LGG) and *Bifidobacterium animalis* (BB-12) shortened the duration of URIs by two days and lowered the severity of infections by 34 percent. The supplements used in the study were powders that could form bacteria by the billions. Scientists believe these beneficial bugs work by lowering the inflammation associated with URIs.

Want to give these a try? Here's what to look for. You can find *Lactobacillus rhamnosus* (LGG) in products like yogurt drinks all over the world, but in the U.S., it's primarily in supplements. Read labels carefully.

And *Bifidobacterium animalis* (BB-12) is found in both yogurts and supplements. Look for the words B. animalis, B. lactis, or B. regularis on labels.

Food combos that clobber colds and fight stress

Ever wonder why you get sicker faster when you're stressed out? It's simple. The more stressed you are, the weaker your immune system. And the more likely you are to catch a cold. So don't let stress eat away at you – eat away your stress instead!

Watch your stress disappear with vitamin C. Vitamin C does more than help you fight colds. This super vitamin serves up a healthy dose of stress relief, shows a study out of Germany. In the study, people who took 1,000 milligrams had lower levels of the stress hormone cortisol and did not experience high blood pressure during a nerve-wracking, public speaking exercise.

Experts say people with high levels of vitamin C in their blood handle mental and physical stress better than people with less vitamin C. They also recover quicker from stressful situations.

A glass of grape juice a day could reduce stress and inflammation and help you live longer! Experts say it's because of the powerful antioxidants in grape juice called polyphenols. Plus, you can buy grape juice fortified with vitamin C, so you can drink it to fight colds, too.

Give your immune system more support with yogurt. Probiotics replace the bad bacteria in your belly with good bacteria. And these powerful organisms fuel your body's cold-fighting defenses.

In preliminary research, probiotics shortened the duration of colds and reduced the number of colds and flu. Experts say more research needs to be done, but it certainly wouldn't hurt you to eat foods loaded with probiotics – yogurts with live and active cultures, and kefir, a tart and refreshing drinkable yogurt.

Snack your way to fewer colds and less stress. A great way to get vitamin C and probiotics is by combining fruits and veggies high in vitamin C with yogurt or kefir. Try these delicious food pairings to lower stress chemicals in your body and fight off colds.

■ Whisk your favorite herbs and spices into a cup of plain yogurt. Or use 1 teaspoon of Worcestershire sauce and a packet of onion soup mix to make a tangy vegetable dip. Enjoy with green and yellow bell pepper slices.

■ Layer sliced kiwis, peaches, and pineapple between dollops of plain or vanilla yogurt to make delightful parfaits. Drizzle with honey.

■ For a super-simple smoothie, toss frozen strawberries in a blender with kefir.

Best foods, worst foods for a stuffy nose

You're in the throes of a miserable cold, and you're beginning to wonder if you'll ever breathe through your nose again. Yes, you will, but first you need to know the foods you eat can either clear up your congestion, or make it worse. Follow these simple suggestions for soothing relief.

Three foods that clear your sinuses. When your nose is stuffed up, reach for these three foods.

■ Drink plenty of water to lubricate your nasal passages and keep you hydrated. Want something with flavor? Go with fruit juices.

■ Eat chicken soup. The soup's hot steam and anti-inflammatory ingredients may help clear you up. Or sip a hot drink like tea with honey and lemon.

■ Snack on chili peppers. Capsaicin, a chemical compound that makes hot peppers spicy, is a natural decongestant.

Foods that make a stuffy nose worse. Your body and some of the foods you eat contain natural substances called histamines. If you have a sensitivity to foods high in histamines, eating them could make your stuffiness worse. Avoiding these three foods may help.

- Boycott alcoholic beverages, especially beer and red wine.

- Don't eat smoked fish like herring and sardines, and stay away from shellfish.

- Forget fermented fare like blue cheese and parmesan, smoked meats, and sauerkraut.

5 teas to help you feel better fast

Throw a tea party when you're down in the dumps with a cold or flu. A warm cup cranks up your immune system, soothes a scratchy throat, and revives your spirits. Reach for one of these.

Breathe easier with peppermint. This refreshing tea breaks up mucus and helps you breathe easier. Experts say it's the menthol in peppermint that acts as a natural decongestant. It also thins mucus and loosens phlegm. As an added bonus, it's soothing and tasty. Buy peppermint tea bags or steep two to three stalks of fresh peppermint leaves.

Try ginger — tropical spice not just for upset stomachs. You may think of ginger as a tummy tamer. But this pungent plant is loaded with natural chemicals that help battle cold viruses. Make your own fresh ginger tea by pouring boiling water over 2 table-spoons shredded ginger root. Steep for 10 to 15 minutes, then strain. Add lemon and honey.

Rev up your immune system with chamomile. In Spanish, this mild, pleasant herb is called "manzanilla" or "little apple." It's that mellow, fruity aroma that makes chamomile sweet to drink during a cold. But it's the herb's antioxidant content that give it cold-busting properties.

Chamomile contains antibacterial compounds called phenols. Phenols rev up the immune system and fight infections associated with colds. Brew a pot with tea bags or dried chamomile flowers. Since it's an herb, chamomile contains no caffeine.

Think "green" to battle germs. Powerful antioxidants make green tea a super hero in the fight against germs. Drinking green tea throughout the day fuels your immune system thanks to its polyphenols, experts say. Five to six cups a day can knock out bad viruses and bacteria. Just watch how much caffeine you're drinking. You can switch to decaffeinated green tea after lunch, but keep in mind it contains fewer antioxidants.

Steep green tea for about 3 minutes max to release the highest amount of antioxidants. And squeeze lemon juice into your cup – the acidity boosts the benefits.

Sit back and relax with pain-relieving spice and honey. This simple tea is a spice and honey powerhouse with its anti-inflammatory and painkilling ingredients. And everything you need is in your pantry. Mix one clove with 1/8 teaspoon powdered ginger, 1/8 teaspoon cinnamon, 1 tablespoon honey, and 2 cups boiling water. Steep for a few minutes and sip slowly throughout the day.

6 healing herbs help you fight infections

Health-promoting herb	What it does to help you fight colds and flu
Astragalus	Revs up your immune system so you're able to fight off infections.
Echinacea	Eases your cold symptoms and shortens the number of days your cold lasts.
Elderberry	Clears up stuffy sinuses, boosts your immune system, and makes colds last less time.
Ginseng (American)	Prevents colds, keeps miserable symptoms to a minimum, and shortens the duration.
Goldenseal	Fights infections by battling bacteria and viruses and helps keep your mucous membranes moist.
Thyme	Safeguards against infections and pumps up your immune system.

Garlic: the 'go to' herb to crush a cold

"Garlic is divine," says New York Chef Anthony Bourdain. And scientists agree with the popular world-traveling author and television personality. Garlic's healing powers make it nothing less than a miracle-worker.

Garlic's medicinal use dates back to ancient times when the Greeks used it for intestinal parasites, the Chinese for depression, and Indian priests for rheumatism and hemorrhoids.

Today, experts suggest eating garlic to crush colds and fend off the flu. Studies show people who took garlic supplements were less prone to catching a cold or endured colds better than those who were given a placebo. And cultures all over the world use garlic preparations to fight the flu.

Researchers say garlic's super powers come from a substance called allicin. Allicin acts like a natural anti-viral, antibacterial, and anti-fungal drug.

The best way to tap into allicin's healing powers is to eat garlic raw. First chop or crush garlic, and then leave it exposed to the air for a few minutes.

Love garlic but can't stand the thought of peeling it? Try this simple trick. Smash a head of garlic with the palm of your hand. Sweep the cloves into a metal bowl. Invert a second bowl over the first like a lid. Shake hard for 10 seconds, and *voilà* — peeled garlic.

But if the thought of throwing back raw garlic makes your eyes water, try sneaking it into your favorite dishes.

- Chop up tomatoes, an onion, fresh cilantro, and garlic for a flavorful batch of homemade salsa.

- Combine minced garlic with coarse salt, red wine vinegar, olive oil, and black pepper for a savory salad dressing.

- Mix a stick and a half of softened butter in a food processor with four cloves chopped garlic until smooth. Add salt and pepper to taste. Spread your homemade garlic butter over toast, asparagus spears, or mashed potatoes.

■ Make your own pesto by combining fresh basil, chopped garlic, and pine nuts in a food processor. Add olive oil, and salt and pepper to taste. Pour over pasta, brown rice, or sautéed vegetables.

■ Dip into homemade hummus by throwing chickpeas, tahini, lemon juice, olive oil, fresh garlic, salt, and cayenne pepper in a food processor until smooth.

One other way to eat garlic raw is to toss into soup or spaghetti sauce at the tail end of the cooking process. You don't want to actually cook garlic, or it will lose its potency.

Fire up your immune system with selenium

Does your immune system need a charge? Try eating canned tuna, whole grains, or a few Brazil nuts. These foods are loaded with selenium, a mineral that helps spring your immune system into action.

Selenium is like a utility player in baseball. The essential micronutrient plays a role in everything from lowering inflammation and keeping your thyroid healthy to fending off cancer and lowering your risk of heart disease.

Experts say selenium acts as an antioxidant, charging up your cells to spread and defend your body against attacks from germ invasions. But researchers also say too much selenium from supplements can block immune cells from doing their job.

Getting selenium from healthy food like mixed nuts, egg whites, and turkey breast serves up a good dose of selenium without the risk.

Fatigue

Best eats for all-day energy

Kick your energy level into high gear

Breakfast. Lunch. Dinner. Repeat. It's the same routine day in and day out. But if you struggle with fatigue, it's time to make a change in your eating habits. Here's why.

Eating three big meals a day zaps your energy, because your digestive tract takes longer to digest them. Grazing on lighter meals and slightly heavier snacks keeps your blood sugar steady and your energy levels stable throughout the day.

The best reason you shouldn't skip breakfast. You know how you fill your gas tank before you go on a road trip? Breakfast is like that first tank of gas — it gets you started and keeps you going throughout your day. Plus, eating breakfast daily battles weight gain and lowers your risk for chronic diseases like diabetes.

Ideally, you should combine lean protein with a whole-grain or fiber-filled food and a healthy fat.

Try a hard-boiled egg with a couple of avocado slices on whole-wheat toast. Or an egg white omelet made with black beans and onions cooked in a little olive or canola oil.

Foods rich in fiber release carbs into your bloodstream gradually, fueling your body with a balanced flow of energy.

A little fruit in the morning like chopped apples and walnuts over oatmeal also delivers a good mix of protein, fiber, and healthy fats.

No-brainer way to feel energized. Think of lunch and dinner as mini meals for fueling your body. Add nutritious snacks mixed with protein, carbs, and fats, and you've got a recipe for all-day energy.

"Meals that are heavy," says Dr. Roberta Anding, clinical dietitian and director of sports nutrition at Texas Children's Hospital, "including greasy foods and foods with a high glycemic load can often contribute to fatigue." High-glycemic foods spike blood sugar levels quickly then send them crashing down.

"Consuming lean proteins," says Dr. Anding, "and quality carbohydrates such as brown rice, sweet potatoes, quinoa, beans, and 100-percent whole-grain breads and crackers can help maintain energy."

Try salmon with grilled asparagus and a whole grain roll, baked chicken breast with salad and quinoa, or a small serving of beef tenderloin with sautéed green beans and baked sweet potato.

For snacks, "avoiding sugary foods such as cookies, candy, doughnuts, cake, and pastries can also be helpful," says Dr. Anding.

Reach for a banana with peanut butter, a pear with yogurt and sunflower seeds, or a yogurt parfait with berries and whole-grain granola.

A drink that kicks your energy level into high gear. No, it's not a Coke or Red Bull or an exotic juice drained from a plant you've never heard of. The magic energy elixir is water – the best way to avoid dehydration, a common cause of fatigue. What's more, water pumps energy-boosting nutrients throughout your body.

And water from fruits and vegetables like melons and cucumbers counts, too. Just make sure you're getting a steady stream throughout the day.

Get back your get-up-and-go with special probiotic

There's hope if you're one of the more than 2 million people in the U.S. with chronic fatigue syndrome. A probiotic strain may calm the inflammation associated with this debilitating disease, renamed Systemic Exertion Intolerance Disease or SEID by the Institute of Medicine in 2015.

An Irish research team tested *Bifidobacterium infantis* *(B. infantis) 35624* on people with ulcerative colitis, psoriasis, and chronic fatigue — all inflammatory conditions. The powerful probiotic lowered blood biomarkers for inflammation in all three conditions.

Scientists have known for years probiotics protect your digestive and respiratory tracts. But they were surprised to find these gut-friendly bacteria also fight inflammation throughout the rest of your body.

You won't find *B. infantis* in your favorite yogurt. You can only get it from supplements. Check labels before you buy.

Deadly dehydration! Are you drinking enough?

Water is the No. 1 drink in America – and rightly so. It's available everywhere from your kitchen sink to your favorite restaurant.

Feeling a bit sluggish? Tap into the pure simple healing power of water to fight fatigue. Without water, your body can get dehydrated, stifling your energy levels and preventing you from performing your best when you're physically active. Dehydration can even make you feel exhausted when you're doing simple chores.

Unfortunately, as you get older, you may become less sensitive to thirst, so you need to be extra careful about staying hydrated. That's why you need to know the warning signs of dehydration, since thirst isn't always the best guide. Ignoring these signs could be deadly. Symptoms like dry mouth and skin, headache, less urine, and dizziness signal you're on your way to being dehydrated. Add extreme thirst, rapid heartbeat and breathing, and little to no urine, and you've got a medical emergency. It's best to make sure you're drinking water throughout the day. It's easy. Start as soon as you roll out of bed.

You don't have to drink water to get the fluids you need for optimal daily energy. Reach for one of these delicious fruits or vegetables. Over 90 percent of their weight is water — cabbage, grapefruit, spinach, broccoli, cantaloupe, celery, cucumber, sweet peppers, radishes, strawberries, tomatoes, zucchini, cauliflower, iceberg lettuce, and watermelon.

Start drinking first thing in the morning. Ever find yourself waking up in the morning with a dry mouth? That's because sleeping for seven or eight hours straight can dry you out. Start your day with a tall glass of water, a great way to dodge dehydration right off the bat.

How to jazz up your H20. Face it – plain water is just plain boring. But you can perk it up with a twist of lemon or lime, or a little fruit juice. Or reach for flavored sparkling water a couple of times a day to break up your routine.

Easy way to make sure you are drinking enough. Make it a goal to fill a pitcher with the amount of water you need in a day, then pace yourself – guaranteed to keep you hydrated and feeling energized.

So just how much water should you pour into that pitcher? You've probably heard this recommendation before – drink eight glasses of water a day. But if consuming eight full glasses of water a day seems a bit excessive, you might be right. Not all experts agree. Some say it doesn't have to be eight glasses, and others say it doesn't even have to be water.

Men should aim for about 15 cups and women around 11 cups of fluids from food, water, and other beverages, suggests the Institute of Medicine. And while scientists agree water is still your best bet for hydration, here's a list of alternatives you might enjoy.

- Guzzle a sports drink after intense physical activity like running for an hour or playing a strenuous game of tennis. Sports drinks replace the electrolytes you lose when you sweat and give you some energy-producing carbohydrates.

- Drink fruit juices that don't contain added sugar. But do so with caution. Fruit juices contain plenty of natural sugars that can add up as empty calories.

- Sip coconut water. This delicious liquid found inside immature coconuts is low in sugar and calories compared to other fruit juices. Some experts say the natural electrolytes make coconut water comparable to sports drinks. But other research says it's no better than water. Either way, if you want a break from water, a glass of coconut water may hit the spot.

- Enjoy a cup of black tea. It will hydrate your body much like water does, suggests a small study published in the *British Journal of Nutrition*. Green tea helps, too.

- Quench your thirst with coffee. Most people think of coffee as a diuretic. But coffee kept regular joe drinkers hydrated similarly to water, shows a British study. But don't pour yourself a cup of java just yet. The small study was done on men who already drank between three and six cups a day. So if you're not a regular coffee drinker, your body may react differently, and a cup of coffee may not be a good substitute for water.

Energy drinks and food bars: don't fall for the hype

Manufacturers market them as safe, quick ways to get an energy fix. But are the ingredients all they're cracked up to be? Experts say no. Here's why.

- They're overloaded with caffeine — enough to make coffee jittery.

- They're chock-full of sugar, about 12 teaspoons in a 16-ounce can. That's enough to spike your blood sugar before it comes crashing down.

- They're brimming with exotic ingredients — most of which aren't regulated by the Food and Drug Administration.

And it's not just energy drinks. Most energy bars are nothing more than candy bars with added protein and sugar, plus vitamins and minerals you already get from a healthy diet. Even more disturbing, most energy bars are sweetened with organic brown rice syrup. Researchers at Dartmouth College discovered that this sweetener contains high concentrations of arsenic.

Bottom line? Don't buy into the hype.

Beef up on B12 for boundless energy

Take advantage of clams, crabs, and mussels if you live near the ocean. They're loaded with vitamin B12, a nutrient you need to fight fatigue.

B12 could win an MVP award for all the ways it helps you stay healthy. It keeps your nerve and blood cells strong, helps make DNA, and prevents megaloblastic or vitamin-deficiency anemia.

Tired and weak? Too little B12 is a hidden reason for chronic fatigue. A deficiency can trigger other symptoms like confusion, depression, memory problems, and numbness and tingling in your hands and feet.

Here are four reasons your B12 levels may be flagging.

Age zaps vitamin B12. The acids in your stomach separate B12 from food as you eat. Then the vitamin attaches to a protein made by the stomach called intrinsic factor, which helps you absorb B12. But as you age, you produce less stomach acid and intrinsic factor, making it difficult for your body to absorb the B12 it needs.

Your medicine cabinet could be the problem. People who have used acid-blockers like Prilosec and Prevacid, and pills for treating peptic ulcers like Zantac, can have trouble absorbing vitamin B12. So can people who take Metformin, a type 2 diabetes drug.

Vegan diets come up short. Your body needs B12 from animal sources. The human body can't use the plant-based form of vitamin B12, shows a study published in the *Journal of Agricultural and Food Chemistry*. That puts vegans and vegetarians at high risk of developing a deficiency.

> Over age 51? Get your B12 from fortified cereals or supplements, recommends the Institute of Medicine. Supplement choices include regular pills, pills that dissolve under your tongue, and nasal sprays. Shots are best if you have a severe deficiency since the vitamin doesn't need to go through your digestive tract to get absorbed.

Chronic diseases destroy B12. Digestive disorders that interfere with absorption like Crohn's disease and celiac disease lead to B12 deficiency. And an autoimmune condition called pernicious anemia, in which your body cannot make intrinsic factor, blocks your ability to absorb B12.

If you remember the days when you had boundless energy, you can get it back. Along with shellfish, reach for these fabulous foods – salmon, trout, rockfish, haddock, and tuna.

Don't start popping B12 supplements just because you feel tired. There's no evidence B12 will boost your energy or athletic performance unless you have an actual deficiency. Your doctor can determine if you are deficient.

Or if you're a meat lover, liver, beef, even a cheeseburger or a beef taco will do the trick. So will low-fat fare like chicken and turkey, as well as fortified cereals and plain yogurt.

3 mighty minerals put more pep in your step

Want to feel invigorated all day, every day? Check out what these three amazing minerals can do for you.

How zinc zaps fatigue. You can feel young for as long as you live. Just make sure you're getting enough zinc in your diet. This important mineral helps boost your immune system and make thyroid hormone. Plus, zinc charges up your energy level. Not enough zinc and your muscles lose strength and tire quickly, and your energy gets zapped during physical activity. Zinc helps remove carbon dioxide from your body when you're active, researchers say. This keeps your muscles from getting tired and boosts your energy.

Turn to the ocean for foods with lots of zinc like oysters, crab, and lobster. Or if you like meat, reach for beef, pork chops, or dark meat chicken.

Can iron rev up your energy? You can't pump iron without iron – or do much else for that matter. Iron is like a delivery truck, transporting oxygen from your lungs to the rest of your body. Not enough iron and your cells start to suffocate, leaving you without energy to get through the day.

Experts say people have a hard time absorbing iron, so they suggest getting it from animal sources like meat, fish, and poultry. Iron from these sources is easier to absorb than iron from plants like legumes and spinach. But one way you can boost your iron absorption from plants is to eat them with foods high in vitamin C like citrus fruits and sweet red peppers.

And remember, getting iron from food is safer than taking supplements. Iron supplements increase the risk of death in older women, suggests the Iowa Women's Health Study. Always check with your doctor before taking an iron supplement.

Magnesium — why you need it to power up your pace. Kick your activity level into high gear with beans, whole-grains, nuts, and leafy greens – foods loaded with magnesium. This magnificent mineral boosts your ability to perform physical activities like walking, suggests an Italian study of elderly women. Your body uses magnesium in over 300 biochemical reactions within your cells, triggering everything from physical energy to healthy brain function.

Pump up your breakfast with mix-and-match power foods

Zinc: eggs, milk, yogurt, cheddar cheese, fortified cereal, baked beans

Iron: ham, turkey, spinach, strawberries, maple syrup

Magnesium: nuts, raisins, black beans, avocado, whole grains

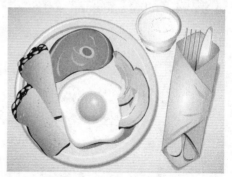

To make sure you're getting plenty of zinc, iron, and magnesium every morning, eat a food from each of the categories.

What to eat to keep your thyroid in check

Your doctor says it's your thyroid. Now what? No need to panic if your fatigue is caused by an underactive or overactive thyroid. Most doctors will send you home with a prescription to help get your thyroid back on track and monitor your thyroid hormones with regular blood tests. But a change in diet may be in order, too. Here's what to eat for a healthy thyroid.

- Main dish – stick with fish, chicken, and turkey. Fish has iodine, and chicken and turkey have tyrosine, nutrients your thyroid needs to pump out the right amount of hormones.

- Side dish – cook up some squash, legumes, whole-grains, lima beans, bell peppers, and sea vegetables like kelp for more thyroid-friendly nutrients plus antioxidants. Antioxidants help keep thyroid problems at bay.

- Snacks – graze on almonds for tyrosine, nuts and seeds for magnesium, Brazil nuts for selenium, and cherries and blueberries for antioxidants.

It's always best to get nutrients from foods instead of supplements. But sometimes you can get too much iodine and selenium from your diet, and that's as harmful as getting too little. Moderation is the key. For instance, one or two Brazil nuts a day are all you need to get your fill of selenium.

GI upsets

Grocery goodies that soothe & comfort

Heal 3 common GI complaints with probiotics

You're used to thinking of bacteria as bad guys, causing illnesses like strep throat, pneumonia, and salmonella poisoning. But some are more like superheroes fighting on the side of good, keeping your digestive tract, immune system, and even your brain healthy. These beneficial bacteria and yeasts are called probiotics – and they're the health wonders of the 21st century. Foods and supplements that contain probiotics can help keep you regular by conquering both constipation and diarrhea, plus manage the symptoms of irritable bowel syndrome!

Clear up constipation without laxatives. As many as one in seven people struggle with mysterious bouts of constipation with no obvious cause. Fiber supplements, laxatives, and stool softeners don't always help, but probiotics might.

Constipation seems to change the makeup of organisms that live in your gut, reducing the amount of beneficial *Bifidobacterium* and *Lactobacillus* bacteria and increasing the numbers of disease-causing organisms, including *Escherichia (E.) coli* and *Staphylococcus aureus*. Probiotics may help by adding beneficial bugs to the mix. Scientists think these good gut bugs pump out compounds that:

- help move stool through your bowels.

- make you more sensitive to the urge to have a bowel movement.

Those theories are supported by the results of 16 studies involving more than 1,000 people from around the world. Probiotics, especially those containing the bacterium *Bifidobacterium, (B.) lactis*, helped relieve constipation – softening stool, moving it through the bowel faster, increasing the number of bowel movements people had each week, and easing gas.

B. lactis comes in many different strains, or varieties, sort of like different flavors of ice cream. Not all will help constipation. But *B. lactis* DN 173 010, the type found in Activia yogurt under the trademarked name *Bifidus Regularis*, may. So might the strain *B. lactis* HN019, sold under the trademarked name HOWARU *Bifido*.

Stops two major causes of diarrhea. Taking antibiotics and traveling abroad both put you at risk for bouts of diarrhea. Luckily, probiotics can often prevent or treat both causes.

■ Antibiotics save lives, but they also disrupt your gut because they kill both good and bad bacteria indiscriminately. The good bugs in your gut normally crowd out the diarrhea-causing ones, like *Clostridium (C.) difficile*. Without them, *C. difficile* can flourish, making you sick. Taking specific probiotics every day while you're on antibiotics seems to keep *C. difficile* in check.

Look for foods and supplements that contain *Lactobacillus (L.) rhamnosus GG* (such as Solgar Advanced Multi-Billion Dophilus); *Lactobacillus (L.) paracasei* DN-114 001 (sold as Actimel and DanActive); or *Saccharomyces (S.) boulardii* (such as FloraStor and other supplements). Take your antibiotics, then wait at least two hours before taking the probiotics. Continue taking them for two weeks after you finish your antibiotic therapy.

■ Taking a supplement that contains the yeast *S. boulardii* or the bacterium *L. rhamnosus GG* while traveling could protect you from Montezuma's Revenge, also known as traveler's diarrhea. People benefited the most from taking 1 gram of *S. boulardii* a day, starting five days before their

trip and continuing until they returned; or 2 billion
L. rhamnosus GG organisms a day (sometimes written as
2 x 109), beginning two days before their trip.

Calm an irritable bowel. Probiotic foods and supplements may
help treat some of the symptoms of irritable bowel syndrome (IBS).
That makes sense, since new evidence links IBS to the overgrowth
of certain bacteria in your small intestine – especially if you have
diarrhea-predominant IBS. No single type of probiotic organism
will cure IBS, but specific ones may relieve specific symptoms.

IBS symptoms	Probiotics that may help	Products that contain it
Overall symptoms	*Bifidobacterium (B.) infantis* 35624	Align
Diarrhea-predominant IBS	*B. infantis* 35624	Align
Abdominal pain	*Bifidobacterium (B.) lactis* DN-173 010	Activia
	B. infantis 35624	Align
	Bacillus coagulans GBI-30, 6086	Schiff Digestive Advantage Gas Defense Formula, Schiff Digestive Advantage Daily Probiotic, others
	B. lactis HN019, aka HOWARU Bifido	Doctor's Best Best Probiotic, Naturade Probiotics, Sedona Labs iFlora Multi-Probiotics, others
Bloating and distention	*B. lactis* DN-173 010	Activia
	B. infantis 35624	Align
Frequency and/or consistency of bowel movements	*B. infantis* 35624	Align
	B. lactis DN-173 010	Activia
	B. lactis HN019, aka HOWARU Bifido	Doctor's Best Best Probiotic, Naturade Probiotics, Sedona Labs iFlora Multi-Probiotics, others

Experts say probiotics are generally safe for treating a range of GI symptoms, especially if you take them under a doctor's supervision. Whatever problems prompt you to try probiotics, be sure to follow the dosage instructions on the label, and take them for at least four weeks before you decide whether or not they're helping.

Are probiotics making you sick?

Gluten hides in the sneakiest places, including probiotic supplements. "Many patients with celiac disease take dietary supplements, and probiotics are particularly popular," says Samantha Nazareth, a gastroenterologist at Columbia University Medical Center (CUMC). Doctors at CUMC noticed that people with celiac disease who took supplements actually suffered more symptoms. This lead them to test the probiotics for gluten contamination.

Out of 22 best-selling supplements, most contained at least trace amounts of gluten. Four had more than just trace amounts — and two of those four were labeled "gluten-free." Experts aren't sure whether such small amounts of gluten can cause problems for celiac sufferers. But if you're one of them and take probiotic supplements, consider stopping them briefly and see if your symptoms improve.

Gluten-free: good for you or waste of money?

Fatigued? Joint pain? Bloating? Celiac disease, an often-misdiagnosed ailment, may be the cause. Only about one in 100 people have this autoimmune disorder, but you might be one of them. Simply cutting gluten from your diet could cure these symptoms.

But that's only true if you actually have celiac disease or non-celiac gluten sensitivity (NCGS), and most people have neither.

- About one out of every 100 people suffer from celiac disease, an autoimmune disease where a protein in gluten triggers an immune system reaction that damages your intestines. Completely avoiding gluten is the only way to treat celiac disease.

- Slightly more people – as many as six out of 100 – may suffer from non-celiac gluten sensitivity, a condition where eating foods that contain gluten brings on abdominal pain, diarrhea, a skin rash, headache, muscle spasms, fatigue, or depression.

Add up the numbers, and only about seven in 100 people have a medical reason to avoid gluten. Instead, most people who eat this way are trying to lose weight or simply think it's healthier.

The hidden dangers of gluten-free foods. They aren't necessarily healthy. Gluten-free foods usually aren't fortified with vitamins and minerals the way regular foods are.

Eating an exclusively gluten-free diet can deprive you of essential nutrients, unless you make a real effort to get those nutrients else-where, from sources such as multivitamins. So not only will you pay more for gluten-free foods, you'll spend money on multivitamins.

Even more serious is the dangerous amount of arsenic in some products. Rice is the main grain used to make gluten-free foods, but it can contain high levels of arsenic. Studies show that people with celiac disease who eat a gluten-free diet consume dangerous levels of arsenic, enough to raise their risks of lung, skin, and bladder cancers.

So who really needs this special diet? People with celiac disease may have no choice but to eat these products and take the risks. But average people do have a choice and should limit the amount of gluten-free foods they eat. Only switch to a gluten-free lifestyle if you have one of these conditions.

■ **Celiac disease.** About 1.8 million Americans have this condition, but 1.4 million don't realize it. Still, that's less than 1 percent of the population. If you have celiac disease, you must cut all gluten, even the smallest amounts, from your diet. Otherwise, your immune system will damage your intestines, limiting your ability to absorb nutrients from food.

■ **Non-celiac gluten sensitivity.** People with this condition suffer from symptoms similar to celiac disease, but without the intestinal damage. Doctors diagnose NCGS by having you eliminate all gluten from your diet, then add it back and see what happens. Doctors may also test your blood for an antibody called IgA-AGA, found in half of all people with NCGS.

■ **Diarrhea-predominant or mixed IBS.** Anyone with this condition should also get tested for celiac disease or NCGS. You're four times more likely to have celiac disease if you also have diarrhea-predominant or mixed IBS. You're also more likely to have NCGS.

Experts aren't sure which comes first – the IBS or the gluten intolerance. Some people with NCGS who keep eating gluten eventually develop bowel inflammation that leads to IBS. And about one in three people with IBS were also sensitive to wheat, in one study. If you're in that group, avoiding gluten may improve your IBS symptoms, too.

Surprising source of gut pain and the no-fuss fix

Gluten gets blamed for lots of gastrointestinal problems, but foods high in FODMAPs (fermentable oligo-di-monosaccharides and polyols) may be the real culprits. Try eating low-FODMAP foods for two weeks and see if your symptoms improve. If so, ask a nutritionist to help you develop a long-term eating plan. Here are some menu ideas.

Breakfast

Coffee (without chicory), gluten-free cereal made from rice or corn (not wheat), almond or rice milk, half grapefruit

Half cup of orange juice, eggs, gluten-free toast, butter, bowl of berries, sliced melon

Lunch

Tuna (canned) on leafy greens topped with olives, olive oil, and balsamic vinegar; glass of iced tea

Sandwich on wheat-free bread of cold cuts; slice of mozzarella, cheddar, or Swiss cheese; and mayonnaise, lettuce, and tomato

Dinner

Roast beef or pork with potatoes, carrots, and sliced bell peppers, seasoned with salt, pepper, and herbs

Chicken or turkey soup made with homemade broth, rice, diced yams, celery, carrots, salt, and herbs

Fish filet topped with shredded Parmesan cheese, quinoa or wheat-free pasta

Snacks

Sherbet, nuts, seeds, grapes, pineapple, tangerines, and gluten-free crackers

Gluten may not be the problem. People with NCGS may not be sensitive to gluten, after all. Some experts suspect that FODMAPs (fermentable oligo-di-monosaccharides and polyols) are the real culprits. Many foods that contain gluten are also loaded with FODMAPs, making it hard to tell what's causing your symptoms. Your gut has a hard time digesting and absorbing these compounds. This gives gut bacteria a chance to feed on them, creating gas, bloating, cramping, and sometimes diarrhea.

To test this theory, people who had been diagnosed with NCGS tried four different diets – low-gluten, high-gluten, low-FODMAP, and whey protein diets. Everyone's GI symptoms improved on the low-FODMAP diet, specifically their abdominal pain, bloating, stool consistency, gas, and fatigue. But cutting gluten from their diets did nothing. And adding gluten back to their diets did not make their symptoms worse. Only FODMAPs had an effect. So before you swear off gluten, take a careful look at other causes.

Secrets to eating healthy on a gluten-free diet

It's hard to get all the nutrients you need when you have celiac disease, but not impossible – not if you eat the right foods in the right combinations.

Celiac disease poses two big challenges – you have to avoid lots of vitamin- and mineral-packed foods because they contain gluten. And the disease can damage your intestines, making it harder for you to absorb certain nutrients. Follow this advice to get the nutrition you need, without jeopardizing your health.

■ **Read the Nutrition Label** on every gluten-free (GF) product you put in your shopping cart. GF diets tend to be high in sugar but low in protein and fiber – not a good combination. Try to choose products that are rich in fiber, low in trans fat, and have little or no added sugar.

■ **Load up on leafy green vegetables.** They're naturally
gluten-free and a terrific source of folate. Following a strict
GF diet can deprive you of this essential B vitamin since
many gluten-containing breads and cereals are fortified
with this vitamin. Leafy greens can help you make up the
difference. Eat them raw, when possible. The heat from
cooking will destroy this B vitamin.

■ **Add a squeeze of lemon or lime juice** to salads, entrées,
and sides to help your body absorb more iron. GF foods
tend to be loaded with phosphorus from corn, soy, and
legumes. Phosphorus binds to iron, calcium, manganese,
and zinc and blocks your body from absorbing them.
Vitamin C can overpower this bond, boosting your iron
absorption in particular. Fresh lemons and limes are the
best sources of vitamin C – even better than grapefruit
and oranges.

■ **Stir fry your dinners in olive oil.** The good fats in olive
oil do a lot of heavy lifting to keep you healthy. They help
you absorb fat-soluble vitamins such as D and A and
improve the way your body handles carbohydrates. Many
GF foods have high glycemic loads because they're made
with rice and potato flour. Eating high-GL foods regularly,
as celiac sufferers do, can lead to high blood sugar, insulin
resistance, weight gain, and a greater risk of metabolic
syndrome, which increases your risk of heart disease,
stroke, and diabetes. The monounsaturated fatty acids
(MUFAs) in olive oil help counteract this effect. On days
when you don't want to stir fry, pour a dash of extra virgin
olive oil on your salads, or use it in place of butter on side
items. Try to eat a little of it at each meal.

■ **Eat foods that boost your gallbladder function**, like artichokes, chicory root, and bitter greens. Herbs and spices
such as turmeric, ginger, sage, and rosemary will do the
same. For some reason, celiac disease keeps your gallbladder
from working as well as it should.

On top of its other challenges, celiac disease causes some people to become lactose intolerant. That's bad news, because celiac sufferers are often short on calcium and more likely to develop osteoporosis. If you can't stomach dairy anymore, talk to your doctor about alternatives such as calcium supplements.

The No. 1 cure for constipation

It fights heart disease, normalizes blood sugar, eases digestion, stimulates weight loss, even improves your mood. But a recent survey shows that fewer than 3 percent of Americans eat enough of it. That's too bad, because fiber could be nature's most perfect food. People who eat a lot of it have a lower risk of dying from – well, anything.

Out of nearly 1 million people, those who ate the most fiber were 16 percent less likely to die over the course of 17 studies than people who ate the least. Folks didn't need to eat a lot of fiber to see big results. For every 10 grams of fiber they ate, their risk of dying dropped 10 percent! Fiber can make living easier, too.

Heal your hemorrhoids. Boosting your intake of fiber and fluid could both prevent and treat hemorrhoids. Struggling with diarrhea or constipation, not drinking enough fluids, and failing to eat enough fiber all put you at risk for hemorrhoids.

The easiest and cheapest fix is to get more fiber and drink more water. This combination makes stools softer and easier to pass. That, in turn, keeps constipation at bay. That's good news for people who already have hemorrhoids, since constipation can worsen their symptoms.

Get regular again. Eating more fiber and drinking more water are the first steps experts recommend for treating constipation. They only suggest laxatives if the fiber-and-water plan hasn't helped after two to four weeks.

Soluble fiber is the kind most likely to treat constipation. It makes stool bulkier, so you have more bowel movements. These foods offer easy, inexpensive, and delicious ways to get more of it.

Food group	Sources
legumes	black, lima, navy, pinto, and kidney beans, as well as chickpeas
vegetables	asparagus, Brussels sprouts, sweet potato with skin
fruits	purple passion fruit, avocado, dried figs, orange
grains	oat bran, oatmeal, oat bran muffins

Fluids — a key part of the equation. Fiber and water go hand-in-hand when it comes to treating digestive problems. In fact, one study found that drinking too little liquid was more likely to cause constipation than eating too little fiber.

Some experts say you should aim to drink 1.5 to 2 quarts of fluid daily. That's roughly seven to nine 8-ounce cups of water or some other liquid each day. Try to limit alcohol. It causes your body to lose fluid, which can worsen constipation.

How to help your body love fiber. Too much fiber plus too little liquid over too short a time period can cause you all sorts of GI grief. Your body needs time to get used to the extra fiber coming in and more liquid to process it.

■ Hold off on increasing your fiber until you have worked your way up to drinking 1.5 to 2 quarts of fluids daily. Then start adding more fiber to your diet.

■ Increase your fiber slowly to give your digestive tract time to adjust. Otherwise, you'll end up with gas, bloating, and even diarrhea. This advice applies to fiber from both food and supplements.

■ Men should try to eat 38 grams of fiber daily and women 25 grams. Don't enjoy counting grams? Then ballpark it by eating two to three servings of whole grains plus five servings of fruits and vegetables every day. This combination should meet your body's fiber needs.

High fiber foods — are you making your IBS worse?

Eating more high-fiber foods may not improve constipation in people with irritable bowel syndrome (IBS). In fact, it could worsen IBS symptoms such as gas, bloating, and abdominal pain.

Some experts say FODMAPs, not fiber, are the problem. Foods rich in fiber also tend to contain lots of FODMAPs (fermentable oligo-di-and mono-saccharides and polyols), which can aggravate IBS.

While high-fiber foods may worsen IBS symptoms, certain fiber supplements may help. Look for supplements made with blond psyllium (Metamucil), partially hydrolyzed guar gum (Nestle's NutriSource Fiber), or calcium polycarbophil (FiberCon).

3 everyday foods that cure constipation

Is constipation a constant in your daily life? Have you tried laxatives, fiber supplements, and folk remedies with no relief? Good news — you can stop searching. Eating these three foods every day is a proven way to get regular.

Olive, not mineral, oil for less straining. Olive oil relieves constipation just as well as mineral oil. Plus, it's full of nutrients and healthy fats that fight inflammation. In one study, constipated people began taking about one teaspoon of either olive oil or mineral oil every day. After four weeks, roughly six out of 10 people were no longer constipated. Surprisingly, the olive oil group had the highest "cured" rate.

Both oils have the same effect – lubricating and softening stool to help it move through your intestines. But unlike olive oil, mineral oil has no nutritional value. Even worse, it's made from petroleum. Olive oil, especially the extra virgin type, is packed with nutrients and health benefits. People in this study saw relief with as little as one teaspoon of oil, but others who tried it on their own used two tablespoons safely and with success.

Kiwi can help you go. This little wonder fruit fits the bill for people suffering from constipation. Kiwi fiber can hold lots of water, which helps soften and bulk up stool so it's easier to pass. But that's just for starters. Kiwis also contain an enzyme that stimulates your colon, helping stool move through your bowels faster. The time it takes stool to move through your colon directly affects how often you have bowel movements. Slower movement equals fewer bowel movements and potentially more constipation.

Research suggests that eating two kiwis each day can treat both regular constipation and constipation linked to irritable bowel syndrome (IBS).

- After eating two kiwis a day for four weeks, half of people with constipation were having more bowel movements and needed laxatives less often.

- Eating two kiwis a day in another study began to ease IBS-related constipation after just one week. People had bowel movements more often, and stool passed through their colons faster.

The best thing about this fruit? It's natural. Unlike laxatives, eating a couple of kiwis doesn't seem to cause any side effects, unless you are allergic to them. The longer you eat them, the more they seem to improve constipation.

MAKE IT

Banish the bloat after big meals

This tiny, bloat-busting fruit can transform your belly. Not only can it treat constipation, it can also banish that bloated feeling you get after eating a big meal.

Kiwis contain an enzyme called actinidin that aids digestion, especially of gluten and heavy, protein-filled foods like red meat, chicken, dairy, and fish.

Kiwis help break down these proteins, moving the food through your stomach faster and easing that overly full feeling. They're particularly helpful for elderly adults who have trouble digesting cheese, fish, and eggs.

So enjoy a guilt-free slice of kiwi shortcake after your next meal. Peel a kiwifruit and slice it into thin, round pieces. Cut a piece of angel food cake in half, crosswise. Cover the bottom half with a layer of kiwi slices and a dollop of whipped cream. Place the upper half of the cake on top. Top this with another layer of kiwi slices and a spoonful of whipped cream.

Bread swap can get you moving again. Rethink your daily bread. Making your sandwiches out of whole-grain rye, not white wheat bread, could relieve constipation. Rye contains a type of fiber called arabinoxylan that gets fermented by bacteria in your colon. That fermentation produces compounds that cause your colon to contract, moving stool along faster and relieving constipation.

Fifty-one people with constipation tested the effects of swapping rye bread for white wheat in their diets. For three weeks, they either:

- ate six slices of whole-grain rye each day, for a total of 30 grams of fiber.

- ate eight slices of low-fiber white wheat bread, for 8.6 grams of fiber.

- or took laxatives.

The rye won, hands down, easing constipation even more than laxatives. If you try rye, add it to your diet gradually. Increasing your fiber too quickly can cause unpleasant gastrointestinal side effects. And drink more water as you bump up your fiber to help your body process the extra roughage.

Best treatment for diarrhea isn't what you think

Bananas, rice, applesauce, and toast (BRAT diet) may be the go-to treatment for an upset stomach. But experts say it isn't the best way to treat diarrhea.

Why BRAT is bad. Doctors once thought high-fiber foods would aggravate GI problems like diarrhea. BRAT contains little fiber, and it's so bland it's unlikely to offend an unhappy stomach. Plus, the foods in it act as binding agents, helping to stop diarrhea by causing constipation. And here's where the problems with BRAT begin.

■ Experts point out that if your diarrhea is caused by a viral or bacterial infection, as most cases are, you should let the diarrhea run its course. This is how your body clears out the toxins making you ill.

■ BRAT foods don't provide many nutrients, and you need good nutritional support to recover from any illness causing your diarrhea.

■ There's no scientific evidence that a BRAT diet helps you recover from diarrhea faster. In fact, there's no evidence backing the diet for any illness.

Gatorade won't work, either. Sports drinks, apple juice, chicken broth, and colas are other no-no's. They all draw more water out of your cells and into your bowels, which can worsen your diarrhea and dehydrate you more.

And none provides enough nutrients to nourish you through a bout of diarrhea. After all, sports drinks were designed to replace the water and electrolytes you lose from sweating, not the wide range of nutrients you lose during an illness.

The best way to survive a case of diarrhea. Here's what experts say you should eat and drink instead.

■ Sip on a product like Pedialyte, CeraLyte, Enfalyte, or Rehydralyte until you can handle solid food – maximum of 48 hours. These are specially formulated to replace the nutrients your body loses during vomiting and diarrhea.

■ If you don't have one of those products on hand, make your own version. Dissolve 1/2 teaspoon of salt, 1/2 teaspoon of baking soda, and 3 tablespoons of sugar in a quart of water.

- Switch to eating solid food as soon as you're able to keep it down. Getting back on solid food will shorten the illness, boost your nutrients, and help protect your intestines from long-lasting damage. Start with complex carbohydrates (such as whole-wheat bread), lean meat, yogurt, fruits, and vegetables.

- Consider taking a probiotic supplement if your diarrhea is the result of taking antibiotics or traveling in a developing country. To learn which probiotics can treat diarrhea, read *Heal 3 common GI complaints with probiotics* in this chapter.

Diarrhea usually goes away on its own in less than a week, but see your doctor if you have a fever, bloody diarrhea, 10 or more loose bowel movements a day, severe dehydration, a weak immune system, or recently spent time in the hospital. These could all signal a more serious illness.

2 ways to stop gut-wrenching attacks

A bout of diverticulitis can lay you out for days and even send you to the hospital. It's enough to make you swear off food. You don't have to dramatically change your diet to avoid another attack. Simply eating more fish, dairy foods, and vegetables could keep your gut from acting up again.

Get more vitamin D. Diverticula are usually painless and harmless, a condition called diverticulosis. But if they become inflamed or infected, it's called diverticulitis. Researchers discovered that people with diverticulosis and low levels of vitamin D are more likely to:

- end up in the hospital due to diverticulitis.

- need surgery to repair the damage from diverticulitis.

■ suffer future attacks of diverticulitis.

The less vitamin D you have in your bloodstream, the more severe your diverticulitis is likely to be, according to this study.

That's not a complete surprise. Plenty of research links low vitamin D levels to other diseases of the colon, including colon cancer and inflammatory bowel disease (IBD). Experts think this nutrient protects your gut, in part, by squashing inflammation, stopping the overgrowth of cells, and keeping the lining of your intestines healthy. It all adds up to natural protection for your colon.

So how much vitamin D do you need? People who had 30 or more nanograms per milliliter (ng/mL) in their blood were much less likely to develop diverticulitis than people with 25 ng/mL. Your doctor can check your vitamin D level with a simple blood test.

Your body makes most of its vitamin D from sunlight, but food and supplements play an important supporting role. People are more likely to end up hospitalized with diverticulitis in parts of the country that get less sun. Give your body extra vitamin D from these top sources.

■ fish, including salmon, trout, tuna, and halibut

■ mushrooms (maitake and morel)

■ milk fortified with vitamin D

Swap meat for vegetables. There's nothing like a thick steak, fresh off the grill – but put down the knife if you have diverticulosis. A 12-year British study found that vegetarians were about one-third less likely to land in the hospital or die from diverticulitis. Other research shows that eating large amounts of red meat makes men more likely to develop diverticular disease. Eating lots of meat may change the types of bacteria living in your gut.

This could weaken the wall of your colon, allowing more diverticula pouches to develop.

The natural fiber in vegetables may help, too. Fiber may not prevent diverticula from developing, but it may prevent them from becoming infected and rupturing, leading to diverticulitis and even death.

In this study, people who ate the most fiber (about 26 grams a day) were 41 percent less likely to end up in the hospital or to die from diverticular disease, compared to those eating the least fiber (less than 14 grams a day).

So here's the moral of the story – if you simply can't give up meat, eat more fiber-rich fruits, vegetables, and whole grains. Among meat-eaters, those who ate the most fiber were less likely to develop diverticular disease.

Taboo foods now safe to eat

You no longer need to swear off nuts, corn, or popcorn if you have diverticulosis. Doctors used to worry that these little pieces of food could get trapped inside diverticula pouches and cause inflammation and infection. Research suggests that doesn't happen.

Not only are nuts and popcorn safe to eat if you have diverticulosis, but people who eat them are also less likely — not more likely — to develop diverticulitis. Nuts are chock-full of nutrients, including inflammation-fighting fats, vitamin E, zinc, and magnesium. Popcorn, on the other hand, boasts magnesium and the anti-inflammatory antioxidant lutein.

Lactose intolerant? You can still enjoy dairy

Good news for people with lactose intolerance – you may not
need to give up ice cream or cheese after all. In fact, experts say
you need to eat dairy foods daily. Sound impossible? Not if you
know how to do it right.

Your body relies on an enzyme, lactase, to break down the lactose
sugar in dairy products. Some people don't have enough lactase
to finish the job. What's left of the sugar ferments in the gut,
causing gas, diarrhea, abdominal pain,
and bloating. People usually develop
lactose intolerance as children, but it
can develop in adults, too, bringing a
sad end to your love affair with
Häagen Dazs.

Lactose is often used
as a filler in capsules
and tablets. Ask your
pharmacist if your
prescription or over-
the-counter medicines
contain lactose.

But it shouldn't. Avoiding all dairy
poses real health hazards. Dairy
products are great sources of calcium,
vitamin D (if they are fortified),
protein, potassium, and other key nutrients. By completely cutting
them from your diet, you increase your risk for osteoporosis and
other chronic health problems.

You may not even be lactose intolerant. Many people who think
they are actually have irritable bowel syndrome (IBS) or inflammatory bowel disease (IBD). The symptoms are very similar. The
difference is, with lactose intolerance, they strike immediately
after eating dairy.

"The symptoms of lactose-intolerance are immediate," explains
Christopher Gardner, professor of medicine at Stanford
University. "If drinking milk makes you uncomfortable, you will
know within two hours. You either have cramps and diarrhea, or
you don't."

If your symptoms come and go, with dairy causing problems on some occasions but not others, you may have IBS or IBD, instead. Your doctor can settle the question with a simple breath test.

If you do have lactose intolerance, experts stress that you should still try to eat dairy every day, for your bones and overall health. Here's how.

- **Start by eliminating all lactose from your diet** to get your digestive tract back to normal. Think beyond the obvious dairy products. Manufacturers use milk byproducts in everything from frozen waffles and lunch meats to soup and salad dressings. Check ingredient lists for words like whey, nonfat milk solids, malted milk, margarine, sweet or sour cream, nougat, casein, caseinates, and curds.

- **Slowly introduce dairy back into your diet,** in small amounts each day. Try drinking 2 ounces of milk four times a day, instead of 8 ounces all in one sitting. And drink it with food. Studies show that lactose-intolerant people can usually handle at least one cup of milk if they drink it with a meal or snack. Don't eat dairy on an empty stomach.

- **Buy lactose-free or lactose-reduced milk.** It has the same nutrients as regular milk but is easier to digest, because manufacturers have added the lactase enzyme directly to it. You can purchase your own lactase enzymes, too. Look for liquids and tablets such as Lactaid or Dairy-Ease.

- **Can't stomach milk?** Try yogurt and hard cheeses like cheddar and Swiss, which have less lactose. Look for yogurt that contains live bacterial cultures. The bacteria help break down lactose.

If all else fails, switch to almond or soy . They're good sources of calcium. Plus, you can use them in place of cow's milk in cooking and baking.

I'm lactose intolerant. Will raw milk help?

Raw milk is no better than regular, pasteurized milk for people who are lactose intolerant. In a recent study, 16 people with lactose intolerance took turns drinking raw, pasteurized, and soy milk for eight days straight. They recorded their symptoms in a diary every day, and scientists gave them breath tests to measure how much undigested lactose was left to ferment in their guts.

Raw milk left as much lactose as pasteurized milk. More importantly, people's symptoms were just as bad after drinking raw milk.

"There was no hint of any benefit," says Christopher Gardner, nutrition expert and professor of medicine at Stanford University. Why? Even though raw milk contains good bacteria, it has the same amount of lactose as pasteurized milk. Only soy milk eased symptoms.

Heart disease

19 ways to clear your arteries

Carbs, proteins, or fats? On this heart-saving diet, you pick — really!

Google search the word "diet" and you'll get over 400 million hits. And if you're concerned about heart health, those hits will include popular plans like the DASH, Ornish, and Mediterranean diets. But one you may not be familiar with is the OmniHeart diet – a plan bursting with awesome, heart-healthy benefits.

Choose from three diet plans. The OmniHeart is actually the umbrella term for three diets, each emphasizing a different macronutrient. The OmniHeart carb diet is similar to DASH in that 58 percent of daily calories come from carbs, 15 percent from protein, and 27 percent from fats. Like the Mediterranean diet, the OmniHeart unsaturated fat diet emphasizes less carbs and more unsaturated fats like canola oil, olive oil, and olive oil spread. The OmniHeart protein diet serves up more protein and less carbs.

All three diets include balanced amounts of calcium, sodium, potassium, magnesium, and dietary fiber.

Battle heart disease and more. In a study titled the Optimal Macronutrient Intake Trial to Prevent Heart Disease, researchers tested OmniHeart against other popular diets. All three OmniHeart diets lowered blood pressure, total and "bad"

LDL cholesterol, and heart disease risk, say scientists. And the higher protein and higher unsaturated fat OmniHeart diets slashed blood triglycerides.

So basically, if you want to eat more carbs, you do so with the OmniHeart carb diet and still reap heart-healthy benefits. Same for the higher protein and higher unsaturated fat diets.

OmniHeart at a glance. Choosing one of the three diets is fairly simple. You just pick the macronutrient – be it carbs, fats, protein – you want to eat more of, and cut down on the other two macronutrients.

All three diets limit the amounts of sweets and sugar you can have. The OmniHeart carb diet allows for the most, but still keeps it under three teaspoons a day. A small cookie and a teaspoon of sugar for your coffee is plenty. Reading nutrition labels for added sugar is a must.

On the OmniHeart unsaturated fat diet, you get almost 10 teaspoons daily of oils and fats. You'll want to measure your oils when you sauté vegetables, use salad dressing, and spread mayo on your sandwich bread. The other two diets keep fats and oils to under five teaspoons daily.

Here's a look at the foods you can eat on the three OmniHeart plans and recommended amounts.

- Feast on fruits and veggies. You can munch on four to seven servings of vegetables and three to six servings of fruits each day. Typical serving sizes include a half cup of cooked vegetables, a cup of salad greens, or one small piece of fresh fruit.

- Graze on whole grains but limit to three to four servings. A serving is a half cup of cereal, a slice of bread, or a half cup of brown rice.

■ Ditch full-fat dairy. Reach for low-fat instead and stick to no more than two servings – a cup of milk or yogurt and 1 1/2 ounces cheese is perfect.

■ Eat protein – but not too much. Even with the higher protein diet, you're limited to 7.6 ounces daily. The other two only serve up to 4 ounces. These proteins can come from fish, poultry, or lean beef, and small servings of nuts, seeds, and legumes.

Calcium pills and heart attacks — should you worry?

You've heard calcium supplements can cause heart disease, but that's only one side of the story. A recent study found that women who took calcium supplements were no more likely to have heart disease than women who took none.

But supplement takers also protected themselves by eating fewer trans fats, smoking less, and exercising more than women who didn't take calcium supplements. So further research is needed to determine whether calcium pills are safe.

Meanwhile, get as much calcium as possible from foods and beverages. If you can't get enough from food, ask your doctor if you need a low-dose calcium supplement.

To make sure you absorb all the calcium you take in, limit calcium robbers like caffeine, alcohol, and salt. And check food and supplement labels to be certain you get plenty of vitamin D, which helps your body use calcium.

---

5 all-star superfoods your heart can't live without

Worried about your heart? These five all-star, artery-clearing foods will hit cholesterol right out of the ballpark. They are delicious, low-cost foods, and they'll keep your arteries slick as a whistle.

Guard your heart with succulent grapes. Snack on the one fruit that lowers blood pressure and cholesterol, protects you against diabetes and cancer, and can even cut your risk of dementia by over 75 percent – believe it or not. What's more, it's cheap and you can get it year-round at any grocery store.

Grapes, both the skins and fleshy insides, are loaded with natural plant chemicals. You've probably read about these powerful chemicals – flavonoids like resveratrol, quercetin, anthocyanins, and catechin. Of all of these, resveratrol does wonders for your heart. And it's in grape juice and wine, too.

Men with high blood pressure who drank Concord grape juice daily for eight weeks slashed their systolic and diastolic blood pressure numbers, shows a Korean study. Scientists say it's the flavonoids in grapes that make cells produce more nitric oxide and relax blood vessels. And that leads to lower blood pressure.

Plus, grape juice flavonoids lowered "bad" LDL cholesterol while raising "good" HDL cholesterol, found a study from Spain.

Serving tip – Here's a cool, refreshing way to eat grapes. Freeze them. Then pop them in your mouth frozen. Or use frozen grapes as edible "ice cubes" in grape juice.

Think of walnuts as the king of the nuts. Their nutritional benefits tower above peanuts, pecans, pistachios, macadamias – even almonds.

That's because walnuts contain the highest amount of polyphenols over all other nuts. And the polyphenols in walnuts protect your arteries, prevent blood clots, and reduce inflammation, suggest researchers.

Seven-a-day is all it takes to combat heart disease, cancer, gallstones, diabetes, and weight gain. Plus, walnuts along with almonds and hazelnuts boost your serotonin levels, a brain chemical. One ounce of these treats daily, which equals seven shelled walnuts, may trigger your serotonin to decrease your hunger, make you feel happier, and improve your heart health.

Serving tip – Spice up your walnuts with this simple recipe. Heat a tablespoon water, 2 teaspoons olive oil, and 1 tablespoon honey over medium heat. Add 2 cups walnut halves and coat. Then sprinkle 1 teaspoon sugar, 1/2 teaspoon salt, 1 teaspoon cumin, 1/2 teaspoon coriander, and 1/8 teaspoon cayenne pepper over the nuts, and stir. Brown slightly and place on a baking sheet to cool.

Slash bad fat with luscious olives. The olive branch is a symbol of peace all over the world. And when it comes to heart health, you can make peace with olives. That's because olives are brimming with oleic acid, a monounsaturated fat that battles heart disease. Experts say olives work by raising "good" HDL cholesterol and lowering "bad" LDL cholesterol. Olives also contain antioxidants that battle fats in your blood and guard against cell damage.

Just make sure you limit them. Olives are packed in brine, and the salt in that brine could raise your blood pressure.

Garlic presses aren't just for garlic. You can use them to mash pitted olives, too. And what can you do with mashed olives? Make tapenade, a heart-healthy spread made with several olive varieties, garlic, capers, lemon juice, olive oil, herbs, and spices. Serve on crusty French bread.

Serving tip – Serve up a savory tapas tray with a variety of olives, crusty whole-grain breads, and low-fat cheeses.

Why you should eat more peanut butter. You may think of peanut butter as a high-fat, high-calorie food. But this American staple is loaded with unsaturated fatty acids and other natural compounds that battle heart disease.

People who ate peanut butter lowered their risk of heart disease, shows the famed Nurses' Health Study. A report within the same study shows women with type 2 diabetes also lowered their risk of heart disease by eating peanut butter. Peanut butter helps by lowering cholesterol and slashing the inflammation that promotes heart disease.

Look for all-natural peanut butter made with 100-percent peanuts and no hydrogenated oils. And stick with only two tablespoons per serving.

Serving tip – How do you reach that last bit of peanut butter at the bottom of the jar? By heating it up. Take the lid off and warm up the glass jar – not plastic – in the microwave on the defrost setting for a few seconds. Then pour over whole-grain pancakes or low-fat yogurt.

Treat your heart to the awesome perks of chickpeas. It's mind-boggling how one humble legume can do so much for your heart. But that's what chickpeas do – they fend off heart disease and serious conditions that trigger heart disease like obesity and type 2 diabetes.

People who eat chickpeas have lower total cholesterol and LDL cholesterol, research shows. In fact, adults who ate chickpeas and hummus were 53 percent less likely to be obese and 43 percent less likely to be over-weight. They also had a 48 percent lower risk of gaining weight and were 51 percent less likely to have high blood sugar levels, say experts.

> Rinse beans right in their can. Over a sink, hold the can upside down and make a few holes on the bottom with a punch can opener, or church key. Turn the can over and completely open the top with a hand-held can opener. Liquid will pour out of the holes at the bottom as you rinse your beans.

A small Iranian study shows overweight people with type 2 diabetes lowered cardiovascular risk factors including fasting blood sugar, fasting insulin, triglycerides, and "bad" LDL cholesterol by substituting two servings of red meat with legumes including chickpeas three days a week. A half-cup of legumes was considered one serving of meat.

Experts credit the natural substances in chickpeas like soluble fiber, vegetable protein, and antioxidants called isoflavones.

Serving tip – Can't get enough hummus? Try making your own. Then fill celery sticks and small, hollowed-out bell peppers with hummus, and serve at your next party. Check out the following recipe and more serving tips.

MAKE IT

Heart-healthy hummus you can't resist

Here's a hummus recipe you and your family will fall in love with. It's simple to make and bursting with flavor and heart-healthy ingredients.

- 1 teaspoon olive oil
- 1 tablespoon lemon juice
- 1/4 cup plain, low-fat yogurt
- 1/4 teaspoon salt
- 1/4 teaspoon paprika
- 1/8 teaspoon pepper
- 3 garlic cloves
- 1 19-ounce can chickpeas, drained and rinsed

Blend all the ingredients in a food processor until smooth. Add more yogurt as needed to reach the consistency you want. Top with chopped nuts, garlic, or parsley. Serve chilled as a dip with sliced bell peppers and zucchini. Or chill, then use as a spread on bagels, whole-grain pita bread, or in place of mayo on a sandwich.

One more reason to cut back on red meat

Beans or beef? Pork or peanut butter? Every day you make decisions on where to get your protein. The latest news about iron might make your decision easier.

You get iron from both meat and plant sources, but your body handles them differently. It's better able to control the absorption from plant or nonheme iron. But iron from red meat, aka heme iron, is another story. Your body absorbs heme iron quicker, which then oxidizes your harmful LDL cholesterol, found an Indiana University study. Once oxidized, LDL can cause inflammation in your arteries and raise your risk for hardening of the arteries, stroke, and heart attack.

Some experts say cutting back on red meat to less than half a serving a day could extend your life. Healthy substitutions include fish, chicken, and turkey, plus plant sources like nuts, beans, low-fat dairy, and whole grains.

Fish that heal and fish that flop

There are plenty of fish in the sea. Some are health-boosting superstars. And some should never be eaten, yet they're sold every day at grocery stores, fish markets, and restaurants.

Sardines, for instance, are one delicious, nutrition-packed food you're probably not eating. They are loaded with memory-saving vitamin D, heart-healing omega-3, fatigue-fighting CoQ10, and more.

A lifetime of eating fish brimming with omega-3 fatty acids like sardines protects men from clogged arteries, shows a Japanese study. The study found the levels of omega-3 are twice as high in Japanese men than in American or Japanese-American men. That could explain why the death rate from heart disease in Japan is surprisingly low.

Eating more fish is a great idea, but you've probably heard about the dangers of mercury – a toxic chemical found in fish and shellfish. But you also know eating fatty, oily fish can help you live a healthier life thanks to their omega-3 fatty acids.

Experts say it's better to eat seafood and reap the health benefits than to skip it altogether. So how do you do that without getting too much mercury? Only eat up to 12-ounces weekly of low-mercury fish, and limit or avoid fish high in mercury.

Consult this easy-to-read chart and reel in the safest, most beneficial catch. Two thumbs up means it's safe to eat. One thumb means it contains moderate amounts of mercury. Seriously limit or avoid fish in the thumbs down column.

Easy guide to fish you should and shouldn't eat		
Two thumbs up	One thumb up*	Thumbs down
Catfish	Cod, Alaskan	Chilean Seabass**
Crab, domestic	Halibut, Atlantic	Grouper**
Herring	Halibut, Pacific	Mackerel (Spanish, Gulf)**
Salmon, Alaskan or canned	Lobster	Marlin
Sardines	Mahi Mahi	Orange Roughy
Scallops	Perch, freshwater	Shark
Shrimp	Sablefish	Swordfish
Tilapia	Snapper	Tuna, canned albacore**
Trout, freshwater	Tuna, canned chunk light	Tuna, Yellowfin**

* Moderate amounts of mercury. Only eat six servings or less per month.
** You can eat three servings or less of these per month. Otherwise, avoid fish in the thumbs down column.

Eggs — the latest wonder food?

Do you have a love/hate relationship with eggs? You love to eat them, but hate that they're loaded with cholesterol. But there's good news. Research now shows they can help raise "good" HDL cholesterol levels, lower blood pressure, plus keep your eyesight sharp, and build up weak bones.

People with normal HDL levels who went on a carb-restricted diet raised their good cholesterol by eating three whole eggs a day, found a small study out of the University of Connecticut. Egg yolks contain phospholipids, a substance that raises your good cholesterol, say scientists.

Additionally, egg whites contain a peptide that lowers blood pressure as much as a low dose of Captopril, a high blood pressure drug, say Clemson University researchers. Peptides are one of the building blocks of protein. And this particular peptide, RVPSL, inhibits angiotensin-converting-enzyme and relaxes your blood vessels, much like the popular ACE-inhibitor prescriptions on the market.

Eating up to one egg a day did not raise the risk of heart disease or hemorrhagic stroke, found a team of researchers who evaluated 17 reports with over 3 million study participants.

But if you have diabetes, be cautious. Scientists also found eating more eggs raised heart disease risk among people with diabetes.

If you don't have diabetes, you can ignore eggs' undeserved bad reputation, and start making these healthy egg recipes.

- ■ Savor egg-guac salad. Combine six cooled and chopped hard-boiled eggs with 4 to 6 tablespoons of your favorite guacamole. Serve over whole-grain toast. Serves 3.

- ■ Try Tex-Mex eggs. Scramble one to two eggs and top with a tablespoon salsa and a tablespoon guacamole. Serve with baked tortilla chips. Serves 1.

■ Go Greek for a great mayo substitute. Mix eight chopped eggs with a half cup 2-percent plain Greek yogurt. A good brand to use is Fage due to its creamy texture and mild taste. Add 1 tablespoon Dijon mustard, 1 teaspoon paprika, 1 tablespoon dill relish, and a dash of salt and pepper. Serve over salad greens with whole-grain crackers. Serves 4.

Jump-start your morning with this juice

Women, take note. Starting your day with a tangy glass of grapefruit juice is great for your heart.

Healthy, postmenopausal women between 50 and 65 years of age who drank two cups of grapefruit juice daily for six months boosted blood vessel flexibility, says a team of French scientists. This flexibility allows blood to flow more freely to the heart.

Researchers say the powerful, heart-healthy substances found in citrus called flavanones are the heroes. Grapefruit juice is especially high in the flavanone naringenin. When study participants drank a beverage without flavanones, their blood vessels showed little to no improvement.

There's a drawback. If you take medication for heart disease, talk with your doctor before drinking grapefruit juice. It can interfere with drugs used to treat high cholesterol and high blood pressure.

Miracle mineral fights deadly disorder

It's called metabolic syndrome, and it's not something you ever want to get. Because if you have it, you've set yourself up for heart disease, diabetes, and stroke.

To be diagnosed with metabolic syndrome, you must have three or more of these conditions – high blood pressure, high blood sugar, low HDL cholesterol and high LDL cholesterol, too much belly fat, and a high level of triglycerides in your bloodstream. But even if you only have one of these conditions, you're already at a higher risk of developing metabolic syndrome.

Experts say this serious condition stems from being overweight or obese and living a sedentary lifestyle. Plus, it's closely linked to insulin resistance, a condition which causes your blood sugar levels to rise.

The best way to fight the syndrome that leads to heart disease and diabetes is to lose weight, get active, and watch what you eat. Foods high in magnesium can help.

Young adults who ate magnesium-rich food or took magnesium supplements were less likely to develop metabolic syndrome than those who consumed less magnesium, found a study published in the medical journal *Circulation*. Another study out of Boston found men and women age 60 who ate the most magnesium-rich foods slashed their risk of metabolic syndrome over those who ate the least amount.

Experts say magnesium works by lowering blood pressure, blood fats, and blood sugar. The mighty mineral also fends off insulin resistance and battles the bulge around your belly.

You can get more magnesium simply by eating foods like bananas, raisins, and almonds. Plus, if you put them all together, you get a yummy treat your heart can't live without. Just slice a banana in half lengthwise. Spread with a little all-natural almond butter and sprinkle with raisins.

GROW IT

Grow good-for-your-heart super sprouts

If you think broccoli is good for you, try broccoli sprouts — broccoli seeds that have been germinated and sprouted over three to five days.

People who ate about 3.5 ounces of broccoli sprouts daily for just one week had lower "bad" LDL cholesterol, while actually boosting "good" HDL cholesterol, found a small Japanese study.

You can find broccoli sprouts in some health food stores, but growing them is simple and fun.

Soak a handful of seeds overnight in room temperature water. Place a thin layer of potting soil in a shallow pan and moisten with a small amount of water. Sprinkle your seeds over the soil, then cover with another thin layer of soil. Cover with plastic wrap and poke a few holes in the plastic for air to circulate.

Keep away from direct sunlight in a warm, dry area. You should see sprouts in about two days. They're ready to eat in three to five days. Grab a bunch and toss in a salad, garnish a bowl of soup, or add to your favorite sandwich.

3 'berry' delicious treats your heart will love

Which fruit has the highest level of antioxidants – those tumor and blood clot fighters? Açaí berries, the exotic little fruit from the Amazon rainforest, popularized in the U.S. on "Oprah."

Unfortunately, this exotic super berry is hard to find in the produce section of your local supermarket, but check the freezer section. Grocers often stock frozen fruit pulp there, perfect for smoothies and cold desserts. Or you could look for açaí powder. The pulp and powder have the highest antioxidant levels over fresh berries, experts say.

And it's not just açaí berries that are loaded with antioxidants. Black raspberries have the second highest amount of antioxidants, and blueberries, blackberries, raspberries, and strawberries are up there, too.

Women who ate blueberries and strawberries at least three times a week lowered their chances of suffering a heart attack, found a study published in the medical journal *Circulation*. The study included over 93,000 women ages 25 to 42. Those who ate the most blueberries and strawberries slashed their heart attack risk by 32 percent. Scientists say it's the anthocyanins, powerful antioxidants that chop bad cholesterol and hike good cholesterol.

Here are a few ways you can enjoy these sweet and tart superfoods.

■ Açaí bowls – Mix frozen açaí fruit pulp in a blender with a banana and pineapple juice. Pour into a bowl. Top with your favorite combination of granola, sliced almonds, strawberries, blueberries, plain yogurt, and spices like nutmeg or cinnamon.

■ Berry sauce – Put 2/3 cup frozen blueberries and 2/3 cup frozen blackberries in a saucepan. Add 1/2 cup water, 3 tablespoons sugar, and 2 tablespoons lemon juice. Bring to a boil, reduce heat, and simmer until the sauce thickens, about 10 minutes. Stir in a pat of butter. Pour your warm berry sauce over pancakes or layer in a yogurt parfait.

■ Black raspberry vinaigrette – Purée 3/4 cup black raspberries. Set aside. Whisk together 3 tablespoons lemon juice, 3 tablespoons red wine vinegar, 1 1/2 tablespoons diced scallions, 1 1/2 teaspoons Dijon mustard, and salt and pepper to taste. Stir in 3/4 cup olive oil until it's well blended. Mix in black raspberries.

Help your heart keep its beat with homemade treat

Wish you could eat something that scrubs the plaque right out of your arteries? You can! Homemade salsa will do the trick. That's because the tomatoes in salsa are rich in lycopene, a powerful antioxidant that's great for your heart and arteries.

Heart-healthy lycopene keeps your arteries clear. Lycopene slashed the risk of both cardiovascular disease and coronary heart disease, say Tufts University scientists who followed over 5,000 people for 10 years. Both diseases have one thing in common — plaque buildup in the arteries that can lead to heart attacks, high blood pressure, and stroke.

Scientists think lycopene blocks the overproduction of harmful molecules called reactive oxygen species. Plus, it reduces inflammation and clotting, lowers total and dangerous LDL cholesterol, and reduces blood pressure.

Eating tomatoes and tomato-based products also lowered the risk of ischemic stroke, the result of a blocked artery in the brain, by 59 percent and stroke overall by 55 percent, shows a study published in the medical journal *Neurology*. The study followed over 1,000 Finnish men ages 46-65 years for 12 years. The men with the most lycopene concentrations in their blood faired best.

> Cutting up tomatoes can leave a juicy mess on your kitchen counters. So the next time you chop tomatoes, place your cutting board inside a cookie sheet. The cookie sheet will collect the excess juices.

Cooked tomatoes boost absorption. So what's the best way to get lycopene, this amazing antioxidant that gives tomatoes their beautiful red color? You may be surprised to learn canned, cooked, juiced, and puréed tomatoes contain more lycopene than fresh off the vine, experts say. These methods release lycopene from plant cell walls and makes it more available to your body.

For even greater absorption, enjoy your tomatoes with a healthy fat like olive oil. People who drank tomato juice with olive oil absorbed more lycopene than those who drank straight tomato juice, found Spanish researchers. And their unsafe LDL cholesterol plummeted six hours after having their oil and tomato juice cocktail. Scientists say it's because lycopene is fat soluble and needs a source of fat to be better absorbed.

Savory salsa in a snap. Here's a savory salsa recipe using canned tomatoes and olive oil – the dynamic duo guaranteed to boost your lycopene and keep your heart healthy and strong.

- 2 10-ounce cans diced tomatoes with green chilies
- 1 28-ounce can whole tomatoes with juice
- 1 cup chopped onion
- 6 cloves garlic, minced
- 2 to 3 chopped jalapeños
- 1/2 lime, juiced
- 1/4 teaspoon salt
- 1/4 teaspoon cumin
- 1/2 cup fresh cilantro (optional)
- 2 to 3 tablespoons olive oil

Purée whole tomatoes in a food processor. Sauté onion, garlic, and jalapeños in olive oil for a few minutes. Add the rest of your ingredients and bring to a boil. Simmer for at least 30 minutes. Serve warm. Refrigerate leftovers for up to two days or freeze.

3 super seeds with 'heart'y benefits

You've heard good things come in small packages. And such is the case with seeds, tiny nutritional powerhouses that reduce your risk of heart disease, lower harmful cholesterol and high blood pressure, and keep your arteries healthy. Here are the three seeds you should be eating.

Fabulous flaxseeds fight for your heart health. King Charlemagne was on to something when he ordered all his subjects to eat the seeds of the flax plant. The wise king knew they were loaded with powerful healers. These healers are fiber, healthy fats, and lignans.

Flaxseeds contain tons of soluble fiber, which guards against high blood pressure and cuts down on harmful LDL cholesterol, experts say. Soluble fiber works by grabbing bile acids and removing them from your body. Bile acids, which help with digestion, are made of cholesterol.

Flaxseeds also contain alpha-linolenic acid (ALA), an omega-3 fatty acid that keeps your arteries slick and your blood flowing smoothly. In fact, omega-3 blocks blood clots from forming, lowers cholesterol and triglycerides, slashes blood pressure, and reduces stroke risk.

Lignans are special plant chemicals that battle cholesterol. People who ate flaxseed bars with a high amount of lignans lowered their total cholesterol by 12 percent and their harmful LDL cholesterol by 15 percent over those who ate flaxseed bars with less lignans, found a small study out of the University of California.

For optimal nutrition, grind the seeds and sprinkle over cereal or yogurt. If you bake your own bread or muffins, mix them into your dough.

Sunflower seeds shut out heart disease. Your friends in Kansas have something to smile about. Known as the Sunflower State, Kansas is one of the top producers of sunflower seeds in the country.

And those seeds are loaded with vitamin E, a powerful antioxidant that stops LDL cholesterol before it forms artery-clogging plaque, say scientists. Vitamin E has other anti-clogging properties, so it makes it easier for your blood pressure to stay down and your heart to pump blood. Plus, it guards against hardening of the arteries, stroke, and heart attack.

What's more, sunflower seeds serve up a healthy dose of polyunsaturated fat (PUFA), the good fats your body needs for maximum health. These PUFAs reduce triglycerides, lower blood pressure, and curtail the buildup of plaque in your arteries.

A great way to eat sunflower seeds is on a salad. Or just grab a handful to nosh on.

Chia seeds chop bad cholesterol. Remember those chia pets you grew as a kid? Bet you didn't know the seeds you used are brimming with powerful heart healers.

Like flaxseeds, chia seeds contain fiber and the healthy fat ALA, which lowers triglycerides and raises good HDL cholesterol.

And if you grind the seeds to make flour, you can battle high blood pressure. People with high blood pressure who ate a little over two tablespoons of chia flour daily for 12 weeks lowered their blood pressure, found Brazilian researchers.

Mix about 1/3 cup chia seeds with two cups of water to make a gel you can add to juices and smoothies. Or use chia flour to bake your favorite homemade breads.

The FDA decision that may save your life

Think twice before you reach for another jelly donut. It's loaded with trans fats – fats that put you at higher risk for heart disease. But a new ruling from the Food and Drug Administration (FDA) is about to change the processed food industry. And it may save your life.

The FDA is banning trans fats from the American diet. Food manufacturers have been adding trans fats to processed foods since the 1950s to boost flavor and increase shelf life. Now the FDA is giving manufacturers until 2018 to phase them out.

It's the partially hydrogenated oils (PHO), the primary source of trans fats, that are no longer deemed "generally recognized as safe" or GRAS, say experts. Studies show these dangerous fats hike your harmful LDL cholesterol and triglycerides, increase the plaque buildup in your arteries, and raise your risk of heart disease.

Harvard researchers believe eliminating trans fats from the American diet could prevent up to one in five heart attacks. That's a quarter of a million less heart attacks and related deaths in the U.S. annually.

Trans fats also occur naturally in meat and dairy foods and in some oils after the manufacturing process, but they're not as much of a health concern.

Until they're completely off the market, read nutrition labels and look for the words "trans fats" and "partially hydrogenated oils" on the following:

- Baked goods

- Coffee creamers

- Crackers, cookies, and cakes

- Frozen pies

- Stick margarines

- Snack foods, including some microwave popcorn

■ Ready-made frostings

■ Refrigerated dough products like biscuits and
cinnamon rolls

Coconut oil — hype or heart-healthy?

Coconut oil is at the top of the food trends list these days. So what's all the fuss about? Here's what you need to know.

Animal studies show virgin coconut oil lowers damaging LDL cholesterol and triglycerides and boosts good HDL cholesterol. Scientists credit coconut oil's natural substances like vitamin E, polyphenols, phytosterols, and lauric acid for its pro-heart benefits.

But experts also warn coconut oil is a whopping 90 percent saturated fat. In comparison, butter is 64 percent and lard 40 percent saturated fat. Olive oil, on the other hand, is mostly unsaturated fat and lowers your bad cholesterol while raising your good cholesterol.

So don't jump on the coconut oil bandwagon. Use it sparingly and for specialty dishes, like Thai food. Otherwise, opt for oils with unsaturated fats like olive and safflower.

High blood pressure

Kitchen cures to the rescue

Make a mad DASH toward this eating plan

Want to slash your blood pressure without drugs? Look no further than DASH – the eating plan proven to lower blood pressure. And you may lose a few pounds to boot!

DASH stands for Dietary Approaches to Stop Hypertension. Researchers with the National Institutes of Health developed the eating plan to help prevent high blood pressure or lower it if it's already too high.

The plan focuses on eating less saturated fat, total fat, and cholesterol and smaller amounts of red meat and sugary drinks. But here's what you get – more fruits, vegetables, whole grains, and low-fat dairy, plus nuts, fish, and poultry. You do get some sweets, just not as many as you may be eating right now.

Plus, you have to eat less salt, which is loaded with sodium, a well-known blood pressure booster. In fact, getting less sodium alone can help lower your blood pressure, but combining it with the DASH plan is even better, say experts.

The DASH diet lowered systolic blood pressure by 7 points in people without high blood pressure and by 11.5 points in people with high blood pressure, shows a study published in the *New England Journal of Medicine*. Systolic blood pressure is the higher number, the one that measures the pressure of blood pushing through your arteries.

And the DASH diet, which promotes more plant protein from nuts, seeds, and legumes, as well as fruits and vegetables, lowers blood pressure and your risk of developing it, found a study published in the *Journal of Human Hypertension*.

Researchers think plant protein works by helping your body absorb more nutrients and less sodium, while relaxing and widening your blood vessels.

Your blood pressure may rise slowly as you age. But here's some great news – scientists say following the DASH diet and eating less sodium will safeguard you in the long haul, not only from a slow rise in blood pressure, but from a higher risk of heart-related death.

Is the DASH plan right for you? Only you and your doctor can decide. But here's an overview of this flexible and balanced eating plan.

- Help yourself to whole grains – they have a whole lotta love for your heart. That's because they're loaded with fiber, protein, calcium, magnesium, potassium, folate, and zinc – nutrients with the power to lower your blood pressure.

- Pile on the veggies. You already know they're good for you. But did you know they serve up 15 percent of the calcium, magnesium, and potassium you need – in addition to fiber, folate, and vitamins A, C, and E? All good for healthy blood pressure – and a healthy body.

- Say yes to fresh fruits. They're rich in potassium, the No. 1 mineral for controlling blood pressure, as well as cholesterol-fighting fiber.

- Discover delicious low-fat dairy. Scientists aren't sure how it works, but they think it's the protein, calcium, magnesium, and potassium in milk, yogurts, and cheeses.

- Don't make meat your main dish. Think of it as a small part of your meal. Eat red meat sparingly, and reach for fish and poultry instead. They're lower in fat, and fish is rich in omega-3 fatty acids, which may help regulate blood pressure.

- Go nuts a few times a week. Nuts, seeds, and even legumes are great sources of protein, magnesium, potassium, and fiber.

- Treat yourself to sweets – but don't go overboard. This will help you save calories for more nutritious foods.

Here's a handy guide for you if your doctor gives you the OK to try the DASH diet. For more details, including portion sizes, go to the website *www.nhlbi.nih.gov*, and search on DASH.

The DASH Eating Plan

The DASH eating plan shown below is based on 2,000 calories a day. The number of daily servings in a food group may vary from those listed, depending upon your caloric needs.

Whole-Grains	**7-8** servings
Vegetables	**4-5** servings
Fruits	**4-5** servings
Low-fat or fat-free dairy foods	**2-3** servings
Lean meats, poultry, and fish	**2** or fewer servings
Nuts, seeds, and dry beans	**4-5** servings per week
Fats and oils	**2-3** servings
Sweets	**5** servings per week

3 superheroes battle high blood pressure

What do breakfast cereals, turnip greens, and cauliflower have in common? Magnesium, a magnificent mineral that puts the brakes on high blood pressure.

You can strengthen your heart muscles – not with exercise, but with this heart-stabilizing nutrient. Magnesium decreases your risk of developing high blood pressure, suggests a four-year study of 30,000 men published in the medical journal *Circulation*. This mineral relaxes blood vessels and regulates two other minerals that affect blood pressure, sodium and potassium, by keeping sodium levels down and potassium levels up.

There's a Bible food that lowers blood pressure — figs! They're chock-full of potassium, and they're the main ingredient in Fig Newtons — a cookie with a fruit filling that helps lower cholesterol, blood pressure, and blood sugar, reduces your stroke risk, and can even help you stay slim. You'll find 95 milligrams of potassium in two cookies.

Magnesium is especially important for people over age 70. That's because senior adults don't eat as many magnesium-rich foods. It's also harder for seniors to absorb magnesium and easier to excrete it in urine.

Magnesium isn't the only nutrient that slashes your risk of having high blood pressure. Researchers say potassium and fiber also play major roles.

Potassium boosts blood flow by relaxing blood vessels, and maintains healthy sodium levels by flushing excess out in your urine.

Fiber lowers high blood pressure risk by cleaning up cholesterol buildup in your blood vessels and flushing it out of your body.

Put them all together and it's like having a trio of superheroes fighting for your heart health.

To get all three nutrients working for you, check out this list of super foods.

■ Check your cereal labels. Many fiber cereals come jam-packed with fiber, magnesium, and potassium. And if you add bananas to your bowl, you get an extra shot of all three.

■ Go green. Reach for turnip greens, mustard greens, or Swiss chard for a whopping dose of fiber, magnesium, and potassium.

■ Roast these veggies. Mix cauliflower florets with artichoke hearts. Not only will you get your fill of fiber, magnesium, and potassium, these two super-healthy vegetables taste great together. Toss them in olive oil and spices, and roast in a 375-degree oven for about 35 minutes. Stir halfway through cooking time.

■ "Berry" powerful blood pressure busters. As if blackberries and raspberries don't have enough powerful nutrients like antioxidants, they're also rich in fiber, magnesium, and potassium. Pick them fresh or buy frozen and add them to your salads and smoothies.

■ Super sauerkraut to the rescue. This tangy-tasting treat comes loaded with probiotics and the terrific trio of fiber, magnesium, and potassium. And making your own fresh kraut is even better for you and easier than you think. Check out *Fun fermented foods are good for your waistline* in the *Weight control* chapter.

7 scrumptious (and healthy) berry recipes you've never tried

You read about berries and antioxidants all the time – how they fight cancer and boost your brain cells. Add battling blood pressure to the list. Fresh or frozen, these sweet little superfoods fight for your heart's health.

People who ate the most blueberries and strawberries over a 14-year period slashed their risk of high blood pressure by 8 percent, found a study published in the *American Journal of Clinical Nutrition*. The findings were actually taken from three different studies of over 150,000 men and women.

Anthocyanins and flavonoids, powerful antioxidants in blueberries and strawberries, boost blood flow, relax blood vessels, and promote heart health. The same holds true for cranberries, blackcurrants, raspberries, and blackberries.

You may already toss berries into your smoothies or top your oatmeal and cereals with them. Lucky for you, these aren't the only ways to enjoy berries. Check out these quick and healthy recipes.

- Toss in blueberries the next time you make a chicken wrap. They will pump up the flavor and the health benefits. Talk about easy, tasty, and healthy.

- Make a strawberry, cucumber, watermelon salad. Simply cut up your fruit, season with lime juice, and top with fresh mint. Refreshing!

- Enjoy this yogurt and blackberry dessert. Simmer 1 1/2 cups frozen blackberries with 1/2 cup water, 1/8 cup sugar, and 2 tablespoons lemon juice. Bring to a boil then reduce the heat for 10 minutes. Stir in a tablespoon of butter. Spoon 1/2 cup plain yogurt into four bowls. Top each serving with your blackberry sauce.

- Try this tangy cranberry sauce. Combine 1/2 cup lemon or orange marmalade with 2 tablespoons grated orange rind, and set aside. Bring a cup of orange juice and 1/4 cup sugar to a boil, then add cranberries. Simmer until the cranberries pop. Remove from heat and stir in marmalade mixture. Cover and chill. Spread on your turkey sandwich.

■ Give raspberries a Mexican twist. Finely dice your berries and mix them into your favorite salsa. Spoon onto your fish tacos.

■ Refresh yourself with berry-sicles. Thread fresh berries onto wooden skewers, 3-inches deep. Spread a thick layer of yogurt on a plate and twirl your berry skewers until they're coated. Place on a cookie sheet covered with waxed paper and put your berry-sicles in the freezer. Enjoy in about 30 minutes.

■ Pop these refreshing berry-yogurt cubes in your mouth. Fill an ice cube tray with dollops of your favorite low-fat yogurt. Drop in some berries. Freeze. Depending on the size of your cubes, you may want to insert a toothpick or popsicle stick.

COOK IT

The surprising soup that's good for your heart

Chicken soup may be good for your soul, but it's gazpacho that's good for high blood pressure. The savory, chilled soup packs in garlic, tomatoes, cucumbers, olive oil, and bell peppers — all brimming with rich nutrients like carotenes, vitamin C, and polyphenols that battle high blood pressure, say researchers in Spain.

To make gazpacho, combine 12-ounces diced, fresh tomatoes with a roughly chopped red bell pepper, cucumber, small sweet onion, and garlic clove in a bowl. Pour in 2 to 2 1/2 cups low-sodium tomato juice, 2 tablespoons sherry vinegar, a dash of hot sauce. Run through a food processor until vegetables are finely chopped and slowly add 1/4 cup olive oil.

Chill in the fridge for four hours. Makes four to six servings.

3 BP-busting juices you didn't know you needed

Drinking red wine or grape juice can be good for your heart, but drinking these three juices could be even better.

You can't beat beet juice. Think of beets as the veggie that lowers blood pressure just like pills. That's because beets contain nitrates, a substance used in heart medications to boost blood flow.

People ages 18 to 85 who drank 8 1/2 ounces of beet juice daily for four weeks dropped their systolic blood pressure by 8 points and diastolic by 4 points, say researchers who conducted a small study in London.

Some study participants were struggling to reach their target blood pressure while on medication. Others had been diagnosed with high blood pressure, but had not yet started taking medication. Beet juice slashed their blood pressure, but two weeks after they stopped drinking it, their blood pressure soared back up.

Researchers say it's the nitrates in beets that should take credit. They convert to nitric oxide in your body, and that relaxes and dilates your blood vessels.

To give beet juice – also called beetroot juice – a try, check the health food section of your favorite supermarket or whole foods shop.

Beet juice may take some getting used to. Start with a small amount and add it to smoothies, other juices, or mix with yogurt.

Scientists say they don't know the long-term effects of drinking beet juice regularly. And they also caution to never stop taking your blood pressure medication without talking with your doctor.

Crank up a healthy heart with cranberry juice. It's sweet. It's tart. And it's the juice with the amazing antioxidants that will drop your blood pressure.

People with normal blood pressure who drank low-cal cranberry juice dropped their blood pressure several points over eight weeks, found a study published in the *Journal of Nutrition.* Cranberry juice also improved several heart disease risk factors like blood sugar, triglycerides, and insulin resistance.

Cranberries are loaded with antioxidants called polyphenols, which include quercetin, anthocyanins, and procyanidins. They all boost heart and blood vessel health – and lower blood pressure.

Could eating out be sabotaging your health?

Eating out regularly may be a risk factor for high blood pressure. People between the ages of 18 and 40 who ate out more than 12 meals a week had slightly raised blood pressure or full-blown high blood pressure, found researchers in Singapore.

If you're a guy, your chances are even higher. Forty-nine percent of the men in the study were more likely to have slightly elevated blood pressure versus only 9 percent of the women.

And scientists made a surprising discovery throughout the study — eating out even one extra meal a week hiked the risk of blood pressure that's slightly higher by 6 percent. Not surprisingly, many people tend to choose foods higher in calories, saturated fat, and salt when they eat out.

The moral of the story? Eat at home more often, where you have control of your salt, fat, and calories.

Power down with pomegranate juice. To the ancient Persians, the pomegranate represented strength. They must have been onto something, because today researchers know the powerful pomegranate serves up a delicious way to strengthen your heart.

People undergoing dialysis lowered their systolic blood pressure by drinking 3 ounces of pomegranate juice three times a week for a year, shows a study in *Nutrition Journal*. People with high systolic blood pressure showed an even greater improvement.

It's because pomegranate juice is rich in polyphenols, which calm inflammation and help your blood vessels dilate and constrict. This helps regulate blood flow. So go ahead, pour yourself a glass. Your heart will thank you!

Should you 'kick the can' to protect your heart?

There's something lurking in your soda can, and it may not be good for your heart. It's called bisphenol A (BPA), a chemical used to line the insides of food and drink cans and glass bottles.

People over age 60 who drank two canned drinks raised their systolic blood pressure by 4.5 points two hours later, found a small study published in the journal *Hypertension*.

BPA acts like the hormone estrogen in your body. When BPA comes in contact with cells that are sensitive to estrogen in your heart and blood vessels, your blood pressure goes up, some experts say.

To cut down your BPA exposure, eat fresh and frozen foods and look for BPA-free containers.

The dangerous drink in your fridge

Tempted to reach for an energy drink? Go ahead — but only if you want your blood pressure to spike. These popular drinks in their cute little 8.3-ounce cans serve up way more sugar and caffeine than your average cola.

Healthy individuals boosted their systolic blood pressure by 10 points and raised their heart rate by five to seven beats per minute after drinking energy drinks, found a small study out of Henry Ford Hospital in Detroit.

And it's not just the sugar and caffeine. Most of these drinks contain taurine, an amino acid that affects your heart and blood pressure.

While healthy people may get away with drinking an occasional energy drink, people with high blood pressure or heart disease should "can" them completely, experts say. Not only can they affect your heart, they may keep your blood pressure medications from doing their job.

Is red wine really good for your heart?

Yes – and no. Red wine is loaded with antioxidants that fend off heart disease, but be wary of alcohol. It won't help lower your blood pressure, Spanish researchers discovered – but drinking too much might make it higher.

What's a wine-lover to do? Try nonalcoholic red wine. Men ages 55 to 75 with an increased heart disease risk who drank about 9 ounces of alcohol-free wine daily for four weeks slashed their blood pressure, found a small study out of Spain. The drop in blood pressure triggered a 14 to 20 percent lower risk of stroke and heart disease.

Nonalcoholic wine is fermented grape juice that goes through an alcohol-removal process. What's left is an alcohol-free beverage chock-full of polyphenols.

It's these polyphenols that lower blood pressure by boosting nitric oxide in your blood vessels, which causes them to relax and dilate. Experts say the alcohol in regular wine may offset the polyphenols.

So when picking a red wine, give an alcohol-free bottle a try. Look for one at your favorite supermarket or order online.

The one drink that keeps you healthy from head to toe

What's the healthiest thing you can drink on the planet? Water — it's the single most important thing to do to maintain healthy skin, hair, and nails. Plus, it regulates your body temperature, heart rate, and blood pressure. Here's how.

When you don't get enough water, your body slips into dehydration. This can happen when you exercise or spend time outdoors on a really hot day. But vomiting or diarrhea can also dehydrate you.

Dehydration can lead to low blood pressure because your blood volume plummets and less oxygen reaches your body's cells.

It can also trigger high blood pressure because if you don't get enough water, your body compensates by retaining sodium.

Your best bet is to drink plenty of water daily. And if you do become dehydrated, seek medical attention immediately.

Easy 'whey' to drink away high blood pressure

What does Little Miss Muffet know that people with high blood pressure don't? To eat her whey, the protein that topples high blood pressure.

Whey is one of the proteins in milk that can be separated and formed into a powder. It's low in lactose, so it's easy to digest if you're lactose intolerant. And it contains all nine essential amino acids.

It's those amino acids that give whey their fighting power. Whey blocks angiotensin-converting enzyme (ACE), a substance in your body that narrows your blood vessels and makes your heart work harder. The blood pressure medicines ACE inhibitors work in a similar way.

Whey also boosts nitric oxide, a substance your blood vessels need to expand.

And it fights two diseases that raise your risk for high blood pressure – diabetes and obesity.

Whey protein powder is easy to find at supermarkets and health food stores. Toss these ingredients in your blender to make the perfect protein shake.

- 3/4 cup fresh or frozen fruit
- 1/2 cup low-fat plain or vanilla yogurt
- 1/2 banana
- 1/2 cup fruit juice, low-fat milk, or almond milk
- 1 to 2 scoops vanilla whey protein powder
- A couple of ice cubes – optional

Sugar just as bad as salt for blood pressure

You know you've got to eat less salt to lower your blood pressure. But did you know the sweet stuff is just as bad? Here's why.

Eating added sugars increases your risk for obesity, diabetes, heart disease, stroke, and other chronic diseases, recent studies show. Scientists are now finding links between added sugars and high blood pressure, too.

Sugar raised systolic blood pressure by a whopping 6.9 points and diastolic by 5.6 points in studies lasting eight weeks or more. Sugar also boosted the number of fats floating around in your blood, which means higher cholesterol levels.

People who drank sugary beverages loaded with glucose and fructose, sweeteners found in high fructose corn syrup, had higher blood pressure, researchers reported in *Hypertension*, an American Heart Association journal.

And if you get too much salt along with too much sugar in your diet, you're just begging for trouble. Blood pressure readings were even higher in people who consumed large amounts of both sugar and salt.

Sugar seems to boost uric acid in your blood, which lowers the amount of nitric oxide in your blood vessels, say experts. Your blood vessels need nitric oxide to remain open and flexible. Sugar may also trigger your body to retain sodium.

Here's what you can do to scale down salt and sugar.

■ Read labels and lower the amount of salt and sugar you eat. The *Dietary Guidelines for Americans 2015* suggests no more than 2,300 milligrams of sodium a day. That's about a teaspoon of salt. Make added sugar no more than 10 percent of your daily calorie intake.

■ Ditch processed foods like canned soups, frozen dinners, lunch meats, instant cereals, and salty snacks. That's where you get most of your sodium.

■ Cut out sugary sodas. Diet sodas did not raise blood pressure, researchers found.

- Adopt the DASH diet, which is low in sodium and includes naturally sweet fruits and vegetables.

- Talk to your doctor about other changes you can make to lower your blood pressure.

COOK IT

Snack your way to lower blood pressure

If you're looking for a healthy, sweet, and crunchy snack, here it is. And with these ingredients, you can snack your way to lower blood pressure. Here's why.

Peanuts have arginine, an amino acid that widens your blood vessels. Walnuts are loaded with omega-3, fiber, and magnesium, all high blood pressure fighters. Plus, flaxseeds slash your blood pressure with their fiber and omega-3.

Dark raisins are brimming with potassium and catechins, powerful antioxidants that boost blood flow. And the flavonoids in dark chocolate promote lower blood pressure and heart health.

Mix the following ingredients in a bowl.

- 1 cup rolled oats
- 1/2 cup peanut butter
- 1/4 cup honey
- 1/2 cup dark chocolate chips or chopped dark chocolate
- 1/3 cup dark raisins
- 1/3 cup flaxseeds
- 1/2 cup peanuts, chopped
- 1/2 cup walnuts, chopped

Chill mixture for 30 minutes. Roll into 1-inch balls and enjoy! Refrigerate leftovers in an airtight container for up to seven days.

Shake the salt habit with heavenly herbs

The tastiest way to eat less salt is to replace it with herbs and spices. You won't sacrifice flavor – really.

People with and without high blood pressure who tasted salty bread and bread seasoned with oregano chose the latter, suggests a small study out of Brazil.

In round one of the study, those with high blood pressure tasted breads with different amounts of salt. Most said they preferred the saltiest sample. But when they tasted a bread containing oregano and less salt, they picked that one over the saltier breads.

Oregano is a great spice to play with because it's cheap and easy to add to your meals. And it's not just oregano. Other herbs and spices can easily replace salt in your cooking.

Spice up your dishes with these world flavors. And make marinades with these herbs and spices plus olive oil for Greek and Italian meals, beer for German fare, and citrus juices for Tex-Mex and Caribbean cuisine.

World cuisines	Herbs and spices
It's all Greek	thyme, dill, basil, parsley, black pepper, marjoram, garlic powder, oregano, lemon zest
Terrific Tex-Mex	cumin, chili powder, cilantro, paprika, onions and garlic (fresh or dried), ground red pepper
Taste of Italy	fresh garlic, basil, oregano, rosemary, flat-leaf Italian parsley
Hint of Asia	curry, ginger, garlic, turmeric, cinnamon, lemongrass, saffron, cardamom, bay leaves
German delights	dill, chives, thyme, bay leaves, borage, parsley, marjoram, white pepper, caraway seeds, juniper berries
Caribbean cravings	cloves, bay leaf, nutmeg, saffron, aniseed, red and black peppers, fresh garlic and onions, allspice, oregano, tamarind
American bites	sage, thyme, parsley, allspice, rosemary, mustard seeds, peppercorn

Indigestion

Natural remedies that put out the fire

4 little-known reasons you should drink water

Water is essential to life. It carries nutrients and flushes out toxins. Amazingly, health professionals are finding more and more ways this refreshing beverage keeps you healthy, including protecting your esophagus – the tube that carries food and liquids from your mouth to your stomach.

Water shields your esophagus from digestive acids. If you have GERD (gastroesophageal reflux disease), you've probably noticed certain drinks, like alcohol and orange juice, can aggravate your symptoms.

Carbonated drinks can also worsen GERD symptoms by causing bloating, which puts pressure on your stomach. This may force acids back into your esophagus. At the same time, fizzy drinks can weaken the sphincter or valve that protects the lining of your esophagus from damaging acids.

Heartburn, or a burning sensation in your chest, is often a sign of indigestion. But indigestion can also be accompanied by abdominal pain, an upset or growling stomach, belching and gas, nausea and vomiting, and a feeling of fullness or bloating.

Drinking water throughout the day will help keep your esophagus clear of digestive juices. But be careful how much you drink with meals. Some health experts say guzzling a lot of liquids with your meal can dilute your stomach contents, making your food harder to digest. Try drinking an hour before or after eating.

Water wins the race to your stomach. If you were to drink half a cup of water and half a cup of lemon juice, the water would reach your stomach faster. That's what happened in one study that also revealed people drinking lemon juice swallowed more often, with smaller amounts of liquid in each swallow. Because it takes acidic drinks longer to reach your stomach, they spend more time in your esophagus where they can cause more damage. This may be a good reason to say "no thanks" next time the waiter asks if you want lemon with that.

H2O waters down acid in your tummy. Water immediately raises the pH of your stomach – reducing acidity in just one minute, according to one study. In the same study, water worked faster than any of the antacids and proton-pump inhibitors tested. Benefits lasted about three minutes.

A tall drink of water helps the medicine go down. If a pill stays in your esophagus too long, it can cause damage. Plus, certain pills may irritate your esophagus even if they don't get caught. These include antibiotics, pain relievers, and drugs for osteoporosis. Drink a full glass of water when taking a pill instead of just a sip to ensure your medicine gets where it's going.

Chew on this — a quick and easy way to reduce acid

In the early 90s, Lee Kuan Yew helped pass a law that made it illegal to import chewing gum into Singapore. He wanted to make the streets cleaner, but what he didn't know then is that chewing gum actually has some health benefits. Compelling research, published since Yew's law was passed, shows chewing gum can be a wonderful remedy against acid reflux.

Reflux is usually worse after meals, but you can improve your symptoms by chewing sugarless gum after you eat. Chewing gum helps wash away acid in your esophagus by stimulating saliva and swallowing.

In three separate studies, people chewed gum for 30 minutes to an hour after eating. Scientists measured esophageal pH before and after and saw a significant decrease in acidity. In one of the studies, chewing gum for an hour helped keep acid away for up to three hours.

Today, no one will be fined for importing chewing gum – even in Singapore. So feel free to try this remedy. It might just do the trick.

> Though chewing gum can protect your esophagus from acid, it sometimes causes uncomfortable side effects. Chomping on gum increases the amount of air you take in and makes you swallow more often. This — as well as ingredients like the artificial sweetener sorbitol in sugarless gum — could lead to gas, bloating, and abdominal cramps.

3 ways to fight a deadly complication of GERD

GERD, Barrett's esophagus, and esophageal cancer have a lot in common. If you leave gastroesophageal reflux disease (GERD) untreated, you could be faced with serious complications such as Barrett's esophagus or esophageal cancer. In fact, Barrett's esophagus, a condition involving damage to the lining of your esophagus, actually increases your risk of developing cancer.

Here are some foods that fight damage and help keep your esophagus healthy.

Vanquish Barrett's with antioxidant-packed veggies. Good news for veggie lovers – dark green, leafy green, raw, and cruciferous vegetables are full of nutrients that may protect against cancer. Eat more foods like broccoli, cabbage, collard greens, kale, spinach, and mustard greens. They're packed with vitamin C and beta carotene – antioxidants that may help combat the damaging effects of GERD and reduce your risk of developing Barrett's esophagus and esophageal cancer.

Give yourself a boost with cancer-fighting berries. Berries are superstar fruits you can use to perk up a salad, jazz up a dessert, or revive a frozen treat. Nutritionists call them superfruits because they are loaded with cancer-fighting antioxidants and nutrients, including vitamins A, C, and E, folic acid, selenium, calcium, beta carotene, lutein, and several anthocyanins.

In one animal study published in *Nutrition and Cancer*, black raspberries, strawberries, and blackberries blocked the growth of tumors by 24 to 56 percent within 25 weeks compared to the animals that didn't eat berries.

Take time for tea to squelch esophageal damage. For some people, tea can be a trigger for reflux symptoms. If it doesn't bother you, you may want to give it a try. Tea contains powerful antioxidants called polyphenols. They fight against esophageal and throat cancer by interfering with the development and growth of cancerous tumors. Green tea polyphenols also keep dangerous cells from multiplying and help your body get rid of toxins and cancer-causing substances.

Studies show coffee is also linked to a lowered risk for esophageal and stomach cancers. Dark-roasted coffee is gentler on your stomach and has less caffeine than light-roasted coffee. People who get heartburn from regular coffee often find dark roasts to be less irritating.

The not-so-hot danger of drinking hot tea

It's probably happened to you before. You got impatient. Or distracted. You thought your tea was cool enough to drink, so you took a big gulp, then had to endure the burning sensation as it traveled from your throat to your stomach. No big deal right? Maybe not. But repeated damage to your esophagus could end up putting your health at risk.

According to a study from China, drinking tea at high temperatures can raise your risk of esophageal cancer. People who drank:

- hot tea (140 to 147 degrees) were about two times more likely to develop esophageal cancer than people who drank warm tea (less than 140 degrees).

- very hot tea (149 degrees and up) were about eight times more likely to develop esophageal cancer than people who drank warm tea.

- a cup of hot tea in less than two minutes were about five times more likely to develop cancer than people who took longer than four minutes.

These effects are not just limited to tea. Other hot foods and drinks can have the same effect. This is because high temperatures damage the protective lining of your esophagus, leaving these cells vulnerable.

Even if you don't want to switch to iced teas and lattes, you can take some extra precautions. Add an ice cube or a little milk to cool your drink faster. Or just wait a few more minutes to let it cool.

Drop pounds and ditch reflux

Your acid reflux flares up when you eat certain foods. But there's another trigger directly linked to your GERD symptoms – your weight. If your body mass index (BMI) shows you're in the overweight or obese range, you're more likely to suffer from reflux no matter what you eat.

High calories, high volume = high chance of reflux? Studies are mixed when it comes to the effect of calories on GERD. One study showed more stomach acid is produced during a high-calorie diet compared to a low-calorie diet. Another says it's really the volume of the meal that counts.

Scientists agree that increased body fat puts more pressure on your abdominal organs. Eating less at a time can reduce pressure on your stomach, while a low-calorie diet can help you get rid of unwanted weight, which will take a load off your tummy.

A low-carb diet relieves GERD symptoms. Some experts think a low-carb diet can help GERD symptoms and reduce acids. This may be because protein and fat take longer to digest, which gives stomach acid something else to do besides sneak back into your esophagus.

Generally, a low-carb diet includes meat, poultry, fish, eggs, and vegetables like asparagus, broccoli, carrots, squash, and cucumbers. Avoid eating a lot of legumes, fruits, breads, sweets, pastas, and starchy vegetables, like corn, peas, and potatoes.

A study published in *Digestive Diseases and Sciences* supports the low-carb diet. The meal plan included less than 20 grams of carbohydrates a day, but you should talk to your doctor first to discuss the best eating plan for you.

Quiet 'silent reflux' with a low-acid diet

GERD sufferers are all too familiar with heartburn. But amazingly, some people with acid reflux never actually experience heartburn. A smaller percentage of people with GERD have another symptom often called "throatburn." Throatburn can be uncomfortable, and it comes with its own list of symptoms. Luckily, a low-acid diet can help relieve the burn.

Throatburn is caused by a condition known as laryngopharyngeal reflux (LPR). This silent reflux develops when stomach acid travels up your esophagus to your throat. Symptoms of LPR include:

- hoarseness

- constant need to clear
  your throat

- sensation of a lump in
  your throat

- chronic cough

- difficulty swallowing

- sore throat

- feeling of mucus sticking in your throat

Hypochlorhydria — a condition in which your stomach doesn't produce enough acid — can actually cause a number of GERD symptoms. Your doctor can run tests to determine if this is the cause of your reflux symptoms.

Though LPR is similar to GERD in many ways, it also differs on several counts. Typically, people with LPR have daytime reflux, or reflux that occurs in the "upright" position.

A low-acid diet appears to be beneficial for symptoms of LPR that are not helped by traditional acid reflux treatment. In one study, people ate from a list of low-acid foods for two weeks. The list included foods like beans, whole-grain breads, chicken, fish, oatmeal, potatoes, rice, skim milk, turkey, and vegetables (excluding onions, tomatoes, and peppers). Bananas and melons were the only fruits on the list. By the end of the study, 95 percent of the people showed improvement.

4 herbal teas that will settle your stomach

The last thing you want to think about is food when your tummy starts giving you trouble. If you can't stomach solids, try herbal teas. Not only will sipping tea help you stay hydrated, some herbs have amazing chemicals that help fight stomachaches.

Chamomile. The stomach-healing power of chamomile starts with the dried white and yellow flower head, which make a soothing tea. Traditionally, chamomile has been used for various digestive conditions including indigestion, gas, diarrhea, stomach cramps, and irritable bowel syndrome (IBS). Scientists think it helps by relaxing muscles that move food through your intestines, getting rid of gas and soothing your stomach.

Make tea by pouring one cup of boiling water over three teaspoons of dried herb and steeping for 10 to 15 minutes. Drink three to four times a day between meals. You can easily find chamomile tea bags in your local supermarket, but they may not be as effective.

Peppermint. Peppermint is a popular flavoring for gum, toothpaste, and teas, but don't be surprised if you hear someone suggest it for irritable bowel syndrome. One study showed that people taking 225 milligrams of peppermint oil in enteric-coated capsules twice a day for four weeks had improved overall IBS symptoms compared with people taking a placebo. A word of caution – large doses of peppermint oil can be toxic.

Peppermint may also help indigestion, stomach cramps, bloating and gas, constipation, diarrhea, nausea from food or travel sickness and postoperative nausea. It works by calming your stomach muscles and improving digestion. It can also relax the valve that keeps stomach acids out of your esophagus, making heartburn worse. For this reason, it is not recommended for people who have GERD.

To make peppermint tea, steep one teaspoon of dried peppermint leaves in one cup of boiling water for 10 minutes. Drink four to five times a day between meals.

> Gassy? You're not the only one. Most people produce about one to three pints of gas daily and pass gas about 14 times a day.

Caraway. Some people once believed caraway seeds made into a potion had the power to keep lovers in love. Today, caraway is more likely to be seen in a pot of sauerkraut than a potion, but it's still used for treating gas and other symptoms of an upset stomach.

To make tea, pour a cup of boiling water over one tablespoon of caraway seeds and allow the tea to steep for at least 10 minutes before straining out the seeds.

Fennel. Fennel helps relieve indigestion, constipation, stomach cramps, bloating, and nausea. You can easily find fennel seeds in the spice aisle of any grocery store. To make tea, put a teaspoon of fennel seeds in a tea pot. Add hot water, steep for about 15 minutes, then strain while pouring.

An 'a-peel-ing' cure for acid reflux

What does Pledge furniture polish, TRESemmé conditioner, and L'Oréal sunscreen have in common? D-limonene. It's an organic compound found in the peels of many citrus fruits, often added to products for flavor and fragrance. Here's the twist — scientists have also discovered that this ingredient may help calm your heartburn.

In one study, people with GERD or chronic heartburn took a capsule containing 1,000 milligrams of d-limonene daily or every other day. After 14 days, 89 percent experienced complete relief of symptoms.

Scientists are not entirely sure how d-limonene helps heartburn, but studies suggest it may protect your stomach wall from digestive acid and support normal peristalsis, the wavelike muscle contractions that move food through your digestive tract. Before taking d-limonene supplements, talk to your doctor to see if they're right for you.

Eat this, not that
for indigestion

skim milk  ✓	Milk makes your stomach produce more acid, plus the fat can relax your lower esophageal sphincter. If you can't give it up, choose skim milk.	**whole milk**  ✗
water 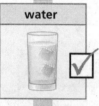 ✓	Carbonated drinks can aggravate indigestion symptoms. Water cleanses your esophagus and reduces the acidity of your stomach.	**soda**  ✗
hummus/pita  ✓	Spicy, greasy foods can irritate your stomach. Instead of chips and salsa, try some hummus with pita bread.	**chips/salsa**  ✗
berries  ✓	High-sugar, fatty foods can be hard on your stomach. Say no to chocolate, and substitute berries for a sweet treat that won't worsen your condition.	**chocolate**  ✗
banana/melon  ✓	Acidic foods like oranges can be a pain for your esophagus and stomach. For relief, switch to low-acid fruits, such as bananas and melons.	**oranges**  ✗

Can the 'sleep hormone' put your heartburn to rest?

You pop a melatonin pill to help you sleep, but you probably never thought to take it for heartburn. Melatonin, sometimes called the "hormone of the night," helps determine when you sleep and when you wake up. One of its lesser-known roles, however, is in digestion.

Melatonin can be found naturally in the lining of your esophagus. It helps protect the passageway to your stomach from stomach acid, free radicals, and stress.

In one study, published in *BMC Gastroenterology*, the combination of melatonin and the proton-pump inhibitor (PPI) omeprazole enhanced heartburn therapy — reducing side effects and healing time. In another study, a melatonin supplement with added vitamins and amino acids led to a 100-percent reduction of symptoms within 40 days. Researchers have examined different melatonin combinations, so talk to your doctor before beginning supplements.

Embarrassing gas? 7 kitchen solutions for the most-common culprits

If you've ever sat in a theater, ridden in an elevator, or enjoyed a night on the town, you know unpredictable gas can be a quick way to ruin a moment. You can avoid those embarrassing situations by paying attention to what you eat. Enjoy these simple solutions to combat even the gassiest ingredients hidden in your food.

Food	Why it causes gas	Solution
Broccoli	Raffinose is a complex sugar found in broccoli, cabbage, asparagus, whole grains, and beans. Your body lacks the enzymes it needs to break down these sugars, so bacteria break it down in your large intestine, causing gases to be produced.	Flavor your food with gas-fighting herbs like ginger or peppermint.
Beans	Soluble fiber can be found in beans, oats, peas, and most fruits. The fiber turns into a gel-like substance in your intestines, which makes it more difficult to break down.	Try a less-gassy variety like black-eyed peas. Before cooking, soak beans overnight in cold water to release enzymes that break down complex sugars.
Milk	Lactose is a natural sugar found in milk, cheese, ice cream, and some processed foods. Some people have a shortage of the enzyme lactase, which makes it difficult to break down the lactose in dairy products.	Switch to lactose-free milk like almond milk.
Onions	Fructose is found naturally in vegetables like onions, artichokes, pears, and wheat and is also used as a sweetener in some drinks. Some people can't absorb fructose properly. Like other sugars, it's digested in the large intestine by harmless bacteria, producing gas in the process.	Cook with gas-fighting seeds like fennel or caraway.
Soda	Carbonated liquids like soda and beer can introduce air into your digestive tract causing belching and gas.	Cut down on the fizz by drinking noncarbonated beverages.
Apples	Sorbitol is found naturally in fruits such as apples, pears, and peaches and is also an artificial sweetener in some diet products.	Switch to fruits with less sorbitol like bananas, melons, and blueberries.
Pasta	Most starches, including corn, wheat, and potatoes, produce gas when digested in the large intestine. Rice is an exception.	Try substituting vegetables in your pasta recipes. Zucchini is perfect for lasagna, or you can roast a spaghetti squash.

Hidden side effects of acid blockers

Hip fractures, heart problems, gastrointestinal disorders? This is not what you had in mind when you started taking your acid blocker. But research shows taking these drugs long-term can have some dangerous consequences.

Antacids bring on B12 deficiency. Older people taking long-term proton pump inhibitors (PPIs), like Nexium and Prilosec, have a greater risk of vitamin B12 deficiency. PPIs block stomach acid that frees B12 from food. In a recent study published in the *Journal of the American Medical Association*, people who took PPIs for more than two years were 65 percent more likely to have low levels of B12.

B12 is found in animal products – meat, fish, milk, cheese, and eggs – but you also get over 100 percent daily value from some fortified cereals. Keep in mind, PPIs can slow down B12 absorption. If you think you're not getting enough of this important vitamin, talk to your doctor.

Inadequate calcium raises risk of hip fractures. Stomach acid also plays a role in bone health by helping your body absorb calcium. Using PPIs for extended periods of time could raise your risk of osteoporosis, bone loss, and fractures – particularly hip fractures.

Calcium supplements can help, but talk to your doctor first. Some supplements, like calcium carbonate, absorb better if your stomach has more acid, so taking them with acid blockers won't do you any good. Calcium citrate and calcium gluconate, on the other hand, work better in lower acidity.

Low mineral levels make stomach problems worse. Studies also show stomach acid affects iron absorption. As with calcium and B12, your body has a hard time absorbing iron if you don't have enough stomach acid. Consequently, you could end up with anemia.

Similarly, PPIs are linked to magnesium deficiency. A magnesium deficiency can lead to gastrointestinal problems, such as diarrhea, Crohn's disease, and intestinal inflammation.

Blood vessel glitches provoke heart problems. Recent studies show PPIs may be related to heart disease risk. One study examined the records of almost 3 million people and concluded that the use of PPIs increased the risk of heart attack.

PPIs reduce the production of chemicals that relax blood vessels and protect arteries and veins. When blood vessels are constricted, blood flow is slowed or blocked. This can lead to high blood pressure and heart disease.

Inflammatory bowel disease

Diet plans that conquer the pain

3 healing vitamins that halt gut pain

ABCs could be your key to beating IBD. Except in this case, it's vitamins A, B, and D versus inflammatory bowel disease (IBD).

Your immune system's main job is to protect you from infections. Autoimmune diseases like IBD pop up when your immune system malfunctions and begins attacking your own cells. Here's what happens.

- Viruses, bacteria, food allergies, and other things in the environment may trigger your immune system to attack your digestive tract.

- Immune cells in your gut release inflammation-causing compounds to fight the invader.

- Once the immune system gets turned on and begins attacking, it doesn't turn off properly. It creates chronic inflammation, which damages your intestines.

That intestinal inflammation is the hallmark of IBD. If it strikes your small intestine, it's known as Crohn's disease. If it attacks your colon and large intestine, it's ulcerative colitis (UC). You don't have to resign yourself to living with either condition.

Research now shows that these three vitamins are essential to curbing IBD.

Vitamin A: the secret to squashing inflammation. It's pretty certain Bugs Bunny didn't have IBD. For one, he's a cartoon character. For another, he was constantly chomping on carrots. Orange vegetables like carrots and sweet potatoes, and green, leafy ones such as spinach and kale are terrific sources of beta carotene, which your body turns into vitamin A. And vitamin A helps squash inflammation.

Researchers gave mice with IBD-type inflammation and intestinal damage a dose of vitamin A to see what happened. Not only did the nutrient calm inflammation in their guts, it also helped heal damaged gut tissue. Scientists say this illustrates how important it is to eat plenty of vitamin-A-rich foods, especially if you struggle with inflammatory problems like IBD.

Keep Crohn's in remission with the sunshine vitamin. Where you live impacts whether you develop Crohn's disease and ulcerative colitis. Living in southern areas lowers your risk. Living in the north raises it. So does moving from the sunny south to the colder north.

It's all tied to vitamin D, the so-called sunshine vitamin. Your body makes most of its vitamin D from sunlight, and southern states get more sun than northern ones. The farther north people live, the lower their blood levels of vitamin D tend to be. Low blood levels make you more likely to develop Crohn's disease and suffer a relapse of it.

Enter supplements. Taking megadoses of vitamin D – 10,000 International Units (IU) per day – may help treat flare-ups of active Crohn's disease. Taking 2,000 IU a day may help prevent a relapse once your Crohn's is in remission.

Vitamin D improves the health of the protective barrier that lines your intestines and keeps it from getting weak and "leaky." Gut barriers get leaky right before a relapse of Crohn's disease.

Talk to your gastroenterologist about whether you need to take supplements, especially in winter, and how much is safe for you.

The B vitamin that heals your bowels. Experts say eating lots of fiber may calm bowel inflammation, but that may not be an option if you have intestinal damage or are in the middle of an IBD flare-up. In that case, here's some good news. Niacin (vitamin B3) supplements may have the same effect.

Good bacteria in your colon thrive on fiber. It helps them produce butyrate, a compound that flips a switch in colon and immune cells, telling them to reduce inflammation. Butyrate also triggers the cells lining your colon to send out cytokines. These help heal the damage caused by IBD inflammation.

But you have to eat lots of fiber to boost your butyrate levels enough to reap these benefits. That's not an option for everyone. Scientists recently discovered that niacin flips the same switches in your gut.

Taking large doses of niacin may have similar healing powers to eating lots of fiber. More research is needed to figure out how much niacin it takes to help IBD, and how safe those doses are. In the meantime, ask your gastroenterologist whether these supplements could help.

The IBD diet that could change your life

Living with inflammatory bowel disease (IBD) is like living on a roller coaster. The ups, the downs, the unexpected turns – you never know when your symptoms will flare up or where you'll be when they do. In the past, experts could only recommend avoiding trigger foods. But recent research reveals a new eating plan that may transform the way you live with IBD.

You experience different symptoms depending on the type of IBD you have, but dietary remedies are often similar. Experts encourage you to drink more fluids and eat less fatty food and fiber as well as dairy if you're lactose intolerant.

But now scientists are honing in on what may be a major component of IBD – gut bacteria. Healthful changes in your diet could impact these bacteria, which may reduce inflammation. Researchers refer to these dietary changes as the inflammatory bowel disease anti-inflammatory diet. But you can just call it the IBD-AID.

Balance your bowels with beneficial bacteria. Eating pre- and probiotics helps restore balance to bacteria in your intestines. If your digestive tract has the wrong proportion of good bugs to bad bugs, it could become unbalanced with an overabundance of harmful bacteria. That's why the IBD-AID advocates foods like these that fight inflammation by balancing your "gut flora."

- fruits and vegetables

- soluble fiber (steel-cut oats, ground flaxseed, lentils, beans)

- good protein and fats (beans, nuts, olive oil, avocado, ground flaxseed, fish, soy)

- probiotics (yogurt, kefir, sauerkraut, kimchi, miso, local honey)

- prebiotics (Jerusalem artichokes, asparagus, leeks)

Root out inflammation-causing bugs. Researchers think some carbohydrates provide food for the bacteria that cause inflammation. The IBD-AID recommends you eliminate refined sugars and certain starches; any foods containing lactose, including milk or cream; and grains, except for steel-cut and rolled oats.

Repair your gut with the right food textures. Bulky, fibrous foods may damage an inflamed or narrow digestive tract. Changing the textures of your foods by breaking them down before you eat can protect your gut and help you absorb nutrients. Many people start the diet by choosing soft foods, using the blender, and avoiding foods with stems and seeds.

For people with an active flare, experts recommend soft, well-cooked, or puréed foods. These foods help heal your gut, which restores balance to your immune system. As your symptoms get better, you can add tender vegetables and firmer foods.

Learn from the success of the IBD-AID study. In a study published in *Nutrition Journal*, all of the people who stuck with the IBD-AID for at least four weeks experienced fewer symptoms. Because of this, they were able to reduce their use of medication.

Cooking secret that can heal your gut

Every time you cook potatoes or rice, then let them cool before eating, you're creating a superstar nutrient called resistant starch 3 (RS3) that helps fight your IBD symptoms.

This starch is different from other nutrients because your body can't digest it normally. Instead, RS3 travels undigested to your intestines where bacteria ferment it. This fermentation produces short-chain fatty acids (SCFAs) like butyrate. Scientists suggest these SCFAs trigger processes that actively help prevent inflammation in the gut.

An animal study found that RS3 reduced the inflammatory lesions of colitis. Although more research is needed, you can ask your doctor if resistant-starch foods are safe for you. If so, try eating more legumes, beans, plantains, and yams as well as cooled potatoes and rice.

Surprise! Bacteria cool the fire of flareups

Virtually from the moment you are born, bacteria and other bugs begin colonizing your gut. Most of the time, they're good for you. Occasionally, they're bad. And the bad ones may be behind inflammatory bowel disease (IBD).

The DNA you inherited from your parents sets the stage for IBD by making you more (or less) likely to develop it. But the microorganisms living in your gut also play a role. Having too many bacteria or yeast in part of your intestine, or having the wrong kind, may trigger the development of this disease.

For instance, ulcerative colitis (UC) may appear when harmful bacteria break down the lining that protects your intestines. These and other bugs then damage your intestinal cells, causing inflammation and triggering IBD.

So what do you do? Fight bad gut bugs with good ones. Scientists now know that certain strains of bacteria and yeast can treat IBD flare-ups and help keep the disease in remission.

> Inflammatory bowel disease doesn't just affect your gut. It also causes depression, fatigue, and social isolation. Good bacteria can help there, too. A new study in mice found that the probiotic VSL#3 didn't lessen inflammation, but it did improve "behavioral" symptoms like these.

Yeast keeps Crohn's disease quiet. People whose Crohn's disease was in remission were more likely to stay in remission if they took 1 gram a day of the yeast *Saccharomyces boulardii*, plus the drug mesalamine. Other studies suggest it could also treat flare-ups. Shop for supplements that contain this yeast, such as FloraStor.

Say so-long to UC troubles with probiotics. Send your ulcerative colitis on permanent vacation. The bacteria in easy-to-find probiotic food and supplements can help keep your UC in remission longer.

■ Taking the probiotic product VSL#3 along with your standard IBD drugs could help put active UC into remission. It may even work better than drugs alone. People in studies found relief when taking between 900 billion and 3,600 billion bacteria daily. VSL#3 is sold in single packets of 450 billion or double-strength of 900 billion, which is by prescription only. So talk to your doctor about the dosage that's right for you.

■ If you're already in remission, try eating dairy products that contain *Bifidobacteria (B.)* with your UC drugs to keep it that way. That worked for people who drank slightly more than 3 ounces of a fermented dairy drink each day made with *B. breve, B. bifidum*, and *L. acidophilus*. Look for these bacteria in supplements or in fermented dairy products like kefir. Lifeway-brand kefir, for instance, contains two out of three of these bacterial strains.

■ Supplements that contain *Lactobacillus GG*, such as Culturelle, may also help keep ulcerative colitis in remission.

Follow the same plan for pouchitis. Sometimes UC damages your intestine so much that you need part of it removed. In that case, surgeons create a pouch in your gut to replace the missing section. If the pouch becomes inflamed, you have pouchitis.

Probiotics could treat this, too. In several studies, VSL#3 helped the majority of people with pouchitis keep their condition under control and in remission for up to one year. Only one in 10 people on VSL#3 had a flare-up of pouchitis in one study, compared with four in 10 people on a placebo.

IBD mistakes even smart people make

Be careful with that glass of ice water, especially when your symptoms flare. Drinking an icy cold beverage can sometimes cause cramps, warns the Crohn's and Colitis Foundation of America (CCFA). Who knew, right? But don't stop there. Here are some other little-known mistakes that could be standing between you and feeling better.

One diet is not right for everyone. If one identical twin has inflammatory bowel disease (IBD), the other twin only has a 27 percent chance of developing Crohn's disease (CD) or a 15 percent chance of ulcerative colitis (UC). This holds true even though their bodies are almost exactly the same. IBD definitely isn't a one-size-fits-all condition.

This quality may also help explain why no one diet is guaranteed to work for everyone with IBD – because even similar bodies may react differently to the same foods. What triggers IBD symptoms in one person may not affect another at all. On top of that, researchers say no particular food or food group has been proven to cause IBD symptoms in everyone.

Eliminating most foods is not the answer. You may be tempted to eat fewer foods to play it safe, but experts warn you may permanently remove too many healthy foods from your diet. Even worse, you can't guarantee you'll remove every food that triggers your symptoms. Fortunately, one study on inflammatory bowel disease has found a promising way to create a more flare-resistant diet with fewer food restrictions.

Researchers recruited people with Crohn's disease in remission and split them into two groups. One group took steroids while the other tried an exclusion diet. After eliminating certain foods, people in the diet group then reintroduced them one at a time. Any food that caused a problem was removed permanently.

With this approach, each participant created a diet individually tailored to preventing his or her flares. The study showed they did better long-term than the people who used steroids.

Want to try this? Talk to your doctor first, so she can help create your personalized elimination diet safely and effectively. Once this diet is complete, you may be able to experiment with other diets to improve your results even more.

Guzzling the wrong sports drinks makes things worse. Canadian research shows that people with active IBD consume more sports drinks and sweetened beverages than people who are in remission. But watch out when your symptoms are flaring. Excess sugar from drinks can trigger more diarrhea thanks to the extra water that is pulled into the intestines. So what should you do?

The CCFA recommends sports drinks during a flare to help you keep hydrated – but only if those sports drinks are low in sugar. They also recommend watered-down fruit juice.

For even more nutrition and hydration, they suggest including vegetable stock as part of soup or added to rice. Adding vegetable stock to rice may be a particularly good idea. A study of more than 2,000 people with IBD found that rice, yogurt, and bananas helped people feel better during a flare.

Watch out for foods with emulsifiers. Have you eaten any polysorbate-80 lately? You may laugh but you probably have. Polysorbate-80 is an emulsifier added to foods to give them the right texture and longer shelf life.

According to recent animal research, emulsifiers like polysorbate-80 may alter the bacteria in your gut, skewing the balance in a way that encourages inflammation in your intestines. The scientists behind the research suggest this process may help raise the odds of IBD and other inflammatory conditions.

> Dish detergents contain emulsifiers just like foods. To make sure these emulsifiers don't get into your foods and drinks, rinse your dishes thoroughly after washing them.

Earlier research also suggests these emulsifiers may play a role in inflammatory bowel disease. That's why some experts advise people with IBD to avoid processed, high-fat foods, because those foods often contain emulsifiers.

Fish oil: a danger to your colon?

Omega-3 fatty acids are well-known inflammation fighters, but beware — too much of them can cause your immune system to malfunction. And that could raise your risk for ulcerative colitis (UC), an autoimmune disorder; or colon cancer if you already have UC, research suggests.

Eating fish and other omega-3-rich foods is fine. The problem begins when you eat four or five of them daily in addition to taking omega-3 supplements.

It's easier than ever to overload, too. More and more foods are being fortified with these "good" fats, including eggs, bread, butter, oils, and orange juice. Ask your doctor how much omega-3 is safe to get from supplements, or focus on getting it naturally from foods.

Joint pain

Foods that fight the ache

Proven pain fighters you should eat every day

Are you eating foods that cause arthritis pain or foods that fight it? Scientists say some foods naturally contain compounds proven to ease joint pain. Discover how they can change your body chemistry and help you feel better.

Seafood suppers that wash away pain. Some fish won't do a thing to relieve arthritis pain, but fish like these carry a special ingredient that can make a real difference.

> Don't have time to buy and prepare frozen or fresh salmon? Canned pink salmon has more than 1,000 milligrams of omega-3 in just 3 ounces of fish.

- Try herring – the tiny fish with superpowers. Eat just one herring fillet, and you get more than 3,000 milligrams (mg) of omega-3 fatty acids. These fish oils make your body produce compounds that reduce inflammation and control pain. Studies have even found they can help ease morning stiffness and tender joints in people who have rheumatoid arthritis (RA). Omega-3 may also battle osteoarthritis (OA) by helping block production of inflammation-causing compounds. But herring isn't the only fish rich in omega-3.

- Savor pain-busting salmon with seasonings. Just 4 ounces of salmon may be packed with up to 3,000 mg of omega-3.

For even more omega-3, whip up a marinade for your salmon, and include oregano as an ingredient. Oregano has more omega-3 than any other spice except cloves. Just one tablespoon of oregano has more omega-3 fats than an entire cup of cooked wild rice.

■ **Experiment with sardines.** Canned sardines are ridiculously convenient, yet they deliver more than 1,000 mg of omega-3 in a 3-ounce serving. Mash them up with one of the following – mustard, olives, tomatoes, hot sauce, or lemon juice. Serve them on crackers, toast, or even a sandwich.

■ **Compare trout to tilapia.** Both rainbow trout and tilapia have omega-3, but they also contain omega-6 fatty acids. These omega-6 fats can make your body crank out compounds that cause inflammation. Although your body can't do without omega-6 fats, most Americans eat far more than they need. Some experts say you can make omega-3 even more powerful if you cut back on omega-6 fats. Foods high in omega-6 include meat and fried foods, as well as corn oil, safflower oil, soybean oil, and any foods containing these oils. Even tilapia and canola oil have more omega-6 than omega-3. Fortunately, a rainbow trout fillet has more than 1,600 mg of omega-3. That's four times as many omega-3 as omega-6.

> Look for foods enriched with omega-3 if you are a vegetarian who doesn't eat fish. You may find them in some brands of juice, yogurt, eggs, and other products.

■ **Pollock – the mild fish with a strong pain-fighter.** Omega-3 fatty acids are not only found in strongly flavored fish like salmon and sardines. A half-fillet of pollock has more than 800 mg of omega-3. Bake or broil it with a sauce to help retain moisture.

- Rainbow smelt – the best tasting fish you've never heard of. A 3-ounce serving of rainbow smelt not only delivers plenty of omega-3, but also more than half the daily value for selenium and vitamin B12. What's more, this fish is easy to prepare, so try it broiled, baked, or grilled.

Surprise! Omega-3 from vegetables, seeds, and nuts. Flaxseeds, chia seeds, and walnuts are all great sources of plant-based omega-3. Mix small amounts of flaxseeds or chia seeds into salad dressings, soup, oatmeal, smoothies, or yogurt. To add even more omega-3, serve your fish or other main dishes with a side of turnip greens, Chinese broccoli, cauliflower, or spinach.

Healthy oils that ease the ache. Flaxseed oil is rich in omega-3, so mix it into your salad dressings to help fight inflammation. But don't stop there. An old kitchen favorite and a new up-and-comer may help as well.

- Extra virgin olive oil battles pain on two fronts. This popular oil doesn't just give you omega-3 – it also delivers oleocanthal, a powerful nutrient that fights the same inflammation-causing compounds as ibuprofen. Oleocanthal may even help fight pain and inflammation like a small dose of painkiller. To make sure you have EVOO that contains oleocanthal, taste a teaspoon of the oil. If it stings the back of your throat when you swallow, you've got oleocanthal. To fight pain with oleocanthal, you need almost four tablespoons of EVOO – nearly 52 grams of fat. That's more fat than a McDonald's

Some seafood is high in mercury, which can be particularly dangerous to young children, pregnant women, and women who may become pregnant. Good examples of seafood low in mercury — but high in omega-3 — include herring, salmon, sardines, rainbow trout, rainbow smelt, pollock, anchovies, mussels, and shad.

Double Quarter Pounder with cheese. To keep your weight from skyrocketing, replace 52 grams of unhealthy fat from your current diet with EVOO. Get creative – use this oil in salad dressings, pasta, vegetables, and more.

■ **Make friends with camelina oil.** Want a healthy oil that doesn't need to be refrigerated? Camelina oil could be right for you. Made from the camelina seed, this oil has more omega-3 than omega-6, plenty of vitamin E, and more healthy monounsaturated fats than flaxseed oil. It also has a 475-degree smoke point, so you can use it when cooking. Camelina oil may not be widely available yet. If you can't find it in local stores, check online.

Common spice blocks arthritis pain as well as drugs

Arthritis is a pain in the neck – and everywhere else in your body. But you can ease the ache of arthritis with this amazing food. Just add one tablespoon of turmeric to your favorite dishes. Couldn't get any easier.

Super-nutrient fights osteoarthritis pain like powerful painkillers. This flavorful spice doesn't just give curry and mustard a golden yellow color. Turmeric contains a powerful phytonutrient called curcumin. When it comes to easing the aches and pains of both osteoarthritis (OA) and rheumatoid arthritis (RA), studies suggest curcumin works just as well as nonsteroidal anti-inflammatory drugs (NSAIDs), like ibuprofen and aspirin.

That may sound too good to be true, especially if you take a painkiller like ibuprofen. But scientists in Thailand put it to the test. They pitted curcumin extract against ibuprofen in a study of 107 people with knee OA. After six weeks, walking and stair climbing ability, as well as pain, had improved just as much in people taking curcumin as in those taking ibuprofen.

But that's just the beginning. A 2010 clinical trial tested a turmeric supplement called Meriva for eight months. Meriva combines the equivalent of 200 milligrams (mg) of curcumin a day with phostphatidylcholine to help your body absorb and use curcumin. By the end of the study, pain, stiffness, and knee function had improved by 50 percent in people with knee OA who took Meriva. And when researchers compared walking speeds from a treadmill test, Meriva takers had improved three times as much as people who used the best available arthritis treatments. Tests showed curcumin helps block inflammatory compounds in the body. Curcumin even reduces cyclooxygenase-2 (COX-2), the compound that celecoxib (Celebrex) blocks to squelch pain. That may explain why Meriva takers used fewer painkillers than people who didn't take Meriva.

Unleash this golden spice on rheumatoid arthritis. A recent pilot study found curcumin may fight the pain, swelling, and joint tenderness of RA at least as effectively as the prescription drug diclofenac. Turmeric also seems to block joint destruction, according to animal research at the University of Arizona in Tucson. Experts add that a "master switch" protein in your joints triggers your body's inflammatory response and helps cause RA joint pain. Turmeric inhibits this protein, and that may be why it helps.

Think outside the box just like Kraft. Kraft Foods recently chose turmeric as one of the new coloring agents to replace artificial dyes in its Kraft Macaroni & Cheese. So why not take a cue from Kraft, and try these ideas for adding turmeric to your own dishes.

- Add a dash of turmeric to your salad dressings.

- Sprinkle turmeric on sautéed vegetables like onions, bell peppers, or cauliflower.

- Add turmeric to rice dishes.

- Sprinkle a bit of turmeric on baked or roasted potatoes.

- Mix a half teaspoon of turmeric into one-quarter cup of olive oil, and brush onto asparagus or corn on the cob.

- Spice up lentil soup or a bowl of chili with a pinch of turmeric.

- Scramble your eggs with a little turmeric or toss some into egg salad.

- Make spicy hummus by mixing curry powder with garbanzo beans.

Gout pain?
A superfood that prevents attacks

Eating just a half cup of cherries over a two-day period reduces risk of gout attacks by 35 percent, a Boston University study discovered. And recently, another study found that Montmorency tart cherry juice concentrate reduced people's levels of uric acid, the main cause of gout pain. So try this.

Eat 10 to 12 fresh cherries every day if you can. But since fresh cherries only last a day or so, you may prefer dried or frozen cherries, cherry juice, or cherry juice from concentrate.

Research suggests sweet Bing cherries may be less effective and take longer to work than tart cherries, so choose Montmorency cherries or juice concentrate for best results. To minimize the tart taste, include frozen or fresh cherries in cereal, yogurt, oatmeal, or salad. Mix tart cherry juice concentrate with other juices to improve the flavor.

Protect yourself from 'bum knees' with one simple change

One vitamin can lower your risk of knee arthritis by 50 percent. For some people, eating a daily handful of almonds may be enough to make a difference. Find out if you – or someone you love – is one of them.

What researchers discovered. A North Carolina study checked people's blood levels for two kinds of vitamin E – alpha-tocopherol and gamma-tocopherol. The researchers discovered that the ratio of alpha to gamma was the most important factor in whether certain people developed knee arthritis. In the study, the African Americans and men with the highest levels of alpha-tocopherol compared to gamma-tocopherol also had 50 percent less risk of knee arthritis.

Research suggests both versions of vitamin E may help fight arthritis, thanks to their antioxidant and anti-inflammatory powers. But the amount of each one in your diet may be more important than you expect, and here's why.

Americans generally get plenty of gamma-tocopherol in their diets, thanks to high intakes of canola, corn, and soybean oils. Although gamma-tocopherol is a more potent inflammation fighter and antioxidant than alpha-tocopherol, the North Carolina researchers have evidence that your body may use alpha-tocopherol more efficiently. They also suggest the body may be designed to use up most of its alpha-tocopherol before using gamma-tocopherol.

Why almonds might bring joy to joints. If the researchers are right, eating almonds may be a smart choice because almonds give you much more alpha-tocopherol than gamma-tocopherol. Surprisingly, many people fall short on overall vitamin E, the researchers say. In this study, African Americans had lower levels of both kinds of vitamin E.

If you aren't getting enough of this vitamin in your diet, almonds, hazelnuts, and sunflower seeds are a good way to start adding more. Just remember, foods like these are high calorie. Since becoming obese would raise your odds of knee arthritis, take no chances. Eat these nuts and seeds in place of other high-fat foods to protect your knees – and control your weight.

Stop arthritis in its tracks

Eat enough vitamin C, and you'll slash your risk of osteoarthritis and gout — or at least keep arthritis from getting worse. Women need 75 milligrams (mg) of vitamin C every day, and men need 90 mg. But that doesn't mean you must eat citrus fruits and juices daily. To make sure you get enough vitamin C, even when citrus isn't an option, eat yummy, citrus-free foods like these.

Food	Mg of vitamin C in 1 cup
Tomato juice, canned	170
Kiwifruit, sliced	167
Pineapple chunks	93
Strawberry halves	89
Papaya	88
Kale, raw, chopped	87
Kohlrabi, raw	84
Broccoli, raw, chopped	81
Cantaloupe balls	65
Cauliflower, raw, chopped	52

Don't miss this: Knee pain linked to a vitamin shortage

Sore joints and muscles? You don't have to live with aches and pains. Easing the discomfort can be as easy as boosting your intake of one simple vitamin.

Your aches and pains can mean you're not getting enough vitamin D. What you don't know really can hurt you, research suggests. A recent study of postmenopausal women discovered that those with the lowest blood levels of vitamin D had the worst problems with joint pain. What's more, another study found that African Americans with lower vitamin D levels were more sensitive to forearm and knee pain. Other research has also linked low blood levels of vitamin D to chronic pain, including muscle pain and other pain that might not be arthritis.

How vitamin D helped people feel better. Several studies suggest vitamin D can help ease your pain. For example, one study examined Europeans who saw a doctor about musculoskeletal pain, which can affect the joints, bones, and muscles. The study participants were also deficient in vitamin D. After taking supplements to boost their vitamin D levels, the participants reported less pain, too. But that's not all.

In Romanian research, nursing home residents with a vitamin D deficiency started eating bread fortified with 125 micrograms of vitamin D every day. After doing this for one year, they not only reported less pain, but also had better walking ability and quality of life.

Vitamin D may even help the pain of rheumatoid arthritis (RA). A study from India found that people with RA who took a calcium and vitamin D supplement with their RA medication got significantly better pain relief than people who only took medication.

The vitamin D risk you should never ignore. Too much vitamin D can be dangerous. Before you start taking vitamin D supplements, ask your doctor if you have a vitamin D deficiency. She can test for this deficiency and create a customized plan to fix your vitamin D shortage, if you have one.

But that doesn't mean you're just stuck waiting. Start eating more foods rich in vitamin D. Good choices include canned salmon or sardines, eggs, rainbow trout, Pacific mackerel, and fortified milk, buttermilk, and even eggnog.

8 foods you should try if you have RA

Are you missing an opportunity to ease your achy joints? People who have rheumatoid arthritis are more likely to have low blood levels of the mineral selenium, experts say. Preliminary research suggests this mineral helps relieve arthritis symptoms by controlling the levels of damaging free radicals, so make sure you get enough selenium in your diet.

Try these eight foods to help rev up your levels of this valuable mineral. Meat and fish lovers can try chicken, pork, and turkey breast, as well as rockfish and canned light tuna. Both vegetarians and carnivores can get extra selenium from Brazil nuts, walnuts, and sunflower seeds.

Grab the garlic to guard against hip arthritis

Why would one twin develop arthritis while the other doesn't? For years, hundreds of female twins participated in a British research project to help answer that question. Scientists recently discovered an eating habit that might make a difference.

Add more onions and garlic to your recipes. The researchers found that twins who ate more garlic, onions, leeks, chives, and shallots were less likely to have hip arthritis.

These vegetables from the allium family contain compounds that may help protect your hip joints. The researchers suggest the compounds called diallyl disulphide (DADS) and diallyl sulphide (DAS) are the most likely candidates.

Laboratory studies have found that DADS and DAS can both squelch enzymes that contribute to osteoarthritis and cartilage destruction. Although the researchers say they can't guarantee eating more onions, garlic, and other allium vegetables will lower your risk of arthritis, there's one delicious way you can find out.

You've heard parsley can help you get rid of garlic breath, but researchers from Ohio State University discovered something even better. Eating a few raw apple slices with your garlicky meal disarms the compounds that cause garlic breath. Other foods that may help include milk, lemon juice, and green tea.

5 delicious ways to eat more of these flavorful veggies. You probably already mix garlic in your mashed potatoes and put onions on your burgers. Now, use these tips to add more of these tasty vegetables to your menu.

- Add leeks or shallots to omelets, risotto, and stews, or simply use them in place of onions in any recipe.

- Make a delicious party dip by combining yogurt with finely chopped garlic and chives.

- Include minced, raw garlic in salsa, cooked eggs, or pizza.

- Toss chopped onions in stir-fries, vegetable soup, chili, and vegetable casseroles.

- Scatter red onions on tacos, salads, or pizza.

Build better joints with broccoli

Some people love broccoli enough to mix it into omelets, while other people avoid it like the plague. But once you read this, you'll want to add broccoli to pasta dishes, soups, stir-fries, and anything else you can think of.

The vitamin you should get every day. Broccoli is packed with nutrients, but its high vitamin K content may be particularly important. According to a Boston University School of Medicine study, even a mild vitamin K deficiency can raise your risk of knee OA.

Experts suggest vitamin K may protect against arthritis for two reasons.

- People who get less vitamin K have higher blood levels of 14 inflammation-causing compounds. That's bad news because inflammation can contribute to the cartilage damage of arthritis.

- Your body uses certain proteins to protect your cartilage. But if you don't get enough vitamin K, these proteins may not be able to prevent damage to your cartilage.

Vitamin K may also be important if you already have arthritis. A recent study of nearly 800 older adults found arthritis got worse more quickly in people with lower blood levels of vitamin K. So eating more broccoli – and other vitamin K-rich foods – may be a smart way to help defend against arthritis. Other good sources of vitamin K include turnip greens, Swiss chard, kale, asparagus, and garden cress. Vitamin K can interact with warfarin (Coumadin) and other blood-thinning medications. If you take one of these medicines, talk to your doctor before adding more vitamin K to your diet.

Protect yourself from arthritis and cancer. Sulforaphane has become famous for helping prevent cancer, but a British study suggests it can also block an inflammation-causing compound that promotes damage to your joints. Yet you can easily miss out on broccoli's sulforaphane if you don't know what makes it and what breaks it.

Sulforaphane doesn't exist until chewing or chopping fresh broccoli causes an enzyme called myrosinase to combine with the broccoli compound glucoraphanin. But boiling or frying destroys myrosinase, so steam your broccoli instead. Steaming may even lead to extra sulforaphane.

Frozen broccoli may also have lost its myrosinase, but you can fix that problem. Jazz up your broccoli with spicy mustard, horseradish, wasabi, raw grated cabbage, watercress, or radish. The myrosinase in these foods can give your broccoli the boost it needs to produce sulforaphane.

Gout relief! 5 forbidden foods you can start eating again

Dried beans and peas, asparagus, mushrooms, and oatmeal probably went right off the menu when you started your anti-gout diet, but new research suggests you may be able to eat them again — if you're careful.

In a recent study, people with gout who ate the most purines were nearly five times as likely to have a gout attack compared with people who ate the least. But which purine-rich foods you choose may be the key.

Another study discovered that people who ate the most purines from animal-based foods faced much higher odds of a gout attack than those who ate the most from plant foods. The reason — plant foods are naturally far lower in purines than animal foods. Experts say the trick is to eat them in moderation.

Is your favorite beverage helping or hurting your joints?

Choosing the wrong beverage could mean years of pain. For example, women who drink at least one sugar-sweetened soda a day were 63 percent more likely to develop rheumatoid arthritis, a recent study discovered.

Yet milk may help some people who already have osteoarthritis (OA). Your beverage choice may even help you prevent gout attacks. Here's the scoop you need to know.

Good news for milk lovers. Women can slow progress of knee OA by drinking nonfat or low-fat milk. A four-year study found that women who drank milk every week developed less joint damage in their knees than women who didn't. Women who drank seven or more glasses a week got the best results.

Why alcohol is a double-edged sword. A British study suggests men who average eight or more beers a week have much higher odds of knee OA than men who drink less. Yet people who drink four or more glasses of wine weekly may lower their risk. The researchers suggest polyphenols in wine may help protect your joints. Just remember, alcohol can increase your risk of cancer and other serious health problems, so experts suggest men limit themselves to two drinks a day, and women should stop after one. One drink equals 12 oz. of beer, 5 oz. of wine, or 1 1/2 oz. of hard liquor.

Be even more careful if you have gout. One or two alcoholic drinks – of any kind– makes you 36 percent more likely to have a gout attack, research shows. Drink more than that, and your risk of an attack is 50 percent higher.

How tea may protect your joints. Preliminary research suggests compounds in green tea may help reduce inflammation and slow the destruction of cartilage. What's more, animals fed green tea polyphenols had lower levels of inflammatory compounds in their arthritic joints.

Why not try drinking two or three cups of green tea a day. Experts suggest you should brew green tea at roughly 175 to 185 degrees. If you don't have a thermometer, bring the water to a boil but wait two to three minutes before pouring.

3 pain-fighting supplements that aren't just hype

Tired of spending your hard-earned money on supplements that are more hype than help? Fortunately, scientists have conducted studies on some arthritis supplements to see if they work. Here are three that passed the test, proving they could help reduce pain and make you feel better.

ASU. Compounds found in avocado and soybean oil called unsaponifiables could make your knee arthritis less painful. When combined into a single supplement, these are called avocado-soybean unsaponifiables (ASU).

A Danish review of studies found that 300 milligrams (mg) taken daily may reduce the pain of knee osteoarthritis (OA). It may reduce the need for painkillers, too.

Studies also show ASU can reduce inflammation-causing compounds in your body, protect cells in your joints, and even promote repair of your cartilage. But finding the right dose can be tricky, and some people allergic to latex may not be able to take ASU safely. Talk with your doctor before trying it.

Indian frankincense. You may remember frankincense as a gift brought to the baby Jesus by the Three Wise Men from the East. Indian frankincense may turn out to be a gift for people with arthritis.

A study of an Indian frankincense extract called 5-Loxin suggests it can start working in as little as seven days and may reduce pain by up to two-thirds within three months. Research shows other extracts of Indian frankincense may also ease pain and improve OA symptoms.

Experts think a compound called Acetyl-11-keto-beta-boswellic acid (AKBA) is the active ingredient in Indian frankincense. Products that successfully reduced arthritis pain in studies contained at least 20 percent AKBA or boswellic acids.

If you'd like to try Indian frankincense, clear it with your doctor. If she approves, check your local health food stores. You may find this remedy under its other name, Boswellia. If you can't find it locally, Boswellia may be available from online and mail order sources like these:

- Amazon *www.amazon.com*

- The Vitamin Shoppe *www.vitaminshoppe.com* (toll-free 866-293-3367)

Fish oil. If your doctor says you need more omega-3 fats than fish can provide, fish oil supplements may be the cheap, easy, natural way to get relief from rheumatoid arthritis symptoms.

A Canadian review of fish oil research found that taking fish oil supplements for three or four months reduces joint pain, morning stiffness, number of painful joints, and use of painkillers in people with RA.

In another study, people with early RA who took at least 3 grams (g) of fish oil a day along with their medication fared better than those who didn't. Fish oil takers delayed having to use stronger medicine and needed fewer NSAIDs to control their pain and inflammation. They were also more likely to achieve remission of their symptoms.

But keep in mind taking more than 2 g of fish oil can suppress your immune system, cause drug interactions and side effects, and affect lab test results. Get your doctor's approval before you start taking fish oil supplements.

Take a tip from the Brits to soothe your joints

Strawberries and cream is a traditional favorite for spectators at the Wimbledon tennis championships in London — and this luscious fruit should be a favorite for you, too. Here's why.

One study found that people with knee osteoarthritis could slow its progression by eating at least 152 milligrams (mg) of vitamin C daily. A cup of strawberry halves provides nearly your full recommended dietary allowance (RDA) of vitamin C. But since 152 mg is more than the RDA, you may need to add an orange to your day to reach that amount. Yet strawberries have more to offer than just vitamin C.

Like cherries, strawberries contain at least one anthocyanin that may help fight pain and inflammation. In addition, lab studies suggest strawberry extracts can inhibit the COX enzymes that promote inflammation in your body.

To make your own version of strawberries and cream, combine strawberries with a little nonfat vanilla yogurt.

Got pain? Beans and grains to the rescue

What do Louisiana and China have in common? Louisiana is famous for red beans and rice, and China serves up mung-bean-and-rice porridge. Bean and grain combos like these are good sources of an inflammation-fighter you can unleash against arthritis and gout today.

If you have rheumatoid arthritis or gout, an overload of inflammation in your body is triggering your pain. One sign of having too much inflammation is high blood levels of a compound called C-reactive protein (CRP).

To lower your levels of CRP, you must reduce inflammation. Beans and whole grains can help. A review of studies suggests a serving of whole grains may lower CRP by 7 percent. The Arthritis Foundation also says high-fiber foods can help lower CRP. Whole grains and beans have plenty of fiber, so both fit the bill.

To get the best results from fiber, grains, and beans, remember these tips.

- Watch out for grains and grain products that aren't whole grains. These include white rice and many breads, pastas, cereals, and baked goods. To find whole grains, check for the Whole Grain Stamp from the Whole Grains Council. If you don't find that, check the ingredient list for terms like whole grain, wheatberries, whole-wheat, whole oats, or whole followed by the name of another grain. Choose brown rice over white rice, and eat foods like popcorn and oatmeal.

- Raise the amount of fiber in your diet gradually so you won't experience gas, bloating, diarrhea, and other unpleasant symptoms.

- Make peace with beans. Some people won't eat beans because they're worried about getting gas, but you can prevent that. Spice up a bean dish with summer savory, change the water several times while cooking dry beans – or try Beano.

Muscles & tendons

Nutrition that heals

Pack in the protein to prevent muscle weakness

If you find it difficult to hang on to your morning coffee cup, get up from your favorite recliner, or even bend down to leash your dog for your afternoon walk, you may be experiencing sarcopenia. This debilitating condition produces a gradual loss of lean muscle and strength and is common as you age.

Where did my muscles go? From the time you reach the age of 50, muscle mass drops an average of 1 to 2 percent each year. You may be all too familiar with the symptoms – trouble moving around and a feeling of weakness. That said, if you don't suffer from this condition, chances are you know someone who does.

The most distressing part of sarcopenia is how much it can upset your quality of life.

- When you're unsteady on your feet, you're more likely to fall, and that puts you at risk for significant injuries.

- Too weak to get up and move around? That can lead to weight gain, which usually means additional health problems.

- If your condition gets bad enough, you could even lose your ability to live alone.

Thankfully, even though sarcopenia affects almost one out of every three people over the age of 60, you can protect yourself with protein and exercise and reclaim your independence.

Protein helps you stay strong in your golden years. The old saying, "You are what you eat," is certainly true when it comes to protein. This nutrient is the building block of your muscles. Without it, your body simply can't stay strong. A Tufts University study reveals that people who gobble up beef, chicken, and other sources of protein have more muscle mass.

If you're older, you need about 1 gram of protein per kilogram of body. For example, at 140 pounds, you would need 64 grams of protein a day – that's less than you'll find in an order of sweet and sour chicken.

But don't binge on your entire quota in one sitting. Nutritionists recommend you eat a little at every meal. Because you don't have the ability to store excess protein, eating protein-rich foods throughout the day will give your body the chance to get the most out of them. For example, you could add egg whites to your breakfast, turkey at lunch, and beans in the evening.

Beef up your body with exercise. There's no getting around it. You'll hang onto your muscles longer if you are active in addition to eating plenty of protein. While you don't have to work out with the passion of a body builder, resistance training such as lifting weights is a good idea.

Fight muscle loss with food. Many nutrients work together with protein to battle for brawn, so make sure you get enough of them by minding your meals.

- Vitamin D is important for maintaining muscle strength and function. If you're deficient here, it could add to your muscle weakness. Canned salmon is a delicious option. It's full of protein and vitamin D.

■ Omega-3 fatty acids encourage protein synthesis, a major part of muscle growth, repair, and maintenance. That would make fatty fish a smart choice since it contains both omega-3 and protein.

■ Protein and other nutrients found in dairy also help with muscle function. Have a hankering for yogurt? Help yourself.

Remember, you're not limited to meat, fish, and poultry to get the protein you need. Beans, peas, and pumpkin seeds can be tasty high-protein alternatives. For a quick snack, grab a handful of almonds to keep you going.

Skip the meat! Get plenty of protein with these pairings

What is the first thing you think of when you hear the word "protein"? Is it meat? Meat is a big deal in the United States. In fact, the average American eats around 270 pounds of meat each year. But maybe you aren't a fan of meat or, for medical reasons, have to cut back. You can get all the protein you need by matching up your veggies and grains to get a complete protein meal.

Complementary proteins complement your diet. When you don't get all the essential amino acids you need, your body is not able to use proteins like it's supposed to. Certain foods have low amounts of essential amino acids or "incomplete" proteins. By combining two or more of them to form complementary proteins, you can get enough essential amino acids into your diet.

Some researchers suggest that combining foods like this isn't necessary as long as you eat a variety of plant-based foods. But others say simply mixing it up may not allow you to get enough of certain essential amino acids because plant-food proteins don't have as many amino acids as animal-food proteins. They argue that a combination of plant-based foods will raise the protein quality of your meal.

What everyone does agree on is that many plant proteins contain more limited amounts of amino acids per serving compared to animal sources. You may find it difficult to get enough essential amino acids without attention to complementary proteins. Luckily, there's an easy way to make sure you get all the nutrients you need.

Why protein combos are the way to go. Legumes, grains, and nuts all contain fiber, which helps you feel full without all the calories. They are packed with B vitamins and minerals such as calcium, iron, zinc, potassium, and magnesium. They are also great for your heart and help lower risks associated with heart disease. Dairy products, especially yogurt and milk, provide vitamin D, potassium, and calcium – important nutrients in maintaining bone mass. They are considered complete proteins, which make them great additions to a vegetarian diet.

How to pair for a protein-packed snack. Whether or not you choose to combine complementary proteins, the most important thing is that you have a nutrient-balanced diet. You don't have to eat complementary proteins at the same meal to get the benefits. As long as you eat them within the same day, you can get a protein-rich diet that is just as healthy as eating meat. For example, legumes provide plenty of the amino acids isoleucine and lysine, but they have less methionine and tryptophan. Grains are the opposite, making them a perfect match for legumes. Here are the best foods to pair for a complete protein meal:

- Grains and dairy

- Grains and legumes

- Nuts or seeds and legumes

How to combine proteins for a complete meal

Protein foods like grains, dairy, legumes, nuts, and seeds have low amounts of some essential amino acids. Get the right amounts of protein simply by serving two types of "vegetarian" fare together. Here are complete protein ideas that you can fit into every meal.

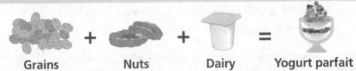

Grains + **Nuts** + **Dairy** = **Yogurt parfait**

Start the day with a parfait. Combine a cup of plain yogurt (13 grams of protein), 1/4 cup of oats (7 g) and pecans (3 g), and a handful of strawberries and blueberries.

23 g protein

Grains + **Legumes** = **Brown rice & kidney beans**

A cup of each of this classic duo is perfect with a tomato for a protein-packed lunch. Add your own seasonings to your rice (5 g) and beans (15 g) for more flavor.

20 g protein

Grains + **Legumes** = **Hummus and pita**

Spice up a half cup of hummus (10 grams of protein) with a tablespoon of chives and sweet green peppers. Serve with a large pita (6 g).

16 g protein

Grains **Seeds** **Legumes** **Dairy** = **Quinoa black bean salad**

Salad doesn't have to be boring. Mix half a head of green leaf lettuce (2 grams of protein) with some high-protein toppings like a half cup of quinoa (4 g) and black beans (8 g), 1/4 cup of feta cheese (5 g), and a tablespoon of sunflower seeds (3 g).

22 g protein

Can a hug make you strong?

Oxytocin is known as the "love hormone" for a reason. This chemical is produced in your brain when you give a hug, have a baby, or gaze into the eyes of your loyal pup. Not surprisingly, it plays a big role in romance and bonding.

Researchers are now discovering a link between oxytocin and muscle aging. The hormone is required for tissue regrowth because it stimulates the release of calcium and activates each protein's specific function — two major contributors of strong muscles. A shortage of the chemical could lead to premature sarcopenia. While cuddling with a loved one probably won't stop your muscles from aging, the FDA-approved prescription drug oxytocin might be a safe way to prevent muscle aging.

3 of nature's best painkillers

When does a hobby become a pain in the elbow or a home project turn into a sore shoulder? It's when you've overused a joint or tendon and it becomes inflamed. Repetitive tasks – like painting a room or raking leaves – can lead to bursitis or tendinitis, two conditions you may want to tackle without medication.

- Bursitis is inflammation of the small, fluid-filled sacs between bones, muscles, and tendons. It often comes from overuse or repetitive stress on a joint, like gardening or playing tennis.

- Tendinitis is most often the result of repetitive motion or injury. It happens more often as you age because, as tendons become less flexible, they are more prone to injury.

Many people take nonsteroidal anti-inflammatory drugs (NSAIDs) for these conditions, making up a multibillion dollar industry. But they don't come without risk. NSAIDs are the most common cause of drug-related death reported to the Food and Drug Administration. You can try natural inflammation fighters and avoid the side effects of pain medicines.

Wash away the pain of inflammation with fish oil. Omega-3 polyunsaturated fatty acids are among the most effective natural anti-inflammatories. These fatty acids, found mainly in fish oil, help stop chronic inflammation triggered by certain immune cells. To test the effects of fish oil supplements on inflammation-related pain, researchers asked 250 people who were using NSAIDs to take 2,400 milligrams (mg) of fish oil a day for two weeks, then reduce the dose to 1,200 mg, while gradually stopping the NSAIDs. The results:

- Fifty-nine percent stopped taking NSAID medication for pain after two months on fish oil.

- Sixty percent reported that their overall pain level had improved.

Eat turmeric to spice up your life and treat inflammation at the same time. Curcumin is a yellow pigment found naturally in turmeric, a plant of the ginger family. An antioxidant and anti-inflammatory, curcumin is often considered a natural alternative to NSAIDs for the treatment of inflammation.

The easiest way to get a boost of curcumin is by eating turmeric. You can add it to vegetable and meat dishes, rice, and soups to add flavor and color. When cooking, be sure to add black pepper to the mix. The piperine found in black pepper helps your body absorb the curcumin.

To get the amount of curcumin taken in recent studies, you would have to eat two tablespoons of turmeric three times a day. The University of Maryland Medical Center only recommends about 1 1/2 teaspoons of ground turmeric powder a day, so you might want to add curcumin supplements. For best results, take 400 to 600 milligrams of standardized powder three times a day.

Try the anti-inflammatory that grows on trees. The salicin in white willow bark works similar to aspirin, but with fewer side effects. Though willow bark extract is more expensive, studies show it may be more effective than celecoxib and aspirin in protecting against inflammation and the harmful effects of oxidative stress.

You can take willow bark in several ways. Tea and capsules are the most popular.

- Dried herb: 1 to 2 teaspoons of dried bark in 8 ounces of hot water, three to four cups daily

- Powdered herb: 240 mg of standardized salicin a day for up to 12 weeks

Talk with your doctor before taking willow bark because it can be dangerous for people taking certain medications, like blood thinners, and those with serious medical conditions like diabetes, asthma, high blood pressure, or gastrointestinal disorders. Likewise, you should never give willow bark to children.

Pick this fruit early to build bigger muscles

The same research team that discovered a compound in apple peels improves muscle size and strength in mice has found another muscle builder — this time in your vegetable garden. Tomatidine, a natural compound from tomato plants, is even more effective in combating muscle loss, increasing strength, and enhancing recovery. So far, tests have only been performed on mice. Although more tests are needed, scientists confirm you can get tomatidine by eating green tomatoes.

Body aches? 3 ways to eat to feel better now

Excruciating pain in every muscle isn't something anyone can see, but if you're suffering with fibromyalgia, you know how it feels. Fibromyalgia is a syndrome no one fully understands. Currently, managing the symptoms is the only treatment available. Because self-care is so essential, it's helpful to know you can ease the pain of fibromyalgia starting in your kitchen.

Vegetarians hold the secret to fibromyalgia management.

Fibromyalgia affects about 5 million people. Amid sleepless nights, morning stiffness, headaches, and leg spasms, sufferers of this syndrome usually experience muscle pain and fatigue. Research suggests a raw, vegetarian diet can help all symptoms of fibromyalgia. One study examined the effects of a low-salt, raw vegan diet on fibromyalgia symptoms. The results were promising.

- People experienced significant improvements in pain, joint stiffness, quality of sleep, and general health.

- Most participants were overweight at the beginning of the study and the raw vegan diet led to significant reductions in body mass index.

Antioxidants — the natural cure for aching, throbbing muscles.

Antioxidants are linked to oxidative stress and fibromyalgia. Oxidative stress causes inflammation and can worsen the progression of disease – including the pain response. Scientists believe antioxidants help decrease oxidative stress by blocking the effects of free radicals.

In a recent study, 50 middle-age women with fibromyalgia took:

- 500 milligrams (mg) vitamin C

- 200 mg vitamin E

- 13 mg *Nigella sativa* seeds (four to five seeds)

After eight weeks of taking the antioxidants daily, their pain scores decreased. It's easy to add antioxidant-rich snacks into your diet. Citrus fruits, berries, and dark green vegetables are high in vitamin C. You can get vitamin E from vegetable oils, nuts, and whole grains.

Stop pain before it starts with tart cherry juice. Doctors encourage fibromyalgia sufferers to exercise to strengthen muscles and improve flexibility. However, exercise can lead to a "fibro-flair" – heightened symptoms and delayed onset muscle soreness (DOMS). Tart cherry juice contains anti-inflammatories and antioxidants, and it can reduce strength loss associated with DOMS. In one study, people drank 10.5 ounces of tart cherry juice twice a day for 10 days. In general, overall pain scores improved, and people with fibromyalgia were able to maintain their strength longer after exercise.

In another study, volunteers drank tart cherry juice five days before, the day of, and for 48 hours following a marathon run. Results showed tart cherry juice is effective for recovery after intense activity.

The reason it's so effective is not completely clear, but researchers have a few theories.

■ Tart cherry juice contains anthocyanins. Scientists think these pigments improve the ability of older adults to resist oxidative damage. To test the theory, people drank about 8 ounces of tart cherry juice twice a day for 14 days. Drinking the juice improved antioxidant defenses and reduced oxidative damage.

■ Another way tart cherry juice may help is by reducing inflammation and muscle damage.

> ## Why this 'cure' will only drive you bananas
>
> Eat a banana if you get a cramp, some people say, but does it actually work? Researchers say no. While bananas can increase your potassium levels, it will take 30 to 60 minutes to take effect — too long for it to do any good. Here's the good news — bananas are still a healthy choice, containing lots of important nutrients besides potassium, like vitamin C, vitamin B6, and manganese.

Stop post-workout soreness with kitchen cures

Cherry juice isn't the only food that can combat sore muscles. From cramps to pain after exercise, there's a food that can help.

Multitalented ginger relieves muscle pain, too. Ginger is used in countries around the world as a spice, condiment, and even an herbal medicine. Due to its anti-inflammatory effect, ginger can reduce muscle pain caused by exercise. Several studies show if you eat ginger before exercise, you'll hurt less later.

- In one study, 36 people took 2 grams of a raw ginger supplement, a heat-treated ginger supplement, or a placebo for 11 days. Muscle pain was significantly reduced in the people taking the ginger supplements.

- In a similar study, ginger decreased muscle pain caused by exercise-related injury to the elbow.

A splash of pickle juice cures cramps in seconds. Cramps are one of the sneakiest kinds of muscle pain. Though scientists are not sure how pickle juice works to stop cramps, studies show it reduces cramps 45 percent faster than if you drink nothing. In one study, published in the American College of Sports Medicine's journal, people drank about 2.5 ounces of pickle juice. Muscle cramps disappeared within 12 to 219 seconds – an average of 85 seconds.

Though pickle juice can help you get rid of muscle spasms fast, the best way to combat cramps is to stop them before they start. Reduce your chances of getting cramps by following these tips.

- Eat foods high in vitamins and minerals, especially magnesium and calcium.

- Drink plenty of water.

- Stretch gently before and after you exercise.

Fast food: the fast track to muscle loss

Chowing down on high-fat meals can disrupt the way your muscles process nutrients, says a study of 12 healthy, college-age men. An increase in diet from 30 percent fat to 63 percent fat changed the muscles' ability to break down and use nutrients. This effect happens surprisingly fast — within just five days.

Other studies say a high-phosphate diet is linked to premature aging, a cause of severe muscle loss. Foods like cheese and pudding contain high amounts of phosphorus, but now some traditionally low-phosphorus foods and beverages have added phosphorus. Look out for:

- iced teas and flavored waters

- carbonated beverages and other bottled drinks

- uncooked meat and poultry products

- breakfast cereal bars

- nondairy creamers

Added phosphorus may be labeled as phosphoric acid, polyphosphate, and other ingredients that end in "phosphate."

Oral health

14 foods that put a smile on your face

Yogurt: a cup a day will keep the dentist away

You've heard of the mind-body connection, but what about the *mouth*-body connection? It may surprise you to learn that problems in your mouth can have a big impact on the rest of your body. In fact, studies suggest that health issues like diabetes, heart disease, and even pregnancy difficulties, are often connected to oral health.

Luckily, a creamy treat you already love can help keep your teeth and gums strong and give you the confidence boost that comes with a clean, healthy mouth.

Yogurt is marvelous for your mouth. Along with tooth-strengthening calcium and protein, yogurt contains millions of "good" bacteria, called probiotics. These are found naturally in your body as well as in foods and supplements. These beneficial microbes help your body by curbing the growth of harmful bacteria, encouraging good digestion, boosting your immune system, and bumping up your resistance to infection.

What a lot of people don't know is that these good guys are also amazingly helpful in your mouth.

- In one study, people took tablets containing probiotic bacteria three times a day. After just eight weeks, scientists saw less plaque buildup and inflammation in gum tissue compared to those who didn't take probiotics.

- Let's face it, bad breath can be embarrassing. But you can fight it by eating plain, sugar-free yogurt on a regular basis. In one study, eating yogurt twice a day for six weeks decreased stinky breath in 80 percent of volunteers.

- Canker sores can make it painful to eat, smile, or even talk. Fortunately, studies suggest probiotics block reoccurring ulcers that appear in the mouth. *Lactobacillus acidophilus* and *Lactobacillus bulgaricus*, two common yogurt probiotics, are warriors when it comes to fighting off bad bacteria that hang out in places like your mouth.

Lactic acid keeps your gums healthy. Like probiotics, lactic acid is made in your body and also found in foods like yogurt. Researchers discovered that foods rich in lactic acid help protect against infection in the spaces between gums and teeth, as well as tissue damage, both telltale signs of gum disease.

A delicious way to meet your dairy needs. Two out of three people in the United States don't meet the dairy requirements set by the Dietary Guidelines for Americans, which is three 8-ounce servings of low-fat or nonfat dairy products daily. You can help give your body the dairy it needs by snacking on a cup of yogurt every day.

Pay attention to ingredients. Avoid common buying mistakes by following these tips to ensure you get the most out of your yogurt.

- Check the sugar content of your yogurt, and beware of fake fruit. You don't want to undo all the good things about yogurt by eating products jam-packed with sugar and artificial ingredients.

- Look for "Live and Active Cultures" on the yogurt label to insure the yogurt contains significant amounts of probiotics. If you don't see this seal, check the ingredient list for *L. bulgaricus, S. thermophilus,* or *L. acidophilus.*

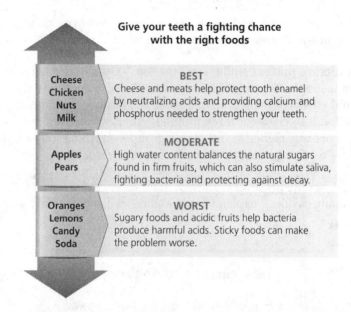

Give your teeth a fighting chance
with the right foods

Cheese Chicken Nuts Milk	**BEST** Cheese and meats help protect tooth enamel by neutralizing acids and providing calcium and phosphorus needed to strengthen your teeth.
Apples Pears	**MODERATE** High water content balances the natural sugars found in firm fruits, which can also stimulate saliva, fighting bacteria and protecting against decay.
Oranges Lemons Candy Soda	**WORST** Sugary foods and acidic fruits help bacteria produce harmful acids. Sticky foods can make the problem worse.

5 cavity-fighting secrets your dentist never told you

You're calm and confident, lounging patiently in the reception area, showing no signs of stress or anxiety as you take in the familiar sounds and smells. Surprise – you're at the dentist. And you're relishing every minute of peace and comfort knowing your mouth will pass every test. Never thought you'd feel that way, did you? But you can, and you can do it without spending a fortune. Here are five natural – and affordable – ways to make you and your dentist smile.

Turn to vitamin D to defeat decay. Vitamin D plays an important role in building and maintaining bone. Scientists have found it also stops the growth of microorganisms and fights inflammation. In reviewing more than 20 studies on almost 3,000 children, researchers concluded that vitamin D can help prevent tooth decay and reduce the number of cavities.

If you love seafood, you have the perfect opportunity to get more vitamin D into your diet. Slip 3 ounces of pink salmon with bones into your next meal, and you'll get 133 percent of your daily value. Tuna and shrimp are also "swimming" in vitamin D.

For a picture perfect smile, say "cheese." Enamel is the hardest substance in the human body, but even it can't stand up to the harmful effects of plaque. In one study, children were given different foods to chew for three minutes. After 30 minutes, the plaque pH was higher in the cheese group – meaning it was less acidic – resulting in lower chances of tooth decay.

"The higher the pH level is above 5.5, the lower the chance of developing cavities," explains Vipal Yadav, lead author of the study.

Are cavities contagious?

Believe it or not, they are. Just like a virus, cavity-producing bacteria can be spread through kissing and sharing drinks and food. Something as simple as tasting your child's food to see if it's too hot can spread harmful germs. Young children are particularly vulnerable to the common bacterium *Streptococcus mutans*.

As an adult, you've probably built up an immunity to many of these microorganisms. But your mouth plays host to more than 500 types of bacteria, so to avoid contaminating anyone else, remember to brush and floss often.

Make strong gums your cup of tea by going green. Up until the 18th century, people believed evil tooth worms crawled into your teeth and caused decay. Thankfully, dentists now know cavities are caused by bacteria feeding on sugar in your mouth and creating acids that dissolve your enamel.

If you drink green tea, you may be arming yourself to fight these germs. In a study, people rinsed twice a day for a minute with mouthwash containing 2 percent green tea. After 28 days, they saw a significant drop in their levels of plaque and gingivitis, showing that green tea promotes healthy gums and reduces plaque buildup.

Wake up and fight cavities with your morning brew. Studies show that drinking coffee can help prevent cavities because it has antioxidant compounds that fight bacteria. It's best to drink it black because adding milk and sugar lessons the antibacterial and anti-cavity effects.

In one study, an extract of *Coffea canephora*, also known as robusta, proved itself a cavity fighter by breaking down sticky microorganisms that cause dental plaque. Robusta is mainly found in instant coffees, espressos, and coffee blends.

Sink your teeth into sugarless gum for a cleaner mouth. Would you believe chewing gum can actually be good for you? In a small study, volunteers chewed gum for up to 10 minutes. Researchers found that some 100,000,000 bacteria were removed from the mouth and trapped in each piece of gum. They theorize that chewing gum daily may help lower the amount of bacteria in your mouth and contribute to long-term oral health.

Latest dental craze may be more fad than fact

Whiten your teeth, eliminate bacteria, strengthen your gums, and even prevent bad breath – in 15 minutes? Advocates of a dental craze called oil pulling say it can do it all. Preliminary studies suggest this ancient Indian folk remedy could be beneficial to your oral health, but not everyone is on board.

Oil pulling involves swishing a tablespoon of sunflower, sesame, coconut, or other edible oil in your mouth for 15 to 20 minutes every day. The theory goes that when you "pull" the oil around your mouth and in between your teeth, bacteria stick to it. When you spit the liquid out, the bacteria go with it.

Some people swish it while taking their morning shower, but if you do this, don't spit it down the drain because it could clog pipes.

3 cheap ways to freshen your mouth

Looking for other natural mouthwash solutions? Gargle baking soda, salt water, or diluted peroxide for 30 to 60 seconds several times a day to fight bacteria and plaque.

- Baking soda is inexpensive and readily available. To make a mouthwash, dissolve one teaspoon of baking soda in a glass of water.

- Salt water is particularly effective for mouth wounds but should not be used long-term. For this rinse, mix 1/4 teaspoon of salt with one cup of warm water.

- Hydrogen peroxide needs to be diluted, so mix one teaspoon of peroxide into a half cup of water. Again, don't use it long-term.

If you don't want to make your own, look for natural, alcohol-free mouthwashes that contain no artificial colors, flavors, or preservatives. Another option is a mouth rinse with xylitol, a natural sugar alcohol that keeps bacteria from sticking to your teeth.

Pull plaque away with coconut oil. Coconut oil seems to be all the rage. Online ads rave that it contains "the healthiest substance on earth," and bloggers claim it can be used for cooking, cosmetics, and improving your health.

Recently, scientists have found that swishing coconut oil may help keep your mouth healthy by fighting plaque formation, which is the primary cause of cavities and gum inflammation. One study reported that oil pulling was just as effective as the antiseptic, anti-bacterial wash chlorhexidine against plaque-induced gingivitis.

Sesame oil helps banish bad breath. In another study, sesame oil worked just as well as chlorhexidine against bad breath and the bacteria associated with it. Other studies with sesame oil had the same results, revealing a significant reduction in the number of *Streptococcus mutans*, a major contributor to tooth decay.

Don't toss out the toothbrush just yet. A technique like oil pulling may be great for developing countries, but in places where commercial products are readily available, is it worth your time? Some people want to go the natural route to avoid the chemicals and alcohol in mouthwashes, which can strip away natural protection and cause dry mouth.

But the American Dental Association (ADA) argues that no studies have provided clear evidence that oil pulling fights cavities, whitens teeth, or improves oral health. Plus they don't mention adverse side effects like diarrhea, upset stomach, or the possibility of inhaling the oil into your lungs. Therefore, the ADA does not endorse oil pulling as a replacement for standard oral hygiene.

And for many dentists, oil pulling does not outweigh the benefits of modern treatment. "It's hard enough to get people to properly brush their teeth, much less to swish an oil for 15 to 20 minutes," says Dr. David Murphy, DDS. "It may be effective, but with easier and less timely products that are more effective, it does not make sense in my mind to recommend oil pulling."

Instead, Dr. Murphy recommends investing in an electric toothbrush and making sure you get proper nutrition. "Overall, the mouth is just a reflection of your body's health," he says.

The absolute best ways to cure cotton mouth

After undergoing radiation therapy to his neck, Joe had a problem. No matter what he did, he couldn't seem to keep his mouth from drying up. He finally resorted to carrying a squirt bottle around with him everywhere he went.

If your mouth has been feeling like the Sahara desert lately, you know how Joe was feeling. Dry mouth can be irritating, but it can also cause dental issues. Know what foods to eat and avoid, and soothe your dry mouth once and for all.

Your mouth should be swimming in saliva. During your lifetime, your mouth produces a lot of saliva – enough to fill a swimming pool, believe it or not. But sometimes your salivary glands don't work right. Xerostomia, or dry mouth, is the result.

Dry mouth is the side effect of more than 400 medications and many diseases, including Sjogren's syndrome and diabetes. You may be surprised to learn that conditions like these can affect the health of your mouth along with the rest of your body.

Dry mouth encourages the growth of bacteria that can cause bad breath. Green tea acts as a disinfectant and deodorant. Swish it around your mouth to temporarily reduce bad breath more effectively than sugarless gum or mints.

Fend off dry mouth by avoiding certain foods. Some ingredients and foods can aggravate dry mouth, leading to cracked lips, infection, and mouth sores. Help your mouth out by dodging these dry-mouth disasters.

- Go easy on caffeine. Coffee, tea, and soda may taste good for the moment, but you'll regret it later when your mouth feels like cotton.

- Steer clear of sticky snacks. Foods like peanut butter and soft bread can stick to the roof of your mouth.

- Limit salt and spice. When your mouth is dry, foods that are salty or spicy can cause pain and make you even more uncomfortable.

- Stay away from dry foods. Biscuits, crackers, and dry snacks absorb moisture in your mouth.

- Avoid alcohol. Alcohol is dehydrating, and your mouth will suffer for it. This includes the alcohol in mouthwash, too.

Mouthwatering tips for a happy mouth. Saliva protects your teeth from decay and allows you to chew and swallow. Follow these tips to add moisture to your mouth and make eating easier.

- Sip water throughout the day. Water thins mucus and makes chewing and swallowing less challenging.

- Chew sugarless gum. Chewing gum or sucking on sugarless hard candy helps stimulate the flow of saliva.

- Eat soft, moist foods. Try blended fruits and vegetables with a high water content, soft-cooked chicken and fish, popsicles, and smoothies.

- Moisten your food. You can do this with broth, soup, sauces, and yogurt.

- Munch on fresh pineapple – it will help thin your saliva. But don't try it if your mouth is sore.

3 natural (and painless) ways to conquer cold sores

Cold sores, also know as fever blisters, can be painful and embarrassing. But perhaps the worst thing about them is their unpredictability. Don't spend your time worrying about your next outbreak. Apply these natural remedies as soon as you feel the tingle to knock out cold sores fast.

Lysine is the first line of attack. If you get these painful blisters, you're not alone. Around 90 percent of American adults have been exposed to the herpes simplex virus, which causes them. Studies show that lysine, an amino acid responsible for tissue repair and growth, battles the amino acid arginine, which helps the herpes virus reproduce. Want to keep cold sores from recurring? Get more lysine, and less arginine, in your diet.

If you're prone to cold sores, experts recommend you get 500 to 3,000 milligrams of lysine a day by eating lysine-rich foods like fish, lean meats, chicken, milk, and cheese. At the same time, reduce the amount of high-arginine foods you eat by limiting chocolate, nuts, seeds, beer, coconut, and grains.

Many foods have both amino acids, so look for foods that are much higher in lysine. Tuna, salmon, cottage cheese, and yogurt are a few examples.

Blackberry extract destroys infection before it begins. You'll spend less time battling blisters with this anti-inflammatory and antiviral compound often used to prevent and treat gum infections. One study showed that blackberry extract inactivated the herpes virus in its early stages. Scientists say the extract can be used topically for herpes infections. It's a cheap remedy, and as an added bonus, you can use it to flavor baked goods and desserts!

Lessen the length of outbreaks with lemon balm. *Melissa officinalis*, more commonly known as lemon balm, is part of the mint family. In one study, participants applied a cream containing 1 percent lemon balm to cold sores four times a day for five days. By the second day of treatment, people applying the lemon balm showed significant improvements compared to those using a placebo cream.

You'll find more tips for using lemon balm in *Get to the root of your skin problems with these 7 herbs* in the *Skin conditions & hair loss* chapter.

Reproductive health

Nutritional know-how for changing times

Give hot flashes the cold shoulder

Celebrity Rosie O'Donnell changed her haircut to make her hot
flashes easier to bear – but you can do better than that. Cut back
on spicy foods, and try these ideas that have already helped
other women.

Cool hot flashes with fruit. Australian researchers discovered that
women who ate the most fruit-rich diet had 20 percent less risk of
hot flashes and night sweats than those who ate the least. This diet
included apricots, strawberries, pineapples, melons, and mangos.

Women who ate the most high-fat foods and sweets actually had
more risk of hot flashes and night sweats. You may fit this high-
fat-and-sugar profile if you eat a lot of cakes, meat pies, cookies,
jam, and chocolate.

Can't really handle eating a lot of fruit right now? No problem.
Another group of women cut their risk of hot flashes and night
sweats by just as much as the fruit lovers, the researchers say.
These women ate a Mediterranean-style diet with plenty of garlic,
salad greens, peppers, mushrooms, pasta, and red wine.

Beat the heat with fabulous seafood. Delicious fish and fish oil
supplements may help reduce the number of hot flashes you have
each day, thanks to their healthy omega-3 fatty acids.

Eicosapentaenoic acid (EPA) may be particularly helpful.
Canadian women who took 500 milligrams (mg) of ethyl-EPA
three times a day for two months reported fewer hot flashes. Fish
like salmon and herring can help you get some of the EPA you
need, so start eating them at least twice a week. Also, ask your
doctor if you can safely take EPA supplements.

Make sage your herbal air conditioner. That sage in your garden isn't just good for cooking. Two studies suggest that taking
sage extract for two or three months may help ease symptoms of
menopause, especially hot flashes and night sweats.

Women who took 280 mg of thujone-free sage extract for two
months experienced 40 percent fewer hot flashes per day, and the
remaining flashes were less
intense. Women who took 120
mg of sage extract and 60 mg of
alfalfa extract for three months
also eliminated or reduced hot
flashes and night sweating.

Sage is generally safe for most
people, but high doses and some
forms of preparation can lead to
seizures, especially in those with
epilepsy or other seizure disor-
ders. Sage supplements may not be right for everyone, and they
may cause side effects or interact with health problems or lab
tests, so talk to your doctor before you try them. Meanwhile, a
mild sage tea might just do the trick.

> Don't want to take a sage pill? Drink sage tea instead. Pour one cup of hot water over either two teaspoons of fresh sage leaves or a heaping teaspoon of dried sage. Steep for 8 to 10 minutes. Strain, sweeten with honey if desired, and drink.

Does soy really work? Soy contains estrogen-like compounds called
phytoestrogens. Although these were once believed to be the
answer to menopause symptoms, research now suggests only some
soy products may help. Studies suggest soy products that provide at
least 15 mg of genistein daily are far more likely to help reduce hot
flashes than products with smaller amounts of this compound.

Before you grab a soy supplement here are three things you should know.

- Some studies suggest soy may raise the risk of Alzheimer's disease, while other studies suggest it may actually improve mental ability.

- Scientists don't know whether phytoestrogens can raise the risk of breast cancer like estrogen does after menopause, so they recommend eating soy foods rather than taking supplements.

- Some experts are concerned soy supplements may have a possible link with the risk of endometrial cancer, but eating soy foods may lower this risk.

Talk to your doctor before trying soy supplements or soy foods, especially if you take MAO inhibitors. If your doctor gives you the green light to eat soy, good foods to try include genistein-rich tempeh, miso, and canned soybeans.

Super seed soothes PMS pain

Don't throw those seeds from your jack-o-lantern into the trash. They could be the key to preventing premenstrual syndrome (PMS). Up to 40 percent of women struggle through a monthly round of symptoms including anxiety, bloating, irritability, depression, headaches, excessive tiredness, and food cravings. But a powerful ingredient in pumpkin seeds may help you avoid all that.

Special iron prevents PMS symptoms. Pumpkin seeds are a surprisingly good source of a special kind of iron called nonheme iron. Recently, a 10-year study of more than 3,000 women found that those who ate the most nonheme iron were less likely to ever have PMS. Nonheme iron may help because it supports brain processes that may fight or prevent symptoms of PMS.

Nonheme iron comes mostly from plants, while heme iron is only found in animal products like meat, poultry, and fish. Your body absorbs far less plant-based iron than animal-based, so you need to eat plenty of nonheme iron to cut your PMS risk.

Pumpkin seeds can help because you get close to 9 milligrams of nonheme iron from just one-fourth cup of seeds. That's more than the recommended daily amount of 8 mg for adults over age 51. Eat them on their own as a snack, or add them to trail mix, smoothies, salads, stir-fries, oatmeal, cereal, muffins, or even pesto.

You may also need other foods to get enough non-heme iron in your diet. Good choices include lentils, white beans, red kidney beans, fortified instant oatmeal, lima beans, prune juice, cooked spinach, black beans, or a baked potato with skin. Some experts even recommend trying iron-fortified cereal if you can't get enough nonheme iron from other sources.

Just remember, you may also be getting heme and nonheme iron from meats, your multivitamin, or other supplement pills. So play it safe – check your supplements, and ask your doctor if any of your medications contain high amounts of iron.

Vitamins give you an edge against PMS. Studies suggest calcium, riboflavin (B2), thiamin (B1), and vitamin D can also help prevent PMS. Fish, low-fat dairy foods, and fortified cereals can help you get more vitamin D and calcium. Fortified cereals also provide a lot of thiamin and riboflavin.

Other thiamin-rich foods include oats, hulled barley, rice, pistachio nuts, pork chops, and hibiscus tea. For more riboflavin, try almonds, roasted turkey breast, feta cheese, and dry milk.

PREPARE IT

The no-hassle way to clean pumpkin seeds

You don't need to spend a lot of time and effort cleaning the seeds that just came out of the pumpkin. Instead of fighting to disentangle the seeds from the pulp, throw the whole mess in a colander, rinse under running water, and follow these steps.

Fill a bowl with warm water, empty the colander into it, and let the seeds soak for a few minutes. Remove any pulp-free seeds that float to the top, and return them to the colander.

Rub the remaining seeds between your hands while keeping them under the warm water. As clean seeds float to the surface, move them to the colander. Keep rubbing pulp-coated seeds and removing clean ones until all the seeds are clean.

Rinse the seeds in the colander under running water one last time. Spread them out on a clean towel or paper towel, and let dry.

Men: painless ways to cut bathroom breaks

Tired of getting up to go to the bathroom several times a night? A "saucy" solution may be just what you need. Studies suggest tasty ingredients in some delicious pasta dishes really can help.

Urinary problems can be a symptom of several conditions, so see your doctor to find out which one you have. If your doctor says it's benign prostatic hyperplasia (BPH) or enlarged prostate, you're not alone. Half of all men over 50 have this problem, but you can do something about it – and fabulous food can help.

Pasta sauce: the right stuff to fight prostate symptoms. A hearty tomato sauce isn't just delicious – it is also a rich source of the powerful prostate defender lycopene. Scientists found that 15 milligrams (mg) of lycopene every day for six months significantly eased prostate symptoms and helped slow the progress of BPH.

Experts aren't sure why lycopene helps, but they suspect its antioxidant powers fight the inflammation and damage caused by free radicals in your prostate. As a result, lycopene may help reduce nagging urinary symptoms. It may also help lower levels of a compound linked to BPH risk.

Although the men in the lycopene study took supplements, you can get 15 mg of lycopene from a half-cup of spaghetti or marinara sauce. You can also enjoy 15 mg of lycopene from tasty options like one cup of canned tomato juice or tomato juice cocktail; a half-cup of canned tomato sauce with mushrooms; or an 8-ounce bowl of tomato soup, minestrone, or tomato rice soup. Other good lycopene sources include sun-dried tomatoes, Manhattan-style clam chowder, and tomato purée.

Add chunky garden vegetables for even better results. Research from the University of California found that men who ate more vegetables had fewer urinary symptoms and were less likely to get BPH in the first place.

To turn plain pasta sauce into garden veggie sauce, you can add the typical vegetables like zucchini, bell peppers, celery, carrots, onions, and garlic, or try new options. Like lycopene, vegetables contain high levels of inflammation fighters and antioxidants to help cut prostate symptoms.

How to stop BPH before it starts. If you haven't developed symptoms of BPH, a number of delicious foods may help you prevent it. For example, try pasta e fagioli, that succulent bean and pasta soup made with olive oil, garlic, tomato paste, onions, and spices.

Research suggests people who eat the most beans and soups lower their risk of BPH by up to 26 percent. And people who chow down on the most onions and garlic cut that risk by up to 60 percent. Eating more citrus fruits may help, too.

Why real men eat more baked beans

Men, the next time you're at a cookout, have an extra helping of baked beans. They have a special nutrient that will protect your prostate.

Zinc is the magic ingredient. Your prostate contains a higher amount of zinc than most other tissues, and studies have shown that men with benign prostatic hyperplasia (BPH) have lower zinc levels compared to men with normal prostates. A diet rich in zinc can help keep your prostate healthy and lower your risk of BPH.

A cup of baked beans supplies 13 milligrams (mg) of zinc — more than the 11 mg recommended daily for men. Other good sources of this essential mineral are oysters, lean beef, turkey, fortified cereals, and pumpkin seeds.

Be better in the bedroom at any age — without drugs

One out of every four men who sees a doctor about erectile dysfunction (ED) is under the age of 40, a recent Italian study discovered. Fortunately, no matter how young you are, drugs and medical treatments aren't your only option. Natural solutions like these can have amazing results.

Why daily pistachios could mean better nights. A small study of men with erectile dysfunction found that eating 3 1/2 ounces of pistachio nuts daily for three weeks improved scores on the International Index of Erectile Function Scale by 50 percent. The scientists also took scans that help measure whether a man has enough unrestricted blood flow to achieve an erection – and one of those measures increased by more than 20 percent in just three weeks.

Eating pistachios also lowered total and "bad" LDL cholesterol while raising the "good" HDL cholesterol. That's important because problems like clogged arteries, heart disease, and high blood pressure account for over 70 percent of ED cases – and cholesterol contributes to these problems. Researchers suggest that eating pistachios may help in several ways.

- Pistachios are a good source of the amino acid arginine, which can help prevent or limit the restricted blood flow caused by hardening or narrowing of the arteries. Arginine not only helps keep arteries flexible on its own, but also boosts nitric oxide, which relaxes blood vessel walls.

- The dangerous molecules known as free radicals cause oxidative stress, which contributes to clogged arteries and decreases the nitric oxide that helps keep arteries flexible. Fortunately, pistachios are packed with antioxidants, which are proven to fight oxidative stress.

If you'd like to try this, keep in mind that the study participants ate 570 calories worth of nuts at lunch every day. Eat your pistachios in place of meat, cheese, or another high-calorie lunch ingredient so you won't gain weight and make ED worse.

"Berry" the problem with artery-opening strawberries. These delicious berries are rich in vitamin C, which helps promote good blood flow. Don't worry if it isn't strawberry season where you live. Frozen strawberries keep longer than fresh, and they're available year round.

Other great sources of vitamin C include kiwifruit, sweet peppers, vegetable juice cocktail, and of course, oranges and orange juice.

Enjoy a second cup of "relaxing" coffee. If you love your morning cup of joe, you're about to love it even more. That's because caffeine may help prevent ED.

Researchers from the University of Texas found that men who drank between 85 and 303 milligrams (mg) of caffeine daily – the equivalent of two or three cups of coffee – were less likely to have erectile dysfunction. The researchers suspect caffeine helps blood vessels relax, promoting the good blood flow needed to prevent ED.

Just be careful to avoid drinks that are high in sugar or calories, because gaining weight can raise your odds of ED symptoms.

Vitamin D may give you a boost in the bedroom, too. Researchers recently discovered that men with ED were more likely to be deficient in vitamin D, especially if their problems were caused by clogged or narrowed arteries. If you suffer from ED, ask your doctor to check your levels.

How to fight ED caused by prostate problems. If you have an enlarged prostate or other prostate conditions, they may interfere with the blood flow needed for an erection. If prostate problems are contributing to your ED symptoms, see *Men: painless ways to cut bathroom breaks* on page 223 for foods that can help, and consider trying a natural supplement like pygeum or saw palmetto.

Studies suggest taking 75- to 200-mg capsules of standardized pygeum extract may ease BPH symptoms if taken for at least one month. You can also try saw palmetto. Studies of supplements have had mixed results, but they may still help some men. Just be aware that saw palmetto can interact with certain medications and it may not be right for everyone.

Check with your doctor before trying either of these supplements to make sure you can take them safely.

Can your prescription cause ED?

The same over-the-counter medicine you use for seasonal allergies could be the reason you have erectile dysfunction (ED). Both Allegra (fexofenadine) and Benadryl (diphenhydramine) can cause this problem. Even worse, diphenhydramine is an ingredient in many combination cold or allergy medicines, so you may not even realize you're taking it.

Many other medicines can cause ED, including prescription heartburn drugs like cimetidine (Tagamet), some types of high blood pressure medicines like clonidine (Catapres), stimulants with mixed amphetamines (Adderall), heart drugs like digoxin (Lanoxin), opiate painkillers like codeine and oxycodone, sleep aids like zolpidem (Ambien), antidepressants like paroxetine (Paxil), and various other medications you might not suspect.

Don't stop taking a prescription drug without talking to your doctor first, because that could be dangerous or even life threatening. Instead, ask your doctor which of your medications may cause ED. You may be able to switch to another one.

Respiratory illnesses

All-star nutrients for better breathing

Breathe easier with 3 super vitamins

Imagine yourself sitting in the sun enjoying a fruit salad chock-full of sliced kiwi, strawberries, and pineapple chunks topped with chopped almonds and sunflower seeds. Sound relaxing? It should, especially if you have trouble breathing. Because you've just loaded up on the vitamins your lungs need to breathe easy.

"C" your way clear to open airways. Looks like vitamin C does more than boost your immunity against colds. It also keeps your airways from tightening during exercise. Experts think it's vitamin C's antioxidant properties that make breathing easier.

When you work out, your body releases inflammatory cells such as histamine, leukotrienes, and prostaglandins, which can narrow your airways. In an animal study, vitamin C decreased the contractions caused by these bronchoconstrictors. About one in 10 people suffers from exercise-induced breathing problems, and surprisingly, almost half of competitive athletes do.

Researchers in several small studies gave people who struggle with exercise-induced asthma (EIA) doses of vitamin C either orally or intravenously. In one study, half the participants breathed easier after taking vitamin C. In another, vitamin C cut down the severity of post-exercise breathing problems.

And it's not just asthma. People with chronic obstructive pulmonary disease (COPD) also felt relief with vitamin C, reports a study out of the University of Utah. Scientists gave COPD sufferers the vitamin intravenously. Participants not only breathed better during exercise, they felt less muscle fatigue, a COPD side effect.

Dodge lung woes with this "D"ivine vitamin. For tip-top lung health, aim to get plenty of vitamin D. Studies show people with low vitamin D levels suffer more asthma and COPD attacks and have a higher risk for contracting pneumonia. Experts believe vitamin D works by boosting the immune system and lowering inflammation in the lungs.

■ When researchers in Israel studied over 21,000 people with asthma, they found those with a vitamin-D deficiency were 25 percent more likely to suffer flare-ups than those in the normal range. Some experts believe raising vitamin D levels in people with severe asthma could even prevent and treat the disease. And this super vitamin may also protect the lungs from developing infections that trigger asthma.

■ Vitamin D slashed COPD flare-ups in people with low D levels, found British scientists. And in people with normal levels of vitamin D, supplements cut the severity and length of COPD attacks.

■ If you're vitamin-D deficient, you're two-and-a-half times more likely to get pneumonia compared to people with high levels, says a study out of Finland.

Breathe easy with this "E"ssential nutrient. It may not be as popular as C and D, but vitamin E is just as important for your lung health.

Both smoking and nonsmoking women over 45 who took 600 milligrams (mg) of vitamin E every other day for 10 years lowered their risk of developing COPD by 10 percent, found a study out of Cornell University and Brigham and Women's Hospital. Vitamin E did not affect asthma in this study.

Vitamin E also guards your lungs from harmful air pollution, suggests a study from the University of Nottingham in England. Scientists say tiny particles and chemicals create damaging free radicals that harm your lungs. But vitamin E acts as an antioxidant, battling this oxidative damage. It also fends off lung inflammation.

Protect your lungs with these healthy foods. While most studies use supplements or intravenous methods to boost vitamin intake, you can get your fill of foods brimming with vitamins C, D, and E by knowing what to shop for.

- You already know citrus fruits and juices like oranges and grapefruit are ripe with vitamin C. Add berries, mangos, kiwi, papaya, pineapple, and watermelon to the mix. Plus, get your fix of vitamin-C veggies with cabbage, spinach, broccoli, green and red peppers, leafy greens, winter squash, cauliflower, and sweet and white potatoes.

- Your body naturally makes vitamin D from sun exposure, but not much, especially as you age. But you can get vitamin D from a number of foods. Fatty fish like tuna, salmon, and mackerel, and other edibles like cheese, beef liver, egg yolks, and mushrooms contain some vitamin D. Plus it's added to fortified milk, cereals, orange juice, and yogurt. Still, it may not be enough, so ask your doctor to check your levels to see whether you need an extra boost.

- Snack on seeds, almonds, and peanuts and you get a mouthful of vitamin E. You also get this lung-friendly vitamin from leafy greens and fortified juices and breakfast cereals.

Why you shouldn't eat apples (and other foods) during allergy season

Here's an all-too-familiar seasonal scenario if you're an allergy sufferer: you're plagued by sneezing, itchy eyes, and a runny nose. You blow your nose, wipe your eyes, and massage your sinuses as you wonder, "Will it ever end?" And then you take a bite out of a piece of fruit like an apple or a peach. And your symptoms get worse. What's going on?

It's called "pollen-food syndrome" (PFS) or "oral allergy syndrome" (OAS). And it happens when you have an allergy to a pollen and then react to a food with similar antigens. Experts dub this allergic response "cross-reactivity" – when your immune system thinks a protein in a pollen is similar to a protein in a food.

An Italian study found people with grass allergies suffered worse reactions to certain foods than people with dust mite allergies. These include peaches, melons, celery, and tomatoes.
A study out of Germany found about 70 percent of people with allergies to birch tree pollens also reacted to eating certain foods like pears, apples, carrots, and nuts.

> Allergic to latex? You may have a problem eating apples, bananas, avocados, or kiwis. These fruits contain proteins similar to those of natural rubber latex that are highly allergenic.

Reactions to these foods can cause itchiness and swelling of the lips, tongue, mouth, throat, and face as well as abdominal pain, cramps, and migraines. Doctors suggest avoiding these foods, especially during allergy season.

But if you can't live without them, these options may help you avoid allergic reactions. Try baking or microwaving the foods to break down the offending proteins. Or substitute canned fruits and vegetables over fresh. You can also peel off the skin. That's where most of the harmful allergen is found.

See the following chart to learn more about the foods that trigger reactions if you have pollen allergies.

Allergic to	May also react to
Ragweed	melons, bananas, cucumbers, zucchini
Birch	pears, plums, apples, peaches, kiwi, cherries, celery, carrots, fennel, parsley, almonds, walnuts
Grass	peaches, melons, oranges, tomatoes, garlic, onions, celery, peanuts, pork, egg whites
Mugwort	melons, carrots, celery, bell peppers, sunflower seeds
Latex	apples, bananas, melons, kiwi, avocado, papayas, potatoes, tomatoes, chestnuts

5 things you never knew about asthma

A lot of people have firsthand experience with asthma – in fact, about 25 million Americans. But some people, even asthma sufferers, don't know the latest medical discoveries. And what you don't know could hurt you.

Caffeine boosts lung function, helping you breathe easy. You may not be able to skip your morning java without dragging all day. But another group of people are drinking coffee for different reasons. Caffeine expands the air passages of your lungs, increasing airflow so you can breathe easier.

Even a small amount of caffeine – less than 5 milligrams (mg) per 2.2 pounds of body weight – appears to help your lungs for up to two hours. That's 320 mg for the average 140-pound person. If you consumed it all in coffee – less than two cups.

Soft drinks aggravate asthma symptoms. Soda has never really had a good reputation. And lately, it's been under fire for its role in some pretty serious health issues, including asthma.

Soft drinks contain additives and sugars that can worsen asthma symptoms. For example, one food coloring, which the United States has now banned, is a known allergen that may intensify asthma symptoms and possibly even cause cancer. The problem is that many people with asthma seem to love their soft drinks. In a study of over 16,000 people, more than 13 percent of participants with asthma drank more than two cups of soda every day.

If you're sensitive to sulfites, avoid dried fruits. But fruit is good for you, right? Well, yes. But if you have asthma, you may be sensitive to a sneaky ingredient that can be found in dried fruit – sulfites.

Sulfites are sulfur-based compounds that are added to foods to boost flavors and preserve freshness. In addition to dried fruit, they can be found in wine, white grape juice, shrimp, maraschino cherries, jams and jellies, and many other products.

Sulfites can cause allergic reactions, especially if you have asthma. About three to 10 percent of people with asthma have a sulfite sensitivity. If you experience chest tightness, stomach cramps, diarrhea, hives, or breathing problems when you eat foods containing sulfite, you too may be sensitive to the additive.

A high-fat diet weakens the effect of inhalers. Studies show people with severe asthma eat more fat than healthy people. Plus Western eating habits – low antioxidants, high fat, and too many processed foods – could raise asthma risk by triggering more inflammation-causing chemicals in your body.

And that's not the only problem. Researchers say saturated fats could reduce your response to inhalers by keeping the drug from reaching your airways.

In one study, an extra 10 grams of fat each day raised the odds of severe asthma by 48 percent. That's about three slices of bacon or one extra slice of cheese pizza.

Let nature help you breathe better

Catch a fish and catch your breath? It's true. Studies show fish oil can protect against asthma and other inflammatory reactions like allergies.

Fish oil is rich in omega-3 polyunsaturated fatty acids, such as eicosapentaenoic acid (EPA) and docosahexaenoic acid (DHA). Scientists think these fatty acids can regulate inflammation by keeping your body from producing substances that trigger an inflammatory response.

Adding fatty fish like salmon, mackerel, and sardines to your diet will give your lungs an extra boost of inflammation protection.

Pycnogenol, an extract taken from the bark of a pine tree, is an herbal ingredient that could also relieve asthma symptoms.

In a six-month study, people took 100 milligrams of pycnogenol in addition to inhaled corticosteroids, half in the morning and half in the evening. More than half of the participants were able to lower the dose of their inhaler medication, and none had to go on a higher dose.

Salt may be a hidden cause of symptoms. At one time, salt was a means of currency. In fact, the word salary comes from a Latin word meaning "salt money." But in today's world, salt is something you want less of, especially if you have asthma. The sodium in salt is the problem – a number of studies show that a high-sodium diet may worsen asthma symptoms, particularly when exercising.

A salt-restricted diet of about 1,500 mg of sodium per day can reduce the severity of exercise-induced asthma. Researchers have found that eating less salt can help out your lungs and reduce symptoms and medication use.

Salt is hidden in processed foods and restaurant meals, so you may find it challenging to restrict it. Choose fresh meats, fruits, and vegetables because they contain the least amount of sodium. Sports drinks are generally high in sodium, so limit them during exercise.

3 oils that harm your lungs — and 2 that heal

Did you know the oils you use for cooking and making salad dressings and marinades can affect your lungs? Oils contain two different forms of vitamin E. And depending on which form is in your favorite oil, you could be hurting or helping your breathing. Here's the lowdown.

Triple threat for asthma. Corn, soybean, and canola oils have a form of vitamin E called gamma-tocopherol. Countries that use these oils have a higher rate of asthma, say researchers. Take the U.S., for instance, where gamma-tocopherol is four times higher in blood plasma levels than in countries that use more olive and sunflower oils. Asthma rates have skyrocketed in the U.S. over the past 40 years, coinciding with the increased use of corn, soybean, and canola oils.

In a long-term study of more than 4,000 adults, a high blood level of gamma-tocopherol was associated with a 10- to 17-percent drop in lung function. That's almost like having asthma, says lead researcher Joan Cook-Mills, an associate professor of medicine in allergy/immunology at Northwestern University. "People have more trouble breathing," she says. "They take in less air, and it's harder to expel."

Cook-Mills believes gamma-tocopherol may increase the activity of a certain protein that leads to inflammation in the airways.

Dynamic duo for your lungs. Olive and sunflower oils do the opposite – they lower lung inflammation and promote healthy lung function. That's because they're rich in alpha-tocopherol, another form of vitamin E.

Countries that use more olive and sunflower oils have the lowest rates of asthma. And in the Northwestern study, people with higher levels of alpha-tocopherol showed the best results when they took breathing tests to measure lung capacity and health.

One delicious way to enjoy more olive oil in your diet is to make your own tangy salad dressing. Here's a recipe you'll keep coming back to.

- 1 sprig fresh oregano or 1 tsp dried
- 1 sprig fresh thyme or 1/2 tsp dried
- 1 minced garlic clove
- 3/4 cup olive oil
- 1/4 cup balsamic vinegar
- salt and pepper to taste

Place the ingredients in a bowl. Mix together and pour into a bottle using a funnel.

4 ways to strike back against COPD

Scientists predict chronic obstructive pulmonary disease (COPD) will become the third leading cause of death globally by 2030. That's enough to take anyone's breath away. COPD is a lethal combination of two lung ailments – emphysema and chronic bronchitis. But taking these simple steps could save you from this debilitating disease.

Fill up on fruit and fish to fix breathing burden. The secret to healthy lungs may be in your daily diet. People with COPD who ate fish, cheese, grapefruit, and bananas had healthier lungs and fewer aggravating symptoms than those who didn't eat those foods, reported researchers at the University of Nebraska.

Another study out of Harvard showed that people who ate a Mediterranean-style diet, rich in fruit, fish, whole grains, and vegetables, slashed their COPD risk in half compared to those who ate a Western diet of refined sugars, processed foods, and cured and red meats.

And a study published in the medical journal *BMJ* found that people who ate more nuts, whole grains, omega-3 fatty acids, and polyunsaturated fats cut their chances of getting COPD versus those who ate processed meats, refined grains, and sugary drinks.

Scientists think the antioxidant and anti-inflammatory substances in healthy foods protect your lungs from COPD.

Stop slurping soft drinks. Think twice before you reach for your favorite soda. An Australian study found that 15 percent of people with COPD drank more than two cups of soft drinks a day. Researchers say the more you drink, the higher your COPD risk. They think the large amount of added sugars in soft drinks promote lung inflammation. Plus, too much added sugar can lead to obesity, a COPD risk factor.

Ban cured meat to beat COPD. Yes, bacon and sausage taste good. But are they worth eating if they sabotage your lungs?

People 45 and older who frequently ate cured meat were more likely to suffer lower lung function and a higher risk of developing COPD than those who did not eat cured meats, found a Columbia University study. For each additional serving they ate per month, they raised their COPD risk by 2 percent.

Scientists say it's the nitrites in cured meats that make them so dangerous. Nitrites damage your lungs much like tobacco smoke does in triggering the development of emphysema.

Enjoy fresh air with ginseng. The Chinese have used Panax ginseng for thousands of years to treat respiratory ailments. And Western medicine may finally be catching up.

Australian researchers found that ginseng acts as an anti-inflammatory and antioxidant for the lungs. It's the natural compounds called ginsenosides that make Panax ginseng so powerful. Ginsenosides help by battling inflammation and lowering the production of harmful oxidants.

Fight a killer disease with zinc

Could your Thanksgiving turkey help you avoid pneumonia? Along with foods like beef, canned pork and beans, and Total Raisin Bran cereal, it just might. The secret is their high zinc content. Research shows that can really make a difference.

- A study of 118 people with pneumonia found that 58 percent of the men and 76 percent of the women had low blood levels of zinc. Most low-zinc patients recovered during their hospital stay, but more than half of them took over two weeks to get better.

■ Nursing home residents with normal zinc levels had fewer bouts of pneumonia than those with low zinc levels, an earlier study found. Those with normal zinc levels who got pneumonia needed fewer antibiotics and recovered more quickly than people with low zinc.

So if you're worried about pneumonia, eat high-zinc foods like the ones listed earlier to help get enough of this mineral. Other good sources include canned oyster stew, pumpkin seeds, and roasted peanuts.

Supercharge your pneumonia vaccine

Nobody wants pneumonia. That's why you get the vaccine. But what if you could supercharge your vaccine simply by eating more fruits and veggies?

That's what researchers found during a study of people 65 to 85 years old. One group ate less than three servings of fruits and vegetables a day, while another group ate five or more. At 12 weeks, they were given the Pneumovax II vaccine, which has extracts of 23 types of *Streptococcus pneumoniae* bacteria.

When your immune system encounters harmful bacteria like these, it produces antibodies that help your body recognize and kill the bad guys. They then stick around to help protect against future attacks. The group that ate extra fruits and veggies had increased antibody activity, which equals extra protection.

Skin conditions & hair loss

33 simple pantry cures

Shrink your healing time with honey

From the Egyptians to the Aztecs to the modern kitchen, honey has made its mark on the world as a wonder food. People have used it for centuries for all kinds of things, including wound healing. But isn't it strange to slather honey all over your skin? The Egyptians didn't think so, and neither do scientists. Recent studies support its therapeutic effects on skin, and now it's your turn to discover the many healing qualities of this thick, golden liquid.

Rich and complex, honey is a blend of proteins, amino acids, vitamins, minerals, and antioxidants. It contains small amounts of vitamin C and several B vitamins as well as minerals like calcium, iron, zinc, potassium, and selenium. No wonder Winnie-the-Pooh was such a fan. All these nutrients add up to some amazing benefits.

Heal a burn or sore five days faster. Research shows honey speeds up the amount of time it takes for wounds to heal – in one study, an average of five days faster than traditional methods. At the same time, it cleanses, eliminates odors, minimizes scarring, and reduces inflammation and pain. Researchers have performed extensive tests on honey, reporting improvements in burns, skin ulcers, and infections. Though it is not a cure-all, scientists say honey is good for many types of skin diseases.

High sugar content, low water content, and acidity in honey prevent the growth of harmful bacteria. But some honey is still more helpful than others. Manuka is a medical grade honey harvested in New Zealand and Australia. It's the only kind you want to put on wounds because, unlike many other honeys, it doesn't lose its effectiveness when exposed to heat and light.

Tell dry, flaky skin to buzz off. Bees are the only insects in the world that make food people can eat. But honey is not just for eating. You can use it to add a glow to your complexion. This sweet substance is a humectant. It keeps your skin hydrated and provides a protective barrier that creates a moist wound-healing environment.

Honey stimulates tissue growth and collagen production. This amazing protein is vital to skin elasticity. But don't go thinking honey is only for your face. It's perfectly safe for other parts of your body like dry feet and elbows.

Watch out for honey "wannabees." Though the urban legend that bees don't sleep is not true, they do put in a lot of hard work. So make sure you're getting the best honey out there.

- Avoid table honeys. They usually have less antibacterial activity than medical grade honey. Plus, studies reveal that many products sold in stores are not actually real honey.

- The Unique Manuka Factor (UMF) reflects the content and purity of manuka honey. To ensure you're getting quality honey, look on the label for a minimum rating of 10 UMF, which is often labeled as "UMF Manuka Honey" or "Active Manuka Honey."

- If you want to know which companies are licensed to use the UMF trademark, go to the Unique Manuka Factor Honey Association's website at *www.umf.org.nz* and click on "Licensees." Manuka honey can be expensive. You want to be sure you're getting the real thing.

- Look for raw, unpasteurized honey that hasn't been filtered and heated, a process that removes a lot of nutrients.

- If you like to eat your honey while you heal, remember it still contains a lot of sugars. Naturally darker honeys like manuka have more antioxidants so lean toward those.

Bee sweet to your skin

It's simple. Just spread a teaspoon of honey evenly over your face and relax for 10 to 15 minutes before rinsing with warm water.

You can also add lemon juice, finely ground oats, mashed avocado, or aloe vera for an extra-nourishing facial.

---

3 delicious ways to get ageless skin

A 50-year-old woman made headlines in early 2015 when she claimed she hadn't smiled or laughed in 40 years to prevent wrinkles. It turns out, she's not the only one who has taken up these extreme measures. Your face is often first to betray signs of aging, but you don't have to stop laughing to enjoy a healthy appearance. Stay happy and youthful with these foods you can easily slip into your busy schedule.

Think "orange" to fight wrinkles. Your skin is your largest organ and the first line of defense against disease. For that reason, anything that damages your skin can be harmful to your overall health. Carotenoids are powerful antioxidants that protect your skin. These pigments are most commonly found in orange foods such as carrots, sweet potatoes, pumpkins, and mangoes. When eaten, carotenoids accumulate in your skin. According to recent studies, people with high levels of antioxidants in their skin have fewer defined wrinkles and signs of premature aging.

Stop sun damage from getting under your skin with olive oil. Getting older is a natural cause of drooping skin, but studies say sun exposure is responsible for 80 percent of evidence that you're not as young as you used to be. Dry skin, brown spots, wrinkles, and loss of elasticity are the red flags of sun damage.

In a study of almost 3,000 people, scientists measured wrinkles, tissue firmness, and pigmentation abnormalities to examine the benefits of eating olive oil. They learned that eating more monounsaturated fatty acids from olive oil lowered risk of severe sun damage in men and women. Two teaspoons or more a day will give you the best results. Don't forget that olive oil isn't just for cooking. You can put it on your skin for an instant moisturizer.

Prevent skin aging with grapes. Prevention is the best way to stop skin aging from environmental factors. To protect against the harmful action of free radicals, eat plenty of antioxidant-rich fruits and vegetables.

Grapes contain a number of nutrients that protect against sun damage, including vitamin C, calcium, phosphorus, magnesium, and iron.

In recent years, scientists have been studying an antioxidant called resveratrol. It's abundant in the skin of red grapes and has unique anti-aging properties. Findings suggest resveratrol may be useful to prevent skin problems associated with aging. However, more studies are needed to find out the best way to get the most from this antioxidant.

In the meantime, keep laughing and don't worry about those wrinkles. Studies show laughter helps to relieve stress and increase blood flow.

What to eat for ageless skin, hair, and nails

Your skin, hair, and nails act as your first line of defense. Keep yours healthy by making sure you get plenty of the right nutrients.

Hair loss
Eggs are a great source of protein, vitamin D, zinc, and iron — all important for healthy hair.

Acne
Strawberries are filled with vitamin C, which helps with collagen building, inflammation, and healing.

Wrinkles
Carotenoids found in mangoes are powerful antioxidants that protect your skin.

Sun damage
Monounsaturated fatty acids from olive oil lower your risk of severe sun damage.

Brittle nails
Beans are full of protein, iron, and zinc, making your nails stronger.

Aging hands: 4 secrets that stop the clock

Just one glance can betray your age. It's not your laugh lines or crow's feet. In this age of Botox and eye lifts, hands are the true reflection of time. Your hands are hard workers, and they are often left unprotected against harsh conditions. Don't they deserve the same tender loving care you give the rest of your skin? Follow these timeless tips for healthy hands you don't have to hide.

Smooth rough, cracked hands with wheat extract oil. It happens every winter. Dry air, hot water, and harsh soaps give you flaky, itchy skin that no amount of lotion seems to be able to conquer. It doesn't help that your natural oil production slows over time, often due to hormones. You don't have to hide your hands away. Use wheat extract oil for soft skin year-round.

The vitamin E found in this oil is good for dry, prematurely aged skin. In a recent French study, women who took 350-milligram wheat extract oil capsules for three months every day experienced a significant increase in skin hydration. And there's more – wheat extract oil applied to your skin will smooth and soften it, as well as reduce roughness and irritation.

The undiluted truth about water and dry skin. You've read it in beauty magazines, but is it actually true that drinking more water can help your complexion? Getting enough water is necessary for your skin, but despite what you read, drinking water isn't going to get rid of dry skin if you're already hydrated.

Your skin is about 30 percent water, so it's no surprise H2O has a direct link to supple, plump skin. If you are dehydrated, drinking water can help skin thickness and density, but keep in mind it won't prevent wrinkles or other signs of aging.

A yellow flower can stop you from getting black and blue. Skin becomes fragile as you age, allowing it to bruise easily. Though staying hydrated can help, drinking more water isn't going to get rid of your "tissue-paper skin." Get help from a flower.

Arnica is a perennial plant with yellow, daisy-like petals. Also called leopard's bane, it reduces inflammation and bruising. You can smooth some on your skin after injury to prevent bruising, but don't put it on broken skin. Arnica is available as a 2-percent essential oil or infused in creams, gels, and ointments. Look for *arnica montana* in the ingredients list.

Spot treat your skin and say "so long" to age spots. Sun damage and constant bruising increase your chances of skin discoloration. But did you know that licorice root may help lighten your skin? You may only think of licorice as candy, but it's actually a perennial with a long history in traditional Chinese medicine. Scientists report that the main ingredients in licorice disperse skin pigmentation and prevent discoloring due to the sun's ultraviolet radiation.

Licorice root, also known as *glycyrrhiza glabra*, can be found in teas, cosmetics, and sweet candies. Licorice extract is available in pharmacies and health food stores. Because this herb can cause serious side effects, talk to your doctor before using it. If he approves, follow dosing instructions carefully.

Are you dehydrated?

Take the hydration test. Pinch the skin on the back of your hand between two fingers and hold it for a few seconds before releasing. Normal skin quickly snaps back. If your skin slowly sinks down to its normal position, you may be dehydrated.

---

4 home treatments that strengthen weak nails naturally

Your fingernails snag on your towel as you're drying off. They chip as you close your car door. You never know if your next trip to the grocery store will be their last.

Lee Redmond holds the Guinness World Record for longest fingernails on a pair of women's hands. She grew her nails for 30 years, eventually reaching a total length of 28 feet 4.5 inches.

Sound familiar? The more you use your hands, the more chances your nails have to get banged up. And if they are already weak, you may be looking at some serious damage. Lucky for you, healthy nails are right at your fingertips.

Battle brittle nails with beef and beans. Tired of dry, weak, easily breakable nails? Forty million Americans know how you feel.

Your nails are made of the same protein as hair – keratin. Keratin requires help from minerals like iron and zinc to stay tough, and deficiencies have a big impact on nail durability.

But there's good news – you can battle brittle nail syndrome with some of your favorite foods. Beef, turkey, chicken, and beans – like pinto, black, kidney, and garbanzo – are full of protein, iron, and zinc. Who knew a juicy burger or grilled chicken sandwich with a side of baked beans could help your nails?

Water your nails. As simple as it sounds, dry nails can be a sign that you need to drink more water. Nails are water resistant, but their hardness has a great deal to do with hydration. Add a long, cool drink of water to your morning routine by taking more than a sip when you pop your daily vitamin and mineral supplement. Staying hydrated will soon become a habit.

Bring healthy back with biotin. Biotin, also known as vitamin B7, is a B-complex vitamin. People who don't get enough biotin often have brittle hair and nails. Biotin strengthens, thickens, and hydrates nails, protecting them from splitting and cracking.

On top of that, biotin assists in the release of energy from carbohydrates, fats, and proteins so you can have more energy and feel healthier.

Biotin is found naturally in meat, egg yolks, milk, fish, nuts, and even some vegetables, including Swiss chard.

This leafy green is also a good source of vitamin A, vitamin C, vitamin E, and vitamin K. You'll get more nutrients from cooked Swiss chard because it's easier to digest and absorb.

Percent Daily Value in Swiss Chard		
	Cooked	Raw
Vitamin A	214	44
Vitamin K	716	374
Vitamin C	53	18
Protein	7	1

Olive oil for dry nails and cuticles. Kitchen remedies aren't all about eating. You can rub on a great nail-saver that's found right in your pantry. Olive oil softens your skin and hydrates your cuticles. This rich oil is excellent for dry to normal skin.

The importance of getting the right nutrients into your diet becomes more apparent as you get older. Hit the nail on the head by making healthy choices.

Get to the root of your skin problems with these 7 herbs

Herbs are the rising stars of natural medicine. In fact, Americans spend billions of dollars on herbal remedies every year. But while the industry is blooming, so are the health claims. Every product promises to heal some sort of ailment. How do you know what to buy? First, try the herbs that are backed by research. Here are seven, scientists say, that can do wonders for your skin.

Tea tree oil. *Melaleuca alternifolia*, or tea tree oil, is often called "first aid in a bottle." It's good for blisters, burns, rashes, acne, and infected wounds. In one study, the participants' acne improved by rubbing on water-based gel with 5-percent tea tree oil for three months. They experienced fewer problems with dryness, irritation, itching, and burning than they did with 5-percent benzoyl peroxide.

Form of herb	How to use it	How often
Essential oil	1 drop oil undiluted directly to cold sores, acne, plantar warts, and corns (cover warts and corns with bandage)	as needed

Witch hazel. This herb comes from the bark and leaves of the *Hamamelis virginiana* shrub. Its wonder ingredient is tannin, an astringent that helps tighten skin. Witch hazel reduces the inflammation associated with acne. It is not recommended for consumption.

Form of herb	How to use it	How often
Extract	1-2 tsp. in 1 cup of water	apply solution 2 times a day
Gels and lotions	look for products with high percentages of witch hazel	follow directions on label

Chamomile. This herb is the staple of bedtime tea, but did you know chamomile also has anti-inflammatory, antibacterial, and wound-healing properties? You can reduce inflammation in your mouth and throat by using it as a gargle. Chamomile's natural chemicals also relieve skin inflammation. Smooth on chamomile cream to soothe tight, dry skin and treat acne, burns, blisters, eczema, and hives.

Form of herb	How to use it	How often
Tincture	30-60 drops in 1 cup of hot water	3 times a day
Cream	buy a product containing 3-10 percent chamomile	follow directions on label
Essential oil	5-10 drops oil in a tub of warm bath water	as needed
Dried flowers	1/4 pound dried flowers in a tub of warm water	as needed
Tea	2-3 Tbsp. dried chamomile in a cup of boiling water	3-4 times a day

Lavender. The word lavender comes from a Latin verb meaning "to wash." The Romans often used *Lavandula angustifolia* for bathing and laundry, but today, many people use it to treat wounds. It heals by stimulating cell growth, killing bacteria, and preventing scarring. Though the essential oil is toxic if taken orally, lavender oil is perfectly safe for treating skin problems like acne, inflammation, and sunburn.

Form of herb	How to use it	How often
Essential oil	1-4 drops oil per tablespoon of base oil (almond or olive oil)	massage into skin as needed
Essential oil	5-6 drops oil in a tub of warm water	as needed for relaxation

Aloe vera. Best known for treating burns, aloe can also help manage acne and eczema as well as soothe rashes, stings, and bites. Research shows aloe vera gel effectively treats small second-degree burns. Plus, in one study, aloe improved symptoms of psoriasis by over 80 percent.

Form of herb	How to use it	How often
Living plant	remove gel from leaf and apply to skin	as needed
Gels and lotions	look for products with high percentages of aloe gel	follow directions on label
Cream	0.5 percent aloe vera	3 times daily for psoriasis

Lemon balm. This herb, also known as *Melissa officinalis*, treats cold sores, or fever blisters, caused by the herpes simplex virus. In a study of 116 adults who applied 1-percent lemon balm extract cream up to five times a day, 96 percent of them reported complete healing after eight days. You will get best results if you apply a compress at the first sign of a cold sore. Lemon balm has also been used topically to treat minor wounds and other skin irritations.

Form of herb	How to use it	How often
Essential oil	5 drops oil per tablespoon of base oil	massage into skin as needed
Essential oil	3 drops oil in a tub of warm water	as needed
Tea	1/4-1 tsp. dried lemon balm in a cup of hot water	up to 4 times daily
Compress	2-4 tsp. dried lemon balm in 1 cup boiling water	apply throughout the day for cold sores

Green tea. Research shows that the polyphenols in this famous herb protect against the effects of ultraviolet radiation and sun damage. In studies on mice, green tea was used topically to decrease premature skin aging and cancer-causing UV damage. Green tea extract acts as an anti-inflammatory and antioxidant and may improve symptoms of rosacea by reducing sensitivity to the sun's UV light.

Form of herb	How to use it	How often
Tea	1 tsp. tea leaves in a cup of hot water	2-3 cups a day (240 to 320 milligrams of polyphenols)
Supplements	100-750 mg. of green tea extract	follow directions on label

Put the brakes on breakouts with 4 acne-fighting foods

"The part can never be well unless the whole is well," wrote Plato over 2,000 years ago. His words still ring true today.

Acne is a skin condition that can cause emotional distress and scar your skin. It's the result of an overproduction of sebum, the oil that lubricates your hair and skin, too many dead skin cells, and bacteria, which trigger inflammation and infection.

Studies indicate certain foods may aggravate acne, like dairy, chocolate, and carbohydrate-rich foods including bread, bagels, and chips. Add more of these anti-acne superfoods to your day and put a stop to the spots.

Eat antioxidants for berry happy skin. Berries are jam-packed with antioxidants and other nutrients that slow the aging process and neutralize destructive free radicals – those pesky guys that cause cell damage and trigger inflammation.

■ Strawberries are filled with vitamin C – an essential ingredient for collagen building. Vitamin C helps control inflammation, stimulate healing, and fight off infection.

■ Goji berries, also known as wolfberries, have been used in traditional Chinese medicine for over 2,000 years. They contain beta carotene, which is converted into vitamin A in the body and fights infection.

■ Blueberries contain lots of fiber, vitamins, minerals, and antioxidants. Antioxidants play a starring role in the prevention of wrinkles and other signs of aging.

Superfruits like blueberries and goji berries have high amounts of flavonoids like anthocyanins. Not only do these nutrients give berries their deep color, but they also fight inflammation and promote good circulation.

Heavenly herb hand sanitizer

For a great-smelling homemade hand sanitizer, all you have to do is mix together:

- 5 drops lavender essential oil

- 5 drops rosemary essential oil

- 30 drops tea tree essential oil

- 1/4 teaspoon vitamin E oil

- 1 tablespoon witch hazel extract

- 1 cup aloe vera gel

Store in a clean container for germ-free hands on the go.

Go nuts over selenium, the inflammation fighter. Brazil nuts are high in antioxidants and are a good source of magnesium, phosphorus, and copper. In a small study, people who ate large amounts of Brazil nuts saw a long-term decrease in markers of inflammation. Selenium is one of the nutrients that helps reduce acne-related inflammation.

Brazil nuts are rich in selenium. In fact, one cup contains 3,643 percent of the daily value (DV). Though selenium protects cells against toxins, too much can cause a condition known as selenium toxicity. Each kernel contains almost 100 micrograms of selenium – about 137 percent of the DV. Don't overdo it. One or two kernels a day is plenty.

> Studies show civilizations untouched by Western culture have fewer instances of acne. Their diets include plenty of fruits, vegetables, and fish.

Zap away zits with a variety of leafy greens. Leafy green vegetables have a reputation for being stocked with nutrients.

- Vitamin A, found in kale and other leafy greens, helps form and maintain healthy skin and soft tissue.

- Zinc repairs tissue and strengthens your body's resistance to infection. Found in spinach and kale, it acts as an anti-inflammatory and antibacterial and may decrease the production of sebum.

- Vitamin E also improves acne in people who have low levels of vitamin E in their blood, research has found. Cook up some Swiss chard or turnip greens for a shot of this beauty vitamin.

Block bacteria with lauric acid. Though you can eat it, coconut oil is more famous for being applied directly to the skin. It is a significant source of lauric acid, which acts as an antibacterial, anti-viral, and anti-fungal. Many studies have examined the potential of using lauric acid for acne. Researchers have found it blocks the growth of acne-causing bacteria.

Coconut oil as a moisturizer is as effective and safe as mineral oil. You can use it as a lotion or put it in a face mask for healthier-looking skin.

Clarifying coconut facial

For an acne-blasting facial for you and a friend, you'll need:

- 30 drops of tea tree oil

- 1 Tbsp. coconut oil

- 1 Tbsp. ground turmeric

- 1 Tbsp. raw honey

- 1 Tbsp. aloe vera gel

Mix ingredients into a paste. Spread evenly over your face and leave on for 20 minutes. Rinse off with warm water and pat dry.

A word of caution — wear an old shirt because turmeric will stain if it gets on your clothes.

Head off hair loss with 5 superfoods

You'll lose between 50 and 100 strands of hair each day, according to dermatologists. That may be true for most people, but perhaps you've noticed a breeze up there where your hair used to be. And, even worse, your brush is beginning to look like a woolly mammoth.

If this is the case, you may be in need of a hair intervention. Don't worry, it doesn't have to be painful. Thinning hair could signal that you need more of certain nutrients. You can solve common causes of hair loss simply by eating more of the right foods. And while you're at it, you'll add shine to your hair and bounce to your step, becoming the envy of every salon.

If your diet is low in several nutrients, you may lose more hair than usual. But this doesn't mean you have to settle for premature hair loss. Try eating more of these fabulous foods and reclaim your "do."

Promote hair growth with an egg. Get hair you'll want to run your fingers through by sinking your teeth into a famous breakfast food you can enjoy any time of day. One scrambled egg has almost half of the protein you need each day. Your mane is made of a protein called keratin, so it's no surprise protein makes your hair stronger and stimulates growth.

More than half of men and women experience hair loss sometime during their lives. Though menopause and pregnancy are often factors for women, lack of nutrients is a big culprit that can affect anybody. Restricting your diet, especially from protein and vitamin D, can lead to hair loss. Fortunately, eggs are a great source of these nutrients, as well as zinc and iron – also important for healthy hair.

Make tresses shine with salmon's omega-3. This fish is swimming in nutrients that help you get shiny, gorgeous hair. To make the most of salmon's nutrients, choose canned.

■ Canned salmon is a good source of calcium, as long as you eat the bones. Low amounts of calcium in your blood can raise your chances of hair loss.

■ Not getting enough polyunsaturated fatty acids like omega-3 and omega-6 increases your chance of hair loss and shedding. Regular canned salmon with skin provides about 2,000 milligrams of omega-3. Stick with this kind and eat a 3-ounce serving twice a week. Skip the skinless variety. It has fewer fatty acids.

■ Salmon also contains niacin, an important B vitamin. It's not only good for your skin, it helps promote hair growth and maintain the cells that make up your hair follicles.

Pay attention to what you were eating before your hair problems began. You may not notice signs of deficiency for two to four months.

Enhance your hair with oysters. Though not all oysters will surprise you with pearls, they will give you the gift of iron and zinc. Some researchers suggest that iron deficiencies are associated with hair loss. This is because iron carries oxygen to cells, including those in your hair. You don't even have to be anemic for an iron deficiency to affect your body.

Signs that you're not getting adequate amounts of zinc are not always obvious, but a deficiency of this mineral may cause hair loss. Oysters have 256 percent of the zinc you need daily.

Keep your hair strong with spinach. Many people associate spinach with iron, but it's also abundant in vitamin A. This nutrient is vital for good vision, a healthy immune system, and cell growth – a key to maintaining healthy skin and hair. That may be why the creator of Popeye chose spinach to be his celebrated superfood.

Spinach also boasts some vitamin C. Getting too little vitamin C could cause dry hair and hair prone to splitting, which encourages hair loss.

Make headway with nutrient-loaded lentils. One strand may not seem that strong, but a whole head of hair combined can bear the weight of two full-grown elephants, says researcher Frédéric Leroy.

To keep hair up to par, you're going to need a lot of support. Lentils are high in protein and low in saturated fat – perfect for vegetarians. These legumes also contain fiber, iron, riboflavin, and high amounts of folate. Riboflavin supports the absorption of other nutrients like protein, folate, niacin, and iron so your body can use the nutrients for healthier skin and hair.

Tricks for runway-ready hair

Styling products are expensive. Before you shell out your hard-earned dough, try some natural options that are probably hanging around your kitchen right now.

Repair your hair with an egg. So you don't particularly like the taste of eggs? You don't have to eat them. While no scientific evidence reports that eggs make your hair grow faster, people have been using them for years to moisturize, repair damage, and add shine.

After applying egg, mayo, or olive oil to your hair, put on a shower cap or cover it with plastic wrap. You can help the moisture soak in by covering your hair with a warm, damp towel.

Thicken your mane with mayo. News flash – there's a way to use mayonnaise that won't end up coming back to haunt your hips. Many people claim putting mayo on their hair makes it look fuller and protects from damaging styling products.

Listen when your hair says, "I'm thirsty." You know the benefits of olive oil for your skin. But olive oil also acts as a natural conditioner, adding moisture to your scalp and hair, leaving it soft and shiny.

How to work it. Choose either one egg, a cup of mayo, or a tablespoon of olive oil, and coat your hair from scalp to tip, leaving it in for 20 minutes before rinsing. When using egg, don't rinse with hot water. Getting scrambled eggs out of your hair is not nearly as fun as eating them.

Three foods, one treatment. Want a triple-action hair treatment? Try all three together. Mix three tablespoons of mayonnaise with one raw egg and a teaspoon of olive oil. Work mixture through your hair from scalp to tip until completely coated. Leave on for 20 minutes and then rinse.

Sleep disorders

Nosh your way to sweet slumber

4 simple snacks sure to help you sleep

So you want to get a good night's sleep without popping pills. Try these delicious snacks. They're loaded with tryptophan, melatonin, and serotonin – substances that encourage a night of sweet dreams.

■ Half a turkey sandwich on whole-grain bread with a glass of tart cherry juice. Turkey is a great source of tryptophan. And carbs from whole-grain bread raise the amount of tryptophan in your brain. Plus, tart cherry juice is rich in melatonin, the body's hormone that triggers sleepiness.

■ Rice pudding with a hot mug of chamomile tea. Warm up your leftover rice with milk, a little sugar, and a splash of vanilla. Rice promotes good sleep, say Japanese researchers, while chamomile is a naturally calming herb.

Packed with nutrients, seeds are known for their great health benefits. But did you know these tasty little snacks can also help you sleep? Pumpkin, sesame, and sunflower seeds are loaded with tryptophan, which triggers serotonin production — two must-haves for a restful night. These seeds also offer up a healthy amount of magnesium, a natural "chill pill." Munch on a handful of seeds before bedtime.

■ Bowl of oatmeal with a warm glass of milk. Eat this breakfast favorite for dinner, and you'll sleep better at night. It even calms restless legs syndrome and painful leg cramps. That's because oatmeal is a rich source of magnesium, a mineral that relaxes restless legs. Oatmeal is also chock-full of melatonin, and milk is a tryptophan treat. Put them together and kiss restless nights good-bye.

■ Kiwi and banana fruit cup. Sleepless nights? Try the cute fruit with the funny name. Studies show people who eat two kiwi one hour before bedtime fall asleep faster, sleep longer, and sleep better. Researchers believe the serotonin in kiwi triggers good shut-eye. Add bananas and yogurt to the mix for their tryptophan boost, and you may nod off in no time.

Are these foods zapping your ZZZs?

What's on your dinner plate may come back to bite you when you go to bed. That's because what you eat at night affects how you sleep.

A whopping 50 million to 70 million Americans struggle with chronic sleep problems. That's three times the number of people who live in Florida.

When you toss and turn because you can't sleep, you're at higher risk for a slew of health problems like cancer, diabetes, depression, obesity, and high blood pressure. Not enough sleep makes you tired, grumpy, and even dangerous. Drowsy drivers cause 40,000 nonfatal injuries and 1,550 deaths a year, says the Department of Transportation.

Knowing what to eat and not to eat could mean the difference between a good night's sleep and a day full of fatigue. Here's what to avoid.

Skip spicy foods. Don't want to spend the night battling heartburn? Then hold the garlic, onions, and tomato sauce. Spicy fare can trigger heartburn, a fiery sleep robber.

And if you think you should reach for peppermint to put out that fire, think again. Some people use this refreshing herb to soothe an upset stomach, but it can also trigger heartburn.

Say no to that nightcap. Sure – that glass of wine may help you doze off, but forget about staying asleep. Alcohol is a powerful sleep aid, say experts, but it only helps you fall asleep for a few hours. After that, you will wrestle with your pillows for the rest of the night. It's because alcohol disrupts sleep homeostasis, your body's internal clock that regulates your sleep/wake cycle.

Cut out your nightly cuppa joe. It's hard to pass up a soothing cup of coffee or tea after dinner. But if you have trouble sleeping, you may want to switch to decaf. The caffeine in your brew can rev up your body for up to seven hours, causing a night of restlessness.

And it's not just the caffeine in coffee and tea. Remember to check labels for pain relievers and cold medicines for added caffeine.

Go easy on steak and fried chicken. You may be trying to fall asleep, but your tummy will be wide awake if you eat fatty or fried foods for dinner. Foods high in saturated fats take more time to digest, making your digestive tract work overtime, robbing you of hours you could be snoozing.

Bite into that BLT for lunch, not dinner. Bacon lovers beware – your favorite sandwich may be what's keeping you up at night. That's because those savory slices of pork contain tyramine, a substance that triggers your brain to stay awake and active.

And it's not just found in bacon. Eggplant, soy sauce, salami, tomatoes, and aged cheeses like Brie and sharp cheddar are also rich sources of tyramine.

Who knew this rice could make you sleepy?

Eat a bowl of Jasmine aromatic long-grain rice for dinner and you may find yourself falling asleep faster. That's what a small study published in the *American Journal of Clinical Nutrition* found.

Experts believe it's because Jasmine rice has a higher glycemic index (GI). Foods with a high GI boost tryptophan and serotonin levels, two brain chemicals you need for healthy sleep. In the study, researchers used small protein portions. They say protein lowers tryptophan levels, so it's better to have a high-GI, low-protein meal.

Researchers experimented with two different meal times and two different types of rice. People ate Jasmine rice one hour or four hours before bedtime. Those who ate four hours before bed slept better. They also tried Mahatma long-grain white rice, which is lower on the GI scale. The long-grain white rice did not induce sleep as quickly as Jasmine.

Can't sleep? Slip into sweet slumber with these 5 herbs

Give your sleeping pills a rest. You can enjoy a night of sweet dreams with a little help from these natural remedies.

Valerian helps you sleep like a baby. The use of valerian as a sedative dates back to Roman Empire days. But even today, studies suggest valerian can help you fall asleep and stay asleep. Research shows people who take 400 to 900 milligrams (mg) of valerian extract up to two hours before bedtime reap the greatest rewards.

But don't expect valerian to work quickly. It could take a few weeks before you see results. And you should talk with your doctor first. Scientists consider valerian safe, but it can interfere with some sedatives and psychiatric medicines.

Catch some ZZZs with chamomile. Herbalists throughout the centuries have said German chamomile is capable of curing anything from muscle aches and pains to tummy troubles. It's also well-known as a calming nighttime supplement for anyone having trouble sleeping.

Experts suggest taking 400 mg to 1,600 mg of standardized extract daily to help you relax. Or brew a tea with fresh chamomile flowers before hitting the hay.

Lavender will get you some shut-eye. Lavender is best known for its sweet fragrance. Most people who try it for insomnia sprinkle a few drops of lavender oil on their pillows and let the aroma lull them to sleep. But researchers have started to experiment with lavender oil as a supplement. An Italian study found 80 mg of lavender oil capsules taken daily calms anxiety and may lead to a better night's sleep.

Another study out of the U.K. found lavender oil supplements eased the jitters in people who watched stressful film clips. So if you have trouble falling asleep after watching a thriller, lavender oil capsules may come to your rescue.

Nod off with lemon balm. Bees love the refreshing herb lemon balm, and so should you. Lemon balm, also known by its botanical name *Melissa*, eases anxiety and sleep disturbances, say researchers who conducted a small study published in the *Mediterranean Journal of Nutrition and Metabolism*. Lemon balm relieved anxiety in 70 percent of participants and restored restful sleep in 85 percent.

Want to drift off with ease? Try tarragon tea. Some people swear by tarragon as a sleep aid even though there's no science to back it up. This aromatic herb, whose name means "little dragon" in French, makes a flavorful tea perfect for relaxing in the evening. Use a teaspoon of dried tarragon per cup of boiling water. Steep for 20 to 30 minutes, then strain. Enjoy before bedtime.

Do your vitamins (or lack of) keep you up at night?

Are you getting too much vitamin C? Not enough B6? The answers to these questions may help you get to the bottom of those sleepless nights.

Experts say too much vitamin C can cause insomnia. Men only need 90 milligrams (mg) and women 75 mg. But some people load up on vitamin C during cold and flu season, throwing back mass quantities every day.

When you consider an 8-oz. glass of orange juice contains 120 mg of vitamin C, it's easy to get your fill from food. And nutritionists say vitamin C from food is always safe. Rich sources include grapefruit, broccoli, sweet potatoes, strawberries, and red and green bell peppers.

On the other hand, not enough vitamin B6 may keep you counting sheep – all night long. This important vitamin helps convert tryptophan to serotonin, two key components of a good night's sleep.

The recommended amount for adults is 1.3 mg of vitamin B6 every day. A baked potato, 3 oz. chicken breast, and a half cup of cooked spinach provides all the vitamin B6 you need for a day. Other good sources include chickpeas, salmon, tuna, beef, turkey, bananas, and sweet potatoes.

2 ways to beat jet lag before you ever take off

You've packed your suitcase, hopped on a plane, and soared across multiple time zones. Now you want to hit the floor running and start your adventure. But you're so tired you feel like you'll never get out of bed. You've got jet lag. Relax – by taking one of these two supplements, you can start beating jet lag before you leave home.

Mellow out with melatonin. You've probably heard of the supplement melatonin and its sleep-promoting properties. In a nutshell, melatonin is the hormone that tells your body clock when to doze off and when to wake up. But when you zoom past several time zones, your body's natural rhythm gets out of whack. By taking melatonin supplements, you naturally reset your internal timer.

Some experts suggest taking between half a milligram and 5 mg one hour before bedtime at your final destination. Others suggest taking 1 to 5 mg an hour before bedtime beginning two days prior to departure and continuing for two to three days after arriving at your final destination.

Catch some Zzzs with pine bark extract. Some scientists say flying causes slight swelling in your brain and body, which aggravates jet lag. A supplement called Pycnogenol made primarily from pine bark extract can help.

Jet lag symptoms lasted only 18 hours in people who took Pycnogenol, but a miserable 39 hours in people who didn't take it, found Italian researchers in one study. In another study, scientists took brain scans of people after long flights and found less swelling in those who took the supplement than those who didn't. Scientists used 50 mg tablets three times a day for seven days starting two days before takeoff.

Zipping across several time zones?

Beat jet lag with this easy meal plan

You can't eat when you're supposed to. You can't sleep when you're supposed to. And you're in Paris. Sigh. It's called jet lag, that feeling of exhaustion when you zoom across several time zones and then can't adjust. To get relief, here's an eating strategy you can try before you fly.

3 days and counting ...

Feast three days before travel, say experts. Gorge on protein during the day, like ham and eggs for breakfast, and chicken or salmon for lunch. Then switch to a high-carb meal for dinner, like whole-wheat pasta or a big bowl of red beans and rice. And drink your cuppa joe in the afternoon.

2 days and counting ...

Eat light today. Stick to foods high in protein during the day, and high in carbs for dinner. Guzzle your caffeinated brew after lunch.

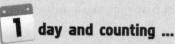

1 day and counting ...

Feast! Just like you did two days ago.

Time to go!

Down your java in the morning if you're headed west, and avoid it if you're flying east. Eat low-cal, high-protein foods throughout the day. Say no to alcohol and yes to water — and lots of it — to avoid dehydration. And if you can, wait to eat breakfast until the morning you're at your destination.

A supplement that helps you sleep if you suffer leg pain

It may start out as pain in the legs and arms during exercise. But as intermittent claudication worsens, the pain can keep you up at night and rob you of a good night's sleep.

Intermittent claudication is caused by too little blood flow in the limbs. That's caused by peripheral vascular disease from plaque buildup.

The supplement propionyl-L-carnitine seems to help soothe the pain and extend the distance people with intermittent claudication can walk. And if it helps relieve pain during exercise, it may keep the pain at bay so you can get some good shut-eye.

Eat like the Greeks for a good night's sleep

Over 22 million Americans suffer from sleep apnea, and many of them don't even know it. It happens when your airways become blocked while you're sleeping, and your brain wakes you up a little so you can catch your breath. In some people, this happens hundreds of times a night. But simple changes, including what you eat, could stop you from losing sleep.

The Mediterranean diet is typically known for keeping your heart healthy, and it may even protect against bone fractures. Scientists can now add another benefit to the list. A small study published in the *European Respiratory Journal* shows obese people with moderate to severe sleep apnea slept better after six months on the Mediterranean diet.

Participants noshed on fish, nuts, fruit, legumes, red meat, potatoes, low-fat dairy, chicken and turkey, unrefined cereals, salads and vegetables, and a daily glass of red wine. They also enjoyed a moderate amount of olive oil and cut down on cream, french fries, butter, margarine, sugary drinks, cakes and cookies, and processed meats. What's more, they walked for up to 30 minutes a day and were treated with CPAP, a device that keeps your airways open while you sleep.

If you're not sure you have sleep apnea, talk with your doctor. The exhausting condition can lead to stroke, high blood pressure, chronic heart failure, depression, and type 2 diabetes. And people with sleep apnea are more likely to get into car accidents.

Want to know the No. 1 way doctors recommend treating sleep apnea? Weight loss. In fact, a small study out of Brazil found obese people who lost weight did not experience as many breathing problems during sleep as those who maintained their weight. Weight loss may give you the rest you've been craving.

Stroke

Diet changes to lower your risk

3 heart-healthy recipes you should toss on the grill today

Grilling can be dangerous. And we're not just talking about the high heat and flames.

Eating charred meat off the grill raises your risk of pancreatic cancer, found a study out of the University of Minnesota. It's because cooking meat at high temperatures burns amino acids and other substances that create heterocyclic amines, cancer-causing chemicals.

But don't sweat it – you don't have to give up grilling completely. Try hobo packets on the following page. They're a delicious way to cook fish and chicken on the grill. And a healthy way to get extra protein, a powerful stroke fighter.

More protein means fewer strokes. You can cut down your chances of stroke a remarkable 26 percent by eating an extra 20 grams of protein each day. That's what researchers in China found. Scientists pored over seven studies, which included 250,000-plus people ranging in age from 30 to 80 to draw their conclusions.

Eat fish five times a week, and you'll cut your chance of stroke by 50 percent. That's what researchers who followed almost 80,000 women ages 34 to 59 found. The women who ate the most fish during the 14-year study were the least likely to suffer a stroke.

Experts also believe eating more protein could lower the number of stroke-related deaths by over 1 million a year around the globe. Some scientists think protein works by lowering blood pressure. But there's a catch. Your protein can't come from red meat like steaks and burgers. Opt for fish, beans, and chicken instead.

Three delicious ways to add more protein to your diet — campfire style. Here's how to make hobo packets. These savory meals are easy to toss together. And you can throw them on the grill or in the oven — your choice. All you need is your meat, vegetables, seasonings, and heavy-duty foil. Seal your meal securely, folding each end of your foil twice. Just make sure there's wiggle room in your packet for heat to expand.

- Cherry tomatoes, purple onions, and chicken chunks seasoned with curry and ginger — is your mouth watering yet? This savory Indian-inspired dish gets even better with chopped mango.

  Protein per 1 cup cubed chicken breast — 43 grams.

- You don't have to go south of the border to spice up a healthy dinner. Jazz up the mild taste of tilapia with cumin and chili powder plus corn, black beans, bell peppers, and chopped tomatoes. Want a little heat? Add chopped jalapeños. And layer tortilla chips at the bottom of your packet.

  Protein per 3 ounces tilapia — 21 grams.

- Treat yourself to trout. This flavorful meal combines carrots, lemon slices, and onions sliced into rings. First, cut up carrots, put them in a foil packet, and dot with butter. Place them on the grill. While they're cooking, stuff your trout with lemons and onions. Salt and pepper to taste. Make another foil packet for the fish and grill until it's flaky — and the carrots are tender, about 20 minutes.

  Protein per 3 ounces trout — 21 grams.

What your daily cuppa joe has to do with stroke — and it's all good!

Confused about whether coffee is good for you? Don't be. Studies show it's the everyday drink that could be lowering your risk of dying from heart disease, stroke, diabetes, and more. And people who drink this hot beverage tend to live longer because of this lower risk.

Men who drank two to three cups daily cut their risk of dying from a stroke by 16 percent and women by 7 percent, shows a study published in the *New England Journal of Medicine*.

Researchers looked at over 400,000 men and women who ranged in age from 50 to 71 at the start of the study. Their findings were the same for caffeine and decaf drinkers. Scientists aren't sure why drinking coffee lowers risk of death, but they suspect it's the thousands of compounds, including antioxidants, in those cups of brew.

Turmeric may heal your brain. A team of German researchers say the spice, one of the ingredients in curry, encouraged nerve cells to repair themselves and to multiply in an animal study. Experts hope their findings lead to a treatment for stroke and Alzheimer's in the future.

And women who drank two to three cups a day slashed their chances of even having a stroke by 19 percent, says a study published in *Circulation*, the American Heart Association's medical journal. Researchers evaluated data for over 80,000 women. Scientists for this study believe it's the antioxidants in coffee that fend off strokes.

So if you're wondering if you should keep drinking your daily dose of java – drink up!

And it doesn't have to be hot. Cold coffee drinks taste great, and they don't have to be loaded with fat and sugar. Here's a delicious way to enjoy a caramel frappuccino. And it's only 50 calories!

Toss a few ice cubes in a blender with a cup of cold coffee and 1/2 cup unsweetened almond milk. Add a little sugar-free sweetener and 1/2 teaspoon of vanilla extract. Blend. Then top with fat-free whipped topping and sugar-free caramel sauce. Makes 2 servings.

PREPARE IT

How to add pizazz to ordinary olive oil

Change the flavor of olive oil by infusing it with dried herbs and spices. Simply add the dried sprigs, leaves, seeds, or peel directly to a bottle of olive oil, cap it tightly, and store in a cool, dark place. The oil will begin to pick up flavor within a few weeks. Try rosemary, red pepper flakes, basil, dill, dried garlic, or cumin.

Infusing works best with dried herbs and spices. Fresh ones, even garlic and citrus peel, contain enough water to grow dangerous bacteria like the one that causes botulism. If you really want to use fresh herbs from your garden, do so wisely. Mix your fresh ingredients, add to the olive oil, and keep refrigerated. Use the oil within one week.

A meal plan proven to add years to your life

You want to eat right, live healthy, and fight heart-related problems like stroke. Then stop eating like an American. Instead, go Greek – and follow the diet that keeps your heart healthy and cuts your stroke risk.

It's known as the Mediterranean diet, which isn't really a diet at all. It's more like an appetizing eating style prominent in Greece and southern Italy where the locals favor fruits and vegetables, fish and poultry, nuts and seeds, pasta, legumes, whole grains, and olive oil.

People who eat this way crush their chances of stroke, shows an Italian study. Researchers followed over 14,000 residents of Molise, a region in central and southern Italy, for five years. They found the more people ate Mediterranean fare and the less they ate butter, red meat, soft drinks, and potatoes, the better their chances of warding off stroke. Healthier foods like those found in the Mediterranean diet lower the inflammation linked to chronic diseases and stroke.

The Mediterranean lifestyle is so heart healthy, the American Heart Association and American Stroke Association have adopted it as one of the primary ways to prevent stroke. Researchers with the associations found people who ate Mediterranean fare supplemented with almonds, walnuts, hazelnuts, and extra virgin olive oil slashed their stroke risk, while people who ate red meat raised theirs.

You, too, can adopt the Mediterranean regimen by making a few simple changes.

First, cut back on red meat, processed and packaged foods, anything fried, and high-fat dairy. Next, think produce, lots and lots of produce. Then stick with fish, chicken, and turkey for your main meats. And remember to pick up beans, garlic, whole grains, nuts, and seeds when you shop.

Here's what a sample day on the Mediterranean diet looks like.

- Breakfast – A medium-size pear or 1/2 cup raspberries or blueberries, 1 cup oatmeal, a handful of walnuts, and 1 cup fat-free milk.

- Snack – Pineapple smoothie made with 1/2 an orange, 1/2 cup pineapple chunks, 6 ounces light yogurt, and ice cubes.

- Lunch – Turkey avocado sandwich using 3 ounces turkey, three avocado slices, 1/3 cup shredded mozzarella cheese,

1 tablespoon light mayo, on two slices whole-grain bread.
Enjoy a cup of grapes on the side.

- Snack – Dip bell pepper slices in 2 tablespoons hummus.

- Dinner – 2 to 3 ounces grilled fish with 2 cups spinach
leaves, a light vinaigrette dressing, and 1 cup whole-wheat
pasta topped with crushed garlic and olive oil.

- Dessert – Light Greek yogurt topped with strawberries.

The one mineral you're not getting enough of — but should be

Sodium makes headlines all the time. Potassium, not so much. Yet this
powerful mineral can save you from suffering a stroke. Here's how.

Postmenopausal women who eat more potassium-rich foods are
12 percent less likely to suffer a stroke than those who eat less,
found a study published in the medical journal *Stroke*. Scientists
studied over 90,000 women from 50 to 79 years of age for 11
years. Those who got the most potassium were 10 percent less
likely to die from stroke than those who got the least.

And more potassium meant a 16 percent lower chance of having
an ischemic stroke, the most common type of stroke. It happens
when an artery to your brain becomes blocked. Experts believe
potassium works by improving blood flow and preventing arteries
from becoming stiff.

The Department of Agriculture recommends women get 4,700
milligrams (mg) of potassium a day. And the World Health
Organization (WHO) recommends 3,510 mg potassium daily to
lower stroke risk.

But some experts believe these goals are too high and not feasible
for Americans because of the link between sodium and potassium

in foods. They say people who get less sodium may not get enough potassium, and vice versa. People who consume more potassium get more sodium. Also potassium-rich foods cost more. And lastly, many experts believe the WHO's recommendations are too far removed from current eating patterns.

The women in the study were able to get an average of 2,600 mg a day. Not quite as high as the recommendations. But still, experts say getting more potassium, even if it's below recommended levels, will cut stroke risk overall, and ischemic stroke by 20 percent in women with normal blood pressure. So it's definitely worth looking into.

Surprising sources of potassium

Don't go bananas to get more potassium. Yes, medium bananas have a whopping 451 milligrams (mg) potassium. But did you know some of your favorite foods have even more? Here's a look at 10 popular, potassium-rich foods.

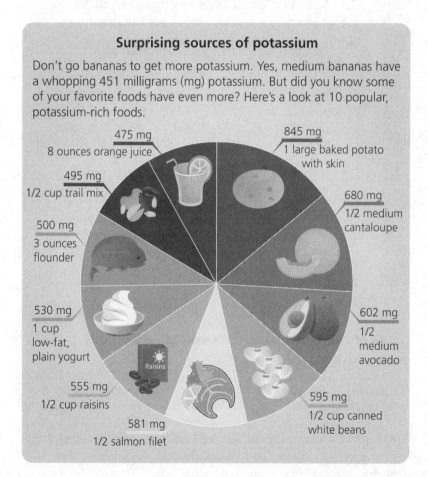

475 mg
8 ounces orange juice

845 mg
1 large baked potato with skin

495 mg
1/2 cup trail mix

680 mg
1/2 medium cantaloupe

500 mg
3 ounces flounder

602 mg
1/2 medium avocado

530 mg
1 cup low-fat, plain yogurt

595 mg
1/2 cup canned white beans

555 mg
1/2 cup raisins

581 mg
1/2 salmon filet

STORE IT

Say good-bye to brown avocados

Avocados turn brown quickly. They can't help it. Once the enzymes on their flesh get exposed to air, it's a downhill battle.

But you can get ahead of the spoiling game with these tips. No matter which one you try, always refrigerate your leftover avocado.

- Some food testers swear by vacuum sealing. So if you have a sealer, try it on your avocados.

- Pour lime juice, lemon juice, or vinegar on the exposed half.

- Place in a sealed container with chopped onions.

- Don't throw away the pit. Put it in the portion you didn't eat.

- Spread a thin layer of mayo over the exposed half, then wrap with plastic wrap.

- Place in lemon water cut-side down. Your avocado may soften and taste a little tart, but this will keep it from turning brown for a couple of days.

5 awesome ways to eat avocados — and cut your cholesterol

It's amazing what you can do with an avocado. And what an avocado can do for you.

This buttery-tasting fruit slashed the bad cholesterol in obese and overweight individuals, found a small study published in the

Journal of the American Heart Association. Doctors placed all participants on three healthy diets to lower cholesterol. While all three diets reduced cholesterol, the participants who ate a Haas avocado daily reaped the biggest benefits. And if you lower your cholesterol, you cut your risk of having a stroke.

It's because avocados are loaded with monounsaturated fatty acids – the good fat your body needs for a healthy heart and squeaky-clean arteries. Plus, they're rich in vitamins, minerals, fiber, and phytonutrients. And if you're worried about the calories, about 227 for one medium Haas, don't be. Simply swap out that 299-calorie donut that's loaded with saturated fats for one of the avocado treats below.

You've probably eaten your share of guacamole over the years. But there's so much more you can do with this versatile fruit. Check out these five easy ways to enjoy avocados every day without making guacamole.

- Creamy avocado dressing – Blend a tablespoon of lime juice, a splash of hot pepper sauce, and one avocado in a food processor. Add 1/2 cup plain Greek yogurt, 1/4 cup low-fat or fat-free mayo, 1 tablespoon chopped red onion, 1 teaspoon minced garlic, 1 teaspoon minced cilantro, and a dash of salt, sugar, and pepper. Process until the dressing is smooth. Pour some over your favorite salad.

- Savory avocado pesto – Add a bunch of basil leaves, 2 avocados, 1/3 cup pine nuts, 1/2 cup grated Parmesan, 2 tablespoons lemon juice, 1 tablespoon minced garlic, and a dash of salt to a food processor. Once your ingredients are finely chopped, pour in 1/2 cup extra-virgin olive oil and purée. Toss with fettuccine.

- Breakfast avo-rrito – Scramble 1 cup egg whites. Place scrambled eggs, shredded cheese, avocado chunks, black beans, and a tablespoon salsa in a tortilla, and roll up.

- Greek avocado salad – Chop a cucumber and 3 avocados, and combine with 1/3 cup feta cheese and 1/2 red onion sliced thinly. In a separate bowl, stir together 1/2 cup olive oil, 1/2 cup red wine vinegar or fresh lemon juice, and 2 teaspoons minced garlic. Slowly pour over your salad and toss gently. Salt and pepper to taste. Chill and serve immediately.

- Avocado cheese melt – Layer your favorite shredded cheese and avocado slices on two slices of whole-grain bread. Add chopped jalapeños for extra zing. Cook like a regular grilled cheese sandwich.

2 essential brain-saving vitamins

What do you get when you top a bowl full of leafy greens with strips of red bell peppers and a handful of broccoli florets? A stroke-fighting salad! That's because your bowl is brimming with the two vitamins you need to slash your risk of stroke.

Bust your stroke risk with B vitamins. A study of 20,000 adults in China found people with high blood pressure who took folic acid supplements along with the blood pressure drug enalapril slashed their risk of stroke over people who took enalapril only. Those who combined the two also lowered their chances of having an ischemic stroke and of suffering a combination of stroke, heart attack, and cardiovascular death.

In a review of studies from China, people who took B-vitamin supplements cut back their stroke risk by 7 percent. Researchers analyzed 14 studies, which included close to 55,000 people to draw their conclusions.

Scientists say B vitamins work alongside drugs that lower homocysteine levels. Homocysteine is an amino acid that triggers strokes and heart attacks when present in high amounts.

Boost your B-vitamins by eating a variety of foods, including beans, fish, papayas, cantaloupe, dark leafy greens, and fortified breads and cereals.

Save your brain with vitamin C. French researchers found people deficient in vitamin C have a higher risk of suffering hemorrhagic stroke, a type of stroke that causes bleeding in the brain. Hemorrhagic stroke is less common than ischemic, but much more deadly.

Experts say vitamin C works by lowering blood pressure and keeping blood vessels healthy.

Before you start throwing back vitamin C supplements, take note. Scientists say they need to do more research to see if vitamin C supplements could help prevent bleeding in the brain. In the meantime, get your vitamin C from food like spinach, strawberries, pineapple, tomatoes, and winter squash – as well as citrus fruits.

7 sneaky ways to shrink your stroke risk

Adding fiber to your diet is easier and tastier than you think – and you'll slash your chances of having a stroke.

An extra 7 grams of fiber added to your daily diet can cut your risk of stroke by 7 percent. That's what a study published in *Stroke*, an American Heart Association journal, says. And a Chinese study of 500,000 people shows eating fresh fruit daily cut stroke risk by 24 percent.

In fact, any amount of extra fiber in your diet will lower your chances of stroke and boost your heart health. Experts think it's because fruit and fiber lower blood pressure, which means less stroke risk. What's more, foods high in fiber keep your body from absorbing cholesterol.

Quick and easy ways to get more fiber

SUNDAY		pour a 10-oz. package of frozen green peas into your soup	14 grams fiber
MONDAY		sprinkle 2 tablespoons chopped dried pears and apricots on your breakfast cereal or dinner salad	4 grams fiber
TUESDAY		spread 2 tablespoons hummus on your morning bagel or lunchtime sandwich	2 grams fiber
WEDNESDAY		try a grain you've never eaten like ½ cup amaranth, quinoa, or pearled barley	2.5 to 3 grams fiber
THURSDAY		savor the sweet taste of two kiwis	4 grams fiber
FRIDAY		snack on 2 tablespoons sunflower seeds	3 grams fiber
SATURDAY		swap a cup of rice for a cup of cauliflower	2 grams fiber

Read this before you take another drink

Drinking too much can lead to stroke. Two or more alcoholic beverages a day during middle age can raise your risk of stroke more than well-known triggers like diabetes and high blood pressure, suggests a Swedish study.

The study followed over 11,000 identical twins for 43 years. Heavy drinkers raised their stroke risk by 34 percent. Those who drank heavily in their 50s and 60s increased their likelihood of having a stroke five years earlier, regardless of other risk factors. In fact, of the identical twins in the study, those who suffered a stroke drank more than their siblings who did not have a stroke.

But how much is too much? The American Heart Association suggests a daily max of two drinks for men and one for women. One drink equals 12 ounces of beer, 5 ounces of wine, or 1 1/2 ounces of hard liquor.

And don't think you can take it easy during the week, then binge on the weekend. Besides stroke, women who throw down four or more drinks and men who guzzle five or more in less than two hours risk alcohol poisoning, liver disease, nerve damage, and more.

PREPARE IT

3 quick and easy fruit hacks

Adding fruit to your favorite recipes makes them tastier and healthier. Check out these quick tips that make tossing in fruit a breeze.

- Want perfectly sliced strawberries? Reach for your egg slicer. Stem your strawberries first. Then slice away like you would a boiled egg. So much easier than using a knife. Not to mention, you get to use your egg slicer on more than just eggs.

- You don't need a pineapple corer to, well, core a pineapple. Use a small biscuit cutter instead. First, cut away the skin. Then slice your pineapple into rings. Lastly, take your biscuit cutter and press into the core of each ring. It should fall right out.

- Stop using a fork to mash your bananas for a bread or muffin recipe. A potato masher will do the job a whole lot easier and quicker.

One really good reason to keep eating cheese

Looks like a little dairy may go a long way to preventing stroke. People in Taiwan who ate dairy foods up to seven times a week lowered their chances of stroke and of dying from heart disease, shows a study out of Monash University in Australia. Researchers, who followed close to 4,000 people ages 19 to 64 for three years, also found people who ate no dairy at all had higher blood pressure and greater body fat – both stroke risk factors.

Scientists think it's the nutrients in dairy food, notably the fats, vitamin D, calcium, magnesium, and proteins, that serve as stroke fighters. Not surprisingly, pairing milk with other nutritious foods, like fortified cereals, also triggers health benefits.

Experts recommend getting dairy once a day or just under five servings a week. A serving equals a cup of milk or about 1 1/2 ounces of cheese.

Brain block — the stunning reason you should skip this snack

Mars bar lovers — beware. The deep-fried version of your favorite candy bar not only affects your waistline, it could cause a stroke.

Men suffered less blood flow to their brains just 90 minutes after eating a deep-fried Mars bar, say Scottish researchers. This drop in blood flow is closely associated with ischemic stroke, the type of stroke that causes a blockage to the brain. And while the drop wasn't significant, it still begs the question — is a high-fat, high-sugar, 1,200-calorie candy bar worth the risk? Probably not.

Instead, reach for a small piece of chocolate. People who ate chocolate regularly lowered their stroke risk by 19 percent over those who ate very little, suggests a study published in *Stroke*, an American Heart Association journal. Eating 2 ounces of chocolate a week could slash your stroke risk by 14 percent.

Tummy troubles

11 ways to quell the queasies

3 ways to soothe your stomach with ginger

A bold-flavored plant with a strong and spicy aroma isn't something you usually associate with relief for a troubled tummy. But this root can actually help relieve a number of stomach problems. If you find the slightly sweet, peppery ginger root too spicy on its own, try these delicious ways to slip ginger into your diet.

Stay regular with ginger tea. Your stomach stays busy. And when it's working properly, you don't even think about it. But when your digestive system starts to act up – or back up – you'll need to act fast to get things moving along. A little bit of ginger can help.

The powerful chemicals found in ginger gather in your digestive tract. That's why ginger is so effective in treating stomach trouble. Ginger moves things along, keeping your internal plumbing running smoothly.

In one study, scientists found 1,200 milligrams of ginger was enough to stimulate the digestive tract. The effectiveness of ginger in preventing vomiting has been attributed to its ability to prevent, break up, and get rid of intestinal gas. Ginger also protects the lining of your stomach from damage.

Making ginger tea is easy, and you can do it many different ways. Here's one way – grate a tablespoon of ginger and put it in two cups of boiling water. Turn off the heat and let it steep for 10 minutes.

Give it a different twist by adding honey, lemon juice, fresh mint leaves, or a cinnamon stick.

Calm your travel troubles with candy. You never know when you or a traveling companion will get car sick. Candied ginger is convenient for unexpected upsets. Just stick some in your purse or travel bag for convenience no matter where you are. You can buy it in stores or make your own. For an easy recipe, check out *On-the-go ginger chews* on the next page.

In one study, ginger worked better than the common motion sickness medicine Dramamine in relieving symptoms of motion sickness. Another study showed the same results in people taking a capsule containing half a gram of ginger powder twice a day for nausea and vomiting during pregnancy. Take it on your next plane trip, cruise, or road trip.

Capsules are also convenient, so if you choose to go that route, 250-milligram capsules up to four times a day is recommended by many doctors.

> Try ginger to put a stop to post-op nausea. Studies show at least 1 gram of ginger is effective for reducing nausea and vomiting after an operation. Every surgery is different, so check with your doctor before trying ginger.

Gingerly ease inflammation with vinaigrette. Oxidative stress can cause inflammation, which may irritate your tummy. Ginger has powerful antioxidants that help reduce oxidative stress by battling free radicals.

Studies showed ginger is rich in zingiberene, bisabolene, gingerols and shogaols – compounds that have antioxidant, anti-inflammatory, and cancer-fighting properties.

Ginger may act as an anti-inflammatory by keeping tabs on calcium levels that influence chemicals involved in inflammation.

Here's a simple way to slip ginger into your meal. Combine the following ingredients in a blender for a tasty salad dressing.

- 1/2 cup olive oil
- 1/4 cup balsamic vinegar
- 2 tablespoons low-sodium soy sauce
- 3 cloves garlic, chopped
- 2 tablespoons honey or brown sugar
- 2 tablespoons minced fresh ginger root
- 1/4 cup water
- 1 teaspoon toasted sesame oil

COOK IT

On-the-go ginger chews

Candied ginger is perfect for when you're on-the-go. Whip up a batch at home, then carry some with you for quick relief from nausea.

- 1/2 pound fresh ginger
- 2 cups granulated sugar
- 2 cups water

Use a spoon to peel the ginger, then slice thinly. Put slices in a pot with enough water to cover and bring to a boil.

Reduce heat and simmer for 30 minutes. Reserve 1/4 cup of the liquid and drain.

Put sugar, 1/4 cup liquid, and cooked ginger slices back in the pot.

Bring to a boil, reduce heat, and simmer for about 20 minutes, stirring constantly. The water will evaporate, and the sugar syrup will crystallize.

Spread the ginger slices on a cooling rack. Once cool, store the pieces in an airtight container for up to four weeks.

Eat to outsmart motion sickness

It's hard to predict, but it's the quickest way to ruin a vacation. Motion sickness. The queasy feeling that comes in waves in your stomach.

You feel the queasiness of motion sickness when your inner ear senses motion, but your eyes can't tell you are moving. And if your inner ear isn't in tiptop shape, you could be suffering even when you're not traveling.

Your balance is determined by your inner ears, eyes, pressure receptors, and sensory receptors that tell your central nervous system how to process information.

You could experience motion sickness when your central nervous system receives conflicting messages – imagine your boss, your mom, and your best friend all telling you to do something different at the same time.

This is what can happen when you read in the car. Your eyes are looking at a fixed object, telling your brain you are sitting still, but your inner ear is sensing movement.

Your inner ears are made up of tiny parts that regulate pressure and monitor direction of motion. If something is wrong with any of these parts, you can have balance problems that lead to symptoms like nausea and vomiting – as well as dizziness. Certain nutrients can help support your inner ears so you can fight the source instead of the symptoms.

Pile on the colorful vegetables. Magnesium is an essential mineral that plays many roles in your body. Early signs of magnesium deficiency include loss of appetite, nausea, vomiting, fatigue, and weakness. A deficiency can also overstimulate your auditory nerve – nerve fibers that carry information from your inner ear to your brain.

Studies show higher intakes of magnesium, vitamin E, vitamin C, and beta carotene help protect against oxidative stress and preserve cells in your inner ears. To get these nutrients, eat colorful veggies like broccoli, spinach, sweet red peppers, and sweet potatoes.

Grab some yogurt and cheese. Magnesium works hand in hand with another important nutrient – calcium. If you have a magnesium deficiency, it may throw off calcium channels in the cells of your inner ears and overstimulate parts of your auditory nerve that receive signals.

Scientists think low calcium levels could be a possible source of inner ear problems. Calcium has an important role in the inner ear, transporting information about sound, movement, and gravity. You can find calcium in cheese, yogurt, milk, as well as nondairy foods like leafy greens and fortified cereal.

Motion sickness Rx: what to eat before you travel

Ever wonder if it's better for your stomach if you eat something before a big trip? Turns out, it may be *what* you're eating that makes the difference.

Research shows a high-protein liquid drink is better than a high-carbohydrate liquid drink for reducing nausea. In the study, people drank either a high-carb beverage, a high-protein beverage, or nothing before being exposed to a rotating drum to simulate motion sickness. Symptoms were most severe in the group that drank nothing and least severe in the protein group.

Experts agree it's important to avoid spicy or large, high-fat meals. Instead, eat frequent light, protein snacks, like low-fat yogurt or trail mix, when you travel.

FOOD POISONING

Which favorite foods put you at risk?

Harmful bacteria and viruses could be lurking in your food. Knowing the most common sources of foodborne illnesses can help you keep your family safe.

Top causes of food poisoning

Salmonella	Norovirus	Campylobacter
Eggs, poultry, meat, unpasteurized milk or juice, cheese, contaminated raw fruits and vegetables	Raw produce, contaminated drinking water, uncooked foods, shellfish from contaminated waters	Raw and undercooked poultry, unpasteurized milk, contaminated water

E. coli	Listeria	Clostridium perfringens
Undercooked beef, unpasteurized milk and juice, raw fruits and vegetables, and contaminated water	Unpasteurized milk, soft cheeses made with unpasteurized milk, ready-to-eat deli meats	Meats, poultry, gravy, dried or precooked foods

Top 10 riskiest foods

Leafy greens   Eggs   Tuna   Oysters   Potatoes

Cheese   Ice cream   Tomatoes   Sprouts   Berries

Fend off food poisoning with 2 magic herbs

You think it will never happen to you. But each year, one out of six people gets some kind of foodborne illness. With odds like that, it's important to do all you can to keep your family safe. Luckily, scientists have discovered two heroes – a spice and an herb – that have the power to stop *E. coli* in its tracks.

While some types of *Escherichia (E.) coli* live in the gut of perfectly healthy people, strains – such as *E. coli O157:H7* – can cause severe cramps, diarrhea, and vomiting. You can get *E. coli* from contaminated water or food. Raw vegetables and undercooked ground beef are the most common culprits. Chemicals in certain spices and herbs, however, kill the bacteria before it can cross your lips.

Cinnamon's secret ingredient. Cinnamon has a long history in cooking and traditional medicine. Its bark is used to make powders, capsules, teas, and liquid extracts. Cinnamaldehyde is the most active bacteria-fighting component in cinnamon essential oil and is especially active against *E. coli* and *Salmonella*.

Most studies use either Ceylon or Chinese cinnamon essential oil, but Indonesian cinnamon is most common in the U.S. and easier to find in stores. These studies demonstrate how cinnamon damages the cell membrane of *Escherichia coli* and reduces the number of harmful bacteria in food.

Results showed significantly less bacteria when cinnamon was added to all kinds of food, including beef and fruit juices. Though researchers have not yet recommended an amount of cinnamon powder to mix with foods, they say cinnamon oil has potential in food packaging and processing.

Mighty mustard to the rescue. Mustard is one of several herbs from the family of mustard plants, which originated in the Mediterranean. Compounds found in mustard powder kill *E. coli*. Although it takes too long for mustard powder to kill bacteria in meats like ground beef, it does the trick for dry-fermented sausage. And it doesn't take a lot of mustard powder to wipe out the harmful bacteria.

"Over a period of two to three weeks," says Dr. Rick Holley, a professor at the University of Manitoba who has been studying the effects of mustard for years, "they essentially eliminate *E. coli O157:H7* and other toxigenic *E. coli* from the meat batters that are used to make these dry sausages." If you're serious about making traditional sausages, mustard powder is something to look into.

5 deadly mistakes you're making in the kitchen

Most people are aware of how easy it is for bacteria to contaminate food during processing or at restaurants, but 25 percent of foodborne illnesses actually start at home. Here are some of the most common food-handling mistakes. Keep your food safe and your digestive tract healthy by avoiding these kitchen no-nos.

Cooking at the wrong temperature leaves behind bacterial survivors. You can't see the bacteria living in your food so it may be difficult to know if your meal is safe to eat. The easiest way to make sure your food is cooked properly is to use a thermometer. Follow these cooking temperatures suggested by the U.S. Department of Agriculture.

Product	Temperature (°F)	Rest time
Beef, pork, veal, lamb	145	3 minutes
Ground meats	160	-
Ham	145	3 minutes
Poultry	165	-

Storing at the wrong temperature provides a comfortable home for germs. Keeping foods in the temperature danger zone – between 40 to 140 degrees – encourages bacterial growth. You want to make sure cold foods stay cold and hot foods stay hot. Set your refrigerator at or below 40 degrees F and your freezer at or below 0 degrees.

Storing leftovers improperly puts you at risk. You can make your food cool faster by putting it in shallow containers. Don't let your food sit out for more than two hours, and be sure to eat your leftovers within four days.

Defrosting on your counter leads to food safety uncertainty. If you defrost your food on your counter, you can't control the environment. Thaw your frozen food in the refrigerator instead of at room temperature so you know it will be below the temperature danger zone at all times.

Reusing your kitchen utensils increases your chances of cross contamination. Keep your meat and produce separate, from shopping to storing to cooking. Here are some tips to avoid cross contamination.

- When preparing your food, use different colored cutting boards – one for meats and one for veggies.

- Never put cooked burgers back on the plate you used for raw burgers. You also don't want to use the same knife or plate.

- If you want to use marinade as a sauce after marinating your meat, boil it to kill the germs.

Organic chicken: will it protect you from deadly bacteria?

Organic chicken. All-natural meats. Free-range poultry. Everywhere you turn, companies are broadcasting "safer," "more-nutritious" chicken. But will organic chicken actually help keep your family healthier?

Organic meat does have a few things going for it. Organic agricultural practices are said to be kinder to the environment as farmers must follow certain rules regarding the use of pesticides and antibiotics. Because of this, eating organic poultry may lessen your exposure to certain pesticides and antibiotic-resistant bacteria. But that doesn't mean you're completely safe from bacterial contamination.

Chicken is a high-risk food – both organic and conventional. In a review of 12 years of research, scientists found that people alerted the Centers for Disease Control to more bacterial outbreaks from chicken than any other meat or poultry product. Among the outbreaks, *Salmonella* and *Clostridium perfringens* were the most common.

Out of three lots tested in one study published in the *Journal of Food Protection*, 60 percent of the chickens had *Salmonella*. Eating organic chicken doesn't reduce the risk of deadly *E. coli* either. Scientists warn that you shouldn't assume free-range or organic conditions will prevent chicken from becoming contaminated.

The bottom line – organic raw poultry is not necessarily safer than other poultry. So buy organic chicken if you think you're getting better-quality meat. But make sure you take all the usual precautions to protect your family from the harmful bacteria it may carry.

Bad bugs you want to avoid at all costs

Stomach flu, traveler's diarrhea, food poisoning – all common names for gastroenteritis, an infection that attacks your digestive tract. The harmful culprits include viruses, bacteria, and parasites, and they can show up anywhere. Protect yourself by being aware of the worst offenders and where they're hitching a ride.

Source	Harmful organism
Contaminated water	Campylobacter jejuni, Escherichia (E.) coli, Entamoeba histolytica, Norwalk virus, Giardia, Cryptosporidium
Contaminated food	Entamoeba histolytica, Norwalk virus
Raw milk	Campylobacter jejuni, Escherichia (E.) coli, Listeria monocytogenes, Salmonella
Raw or undercooked meat, poultry, eggs, or shellfish	Campylobacter jejuni, Escherichia (E.) coli, Listeria monocytogenes, Salmonella, Vibrio parahemolyticus, Norwalk virus
Garlic in oil, improperly canned foods, vacuum-packed and tightly wrapped food	Clostridium botulinum
Unpasteurized apple juice or cider	Escherichia (E.) coli
Uncooked fruits and vegetables, raw leafy vegetables	Listeria monocytogenes, Escherichia (E.) coli
Soft cheese, improperly processed ice cream	Listeria monocytogenes
Dairy products	Salmonella
Foods left for long periods in steam tables or at room temperature	Clostridium perfringens
Improper food processing or handling	Shigella, Staphylococcus aureus
Unwashed hands of people who have the virus; sharing food, drink, or utensils with infected people	Astrovirus, Rotavirus
Person-to-person contact	Norwalk virus, Giardia, Cryptosporidium

Wash away stomach woes naturally

If you were thrust into a reality show where you had to survive out in the wild, it's nice to know you could go weeks without food – especially if you have absolutely no survival skills. But you wouldn't make it long without water. Water is perhaps the most essential nutrient in your body and is particularly important to good digestion – and a tranquil tummy.

H2O keeps everything moving along. Your body can't absorb all the nutrients it needs if you don't have a strong, working digestive system. Water helps transport food through your digestive tract and also helps break it down so your body can absorb the nutrients.

Water also plays an important part in eliminating waste. Believe it or not, you can easily lose two to three quarts of water a day just through breathing, sweating, and using the bathroom. If you don't replace that, you'll end up dehydrated. Then your colon will steal fluid from the stools passing through to try and keep your body in balance. The result? Uncomfortable – maybe even painful – constipation.

Fluids are just what the doctor ordered. Whether you're sick from food poisoning, the flu, or just plain indigestion, water should be part of your recovery plan. Drinking water is critical during bouts of diarrhea and vomiting as it helps restore lost fluids.

And if you happen to eat a bad taco at lunch, water can help relieve your upset stomach by flushing out the offending germs. So even if your stomach is queasy, try to drink clear liquids, including water, as often as possible throughout the day.

Ulcers

Quick fixes to end the suffering

Switch to a breakfast that's easy on your tummy

Crispy bacon, buttered toast, a big bowl of your favorite cereal. Breakfast has never been so interesting – or tasted so good. But if you have an ulcer, the thought of sizzling bacon or cold milk may have you cringing. Certain foods can irritate an already sensitive stomach. Switch to a breakfast that fights the most common cause of ulcers and is easy on your tummy.

Scientists once thought that stress and spicy foods caused ulcers. Now they know the bacterium *Helicobacter pylori (H. pylori)* is the culprit for over half of peptic ulcers – ulcers that form in your esophagus, stomach, or first part of your small intestine. *H. pylori* weakens the lining that protects your stomach and intestines from acids, which can lead to damage.

Though your breakfast won't cause ulcers to develop, it can aggravate your sores. Eating a probiotic-packed food like yogurt can save you from discomfort and speed up the healing process.

Probiotics banish bad bacteria from your gut. Although the antibiotics for treating *H. pylori* are usually effective, they kill good bacteria, too, and often cause side effects, like diarrhea. Probiotics help by balancing the microbes in your gut and replenishing the good bacteria.

Many studies agree that probiotic treatment is effective in reducing *H. pylori* and associated stomach inflammation. The probiotics used in recent studies include *Lactobacillus* strains and *Bifidobacterium* strains, and in one study, *Streptococcus thermophilus*. These strains can also be found in many yogurts.

Eat your way to a healthier stomach with a yogurt parfait.
Clinical studies found that yogurt containing certain *Lactobacillus* strains improves inflammation caused by *H. pylori*. A study of almost 500 healthy people revealed less *H. pylori* in those eating yogurt more than once a week compared to those who ate none.

Probiotics work against *H. pylori* by producing bacteria-fighting agents and antioxidants. They can change the pH of your stomach, providing unfavorable conditions for the bacteria. They may also stimulate production of mucus, which acts as a barrier to protect the lining of your stomach.

Yogurt provides an ulcer-blasting breakfast with its probiotics, but it also has nutrients that help keep your stomach strong. Yogurt contains the antioxidants vitamin C and zinc, which have anti-ulcer and anti-inflammatory properties.

A parfait wouldn't be complete without fruit and toppings. Strawberries and blueberries have fiber and vitamin C, and almonds and rolled oats both contain fiber and vitamin E.

Fiber helps keep your digestive system running smoothly, and studies show it's effective in preventing some ulcers. Vitamins C and E help heal ulcers, possibly by increasing the effectiveness of antibiotics.

When shopping for yogurt, look for the specific probiotics in the ingredients list or for the "Live & Active Cultures" seal to make sure you get the benefits of the probiotics. This seal means the yogurt contains *Lactobacillus bulgaricus* and *Streptococcus thermophilus*.

PREPARE IT

Overnight berry muesli

No one wants to wake up in the morning and search for food that's gentle on your stomach, yet pleasing to your taste buds. Good news — you can make muesli the night before and have a no-fuss breakfast.

Muesli is a cereal that originated in Switzerland. It usually contains oats, nuts, and fruit. This recipe uses yogurt to soften the oats and make the dish creamy and delicious.

- 3/4 cup plain yogurt
- 1/2 cup rolled oats
- 1/2 cup blueberries or sliced strawberries
- 1 tablespoon chopped almonds

For preparation the night before, stir yogurt and oats into a medium bowl, then cover and refrigerate overnight — at least 8 hours.

When you're ready to eat, mix in berries and top with almonds.

A juicy way to put out the fire

You're eating all the right foods, but your stomach is still in a constant state of protest. What are you doing wrong? Maybe the answer lies in your cup. If you don't pay attention to what you're drinking, you could be making your ulcers worse.

Drinks like milk and acidic fruit juice can irritate your stomach. Swap these drinks for cranberry juice to relieve discomfort and fight ulcers.

Milk was once a popular remedy for ulcers because it provides temporary relief by coating the stomach lining. But milk also stimulates the production of stomach acids, which aggravate ulcers. Acidic juices like orange juice and grapefruit juice can also irritate your stomach.

Cranberries are known for their role in preventing urinary tract infections and bladder diseases, but some studies show they also fight the bacterium *Helicobacter pylori (H. pylori)*, a known cause of ulcers. Cranberry juice stops cells necessary for *H. pylori* growth and keeps the bacteria from sticking to your stomach lining.

In one study, people drank 8 ounces of cranberry juice or another beverage for 90 days. The cranberry juice suppressed *H. pylori* infection in 14 percent of the cranberry group versus 5 percent in the other group.

Cranberry juice also has vitamins C and E. When added to standard ulcer therapy, these vitamins speed up the healing process.

When you shop for cranberry juice, avoid juice cocktails. Cranberry juice cocktail is only about 26 to 33 percent pure cranberry juice and is sweetened with fructose or an artificial sweetener.

Feast on fiber to fight ulcers

Lunchtime can be a sore point if you get an ulcer, but having ulcers doesn't mean you have to settle for a bland diet. Get creative – a fiber-rich salad full of your favorite fruits and veggies is an easy meal that doubles as a defense against ulcers.

While fiber won't cure an ulcer, it can keep your tummy happier by helping food move along. Sluggish digestion along with *H. pylori* encourages ulcers to form.

A Canadian study showed fiber has protective effects against ulcers in the upper small intestine, also known as duodenal ulcers.

Soluble fiber, found abundantly in legumes, is most effective at lowering your risk. Legumes include dried beans and peas, peanuts, and lentils.

Also found in oats, barley, fruits, and vegetables, soluble fiber draws water into your digestive tract. This slows down the digestive process, making sure you don't get too much of certain nutrients like starch and sugar.

Insoluble fiber is found in fruits and vegetables, especially the peel, and whole grains. It speeds up digestion, acting as a natural laxative.

For digestive health, doctors recommend 25 to 30 grams of fiber a day, but the average American gets only half of this. To slip more fiber into your diet, check out this recipe for a roasted sweet potato and black bean salad. A cup of sweet potatoes contains 8 grams of fiber, and a cup of black beans has over 12 grams.

COOK IT

Roasted sweet potato and black bean salad

It's lunchtime again, which means round two for your ulcers. Satisfy your stomach with a delicious meal loaded with fiber. It also has the added boost of olive oil. According to studies, olive oil helps ulcers heal and fights inflammation.

- 2 large sweet potatoes, cut into 1-inch chunks
- 1 can black beans, rinsed and drained
- 1 tablespoon olive oil

Heat oven to 375 degrees. Toss sweet potato chunks with olive oil and your favorite seasonings. Bake until tender, about 15 minutes. Let cool. In a bowl, combine sweet potatoes and beans. Serve on top of your favorite leafy greens. Serves 4.

Trade your morning brew to block tummy pain

Over half of American adults drink coffee every day. But coffee, both caffeinated and decaffeinated, stimulates acid production and can aggravate your stomach, causing irritation and inflammation.

Gastritis is inflammation of the stomach lining, often caused by *Helicobacter pylori* infection. If left untreated, gastritis can lead to ulcers and, in some cases, stomach cancer. Your chances of getting chronic gastritis or *H. pylori* infection increase as you get older, but you can easily switch your morning coffee with gastritis-fighting green tea to reduce your risk.

Here's what studies found.

- Green tea drinkers had a lower risk of developing gastritis or stomach cancer.

- Too many free radicals in your body promote inflammation. Antioxidant polyphenols contained in green tea scavenge free radicals, preventing inflammation.

- Studies on mice show drinking green tea before getting an infection prevents inflammation and damage to the stomach lining, while drinking it after lessens the effects of gastritis.

- High amounts of the beverage was associated with the prevention of chronic gastritis. People in the study drank 10 cups, but watch how much you drink. Too much caffeine could cause unwanted side effects, including anxiety and an irregular heartbeat. You also don't want to drink green tea on an empty stomach because the tannic acid could cause stomach irritation, nausea, vomiting, and liver damage.

Anti-ulcer meal planning made easy

Some foods can take you from bad to worse when you have an ulcer. Highly seasoned, high-fat meals can irritate your stomach, but these vegetables can heal. And they're easy to remember, just think "ABC." Chop up your veggies, add some flavor, and stir-fry to tie it all together. You'll have a great meal that will help fight ulcers and keep them from coming back.

Artichokes heal an aching gut. Artichokes have a long history of treating conditions like nausea and indigestion. Recent studies confirm the ulcer-fighting potential of artichokes. They stimulate the production of stomach mucus, which protects the lining.

Artichokes protect against ulcers another way – fiber. It helps keep your digestive system running smoothly. One medium artichoke contains over 40 percent of your daily value of fiber.

Once you know how to prepare them, artichokes are not so scary. Canned artichokes are the easiest way to go, but you don't want to buy only artichoke hearts because you'll miss out on all the great benefits the leaves have to offer.

If you want to use fresh artichokes, follow these four easy steps.

- Chop off the stems and the top inch of the bud.

- Remove the tough outer leaves until you reach the soft, pale green leaves.

- Cut artichokes in half, lengthwise, and remove the choke, which is the fuzzy part in the middle.

- Stir fry the artichokes with the rest of your veggies.

Beat bad bacteria with vitamin-filled broccoli. Studies show sulforaphane, a chemical found in broccoli and broccoli sprouts, helps destroy *H. pylori*. Adding vitamins C and E to your ulcer therapy can also help your body fight *H. pylori*. In a recent study, people took 500 milligrams of vitamin C and 200 IU (international units) of vitamin E twice a day for 30 days with good results.

Scientists think these vitamins speed up the healing process by increasing the effectiveness of antibiotics, minimizing stomach damage, and strengthening your immune system.

Fruits are famous for their vitamin C, but don't forget about vegetables. Many are also packed with C and are less acidic. One cup of broccoli contains 135 percent of the vitamin C you need each day and 4 percent daily value of vitamin E. Broccoli is also a good source of vitamin A and fiber.

Despite what you may have heard, you *can* use olive oil to stir-fry. Just make sure it's standard or pure olive oil — not virgin or extra-virgin. Olive oil has anti-inflammatory properties and protects against nonsteroidal anti-inflammatory drugs (NSAIDs) linked to ulcers.

Cabbage gets an A+ in stomach healing. In early studies, scientists noted a connection between cabbage juice and peptic ulcers. Today, research supports the theory that cabbage helps stop stomach damage caused by ulcers. One way it does this is through sulforaphane, which kills *H. pylori*.

Scientists have also suggested that vitamin A helps prevent ulcers from forming in your upper small intestine. Cooked cabbage has 20 percent daily value of vitamin A. It's also an excellent source of vitamin C and fiber.

Make your belly better and your taste buds happier. Ginger and garlic irritate some people's stomachs, but if they don't bother you, look to them for extra protection.

- Ginger can thicken the lining of your stomach, lower acidity, and reduce ulcers caused by aspirin. Chemicals found in ginger seem to have anti-inflammatory and antioxidant properties.

- Allicin fights bacteria, including *H. pylori*. It can be found in garlic oil or powder but not in fresh garlic until it is crushed. A medium-size clove of garlic will do the trick.

These three vegetables can make some people gassy. To minimize gas and help with digestion, eat slowly and chew food thoroughly. If needed, you can take digestive enzymes like Beano that help your body digest foods.

STORE IT

3 veggies you're storing wrong

Keep your veggies at their freshest by knowing the best way to store them.

- Artichokes. You can keep artichokes moist by sprinkling a few drops of water on them before storing in a plastic bag in your refrigerator. Don't rinse or trim before storing.

- Broccoli. Refrigerated broccoli can last up to a week, but you can extend its life and revive limp broccoli by trimming the stalk and placing it in an inch of water in your fridge overnight.

- Cabbage. Store cabbage in a plastic bag in your refrigerator. Once you chop the head of the cabbage, it will lose its freshness and vitamin C content quickly so be sure to eat it within a few days after cutting. Once cut, you can wrap it tightly to preserve the vitamin C.

Honey can heal your belly pain

Having a stomach ulcer doesn't mean you have to deny your sweet tooth. You can sweeten your goodies with the food that has scientists buzzing – manuka honey. A diet high in sugar can make your stomach produce more ulcer-irritating acids. Honey is gentler on your tummy, and it's thicker and sweeter so you can use less. Enjoy the taste and let its nutrients heal you from the inside out.

Studies show manuka honey is a promising treatment for stomach ulcers. It kills *Helicobacter pylori*, the most common cause of peptic ulcers. Scientists think honey promotes healing, stimulates new tissue growth, and acts as an anti-inflammatory.

Raw honey also contains large amounts of compounds such as flavonoids and other polyphenols, powerful antioxidants. In an animal study, honey reduced the number of ulcers and protected the stomach lining.

When using honey for wound-healing, make sure you get high-quality honey. It's better at fighting off bacteria. Manuka honey comes from New Zealand and is one of the highest quality honeys. It is fairly expensive, and you can buy it online. Find out more about manuka honey for wound healing in the chapter *Skin conditions & hair loss*.

Urinary problems

Dodge the dangers with superfoods

3 natural ways to conquer a leaky bladder

If you have trouble with incontinence, you know how stressful it can be not knowing if you'll get more than you bargained for every time you leave home. Here are three natural ways to make sure you don't "go" unexpectedly when you're on the go.

Depend on vitamin D to strengthen muscles. Incontinence is nothing if not unpredictable. You can lose bladder control when you bend over to plant flowers in your garden, laugh at something your grandkids said, or simply sneeze. Childbirth, obesity, and aging all contribute to weakened pelvic muscles. Vitamin D just might be your muscles' knight in shining armor.

Vitamin D strengthens your muscles and gives your bladder a better chance of staying strong under pressure. One study, using data from the National Health and Nutrition Examination Survey (NHANES), linked higher vitamin D levels to a lower risk of pelvic floor disorders in women.

The federal Food and Nutrition Board recommends 600 international units (IU) of vitamin D for people up to 70 years old and 800 IU for those older than 70. One of the best sources of vitamin D is fish, with catfish, herring, salmon, trout, halibut, and mackerel boasting high levels. For instance, one 3-ounce serving of canned pink salmon contains about 530 IU of vitamin D.

Limit saturated fat to keep your bladder in check. Steak, bacon, buttery biscuits – are these tempting foods a regular part of your diet? If so, you're like most people who eat way too much saturated fat compared to polyunsaturated fat. And that could be one of your problems.

In a study of 2,060 women, scientists found that women who ate over twice the amount of saturated fat as polyunsaturated fat were more likely to suffer urinary incontinence. And the more fatty foods they ate, the more severe their incontinence.

Researchers think that overloading your diet with saturated fat may contribute to bladder inflammation, one cause of urge incontinence. Foods like beef, pork, cheese, whole milk, butter, and palm oil are high in saturated fat, so try to limit those. At the same time, balance your meals and snacks with polyunsaturated-fat foods like fatty fish, flaxseed, walnuts, and sunflower seeds.

Drink more water for less leaking. "If I don't drink a lot of water, I won't run to the bathroom as often." This type of thinking seems to make sense, but it can make your symptoms worse, experts say. In fact, you could end up with constipation, bladder irritation, or infection.

Drinking enough water will make your urine less concentrated, which reduces irritation and urgency. Plus it will lessen the odor if an accident occurs. Try to drink at least six cups of fluids every day. If you are prone to accidents at night, don't drink anything two to four hours before you go to bed.

Shedding pounds is a proven way to improve incontinence. Extra weight can put pressure on your bladder, raising your chances of leakage. That's why experts recommend losing 5 to 10 percent of your body weight if you're overweight.

5 drinks that bother your bladder

Are you always hurrying to the bathroom everywhere you go? One simple dietary change could transform the way you shop, dine out, and visit with friends.

Simply eliminate these bladder-irritating drinks that cause you to fill up fast. Then you can bring them back one by one to find out which beverages need to stay on your no-go list.

- Caffeinated coffee is a diuretic, making you have to go more often. If you can't live without your daily cup of joe, limit it to less than 2 cups.

- Alcohol also acts as a diuretic and can interfere with bladder control.

- Acidic fruit juices, including cranberry juice, can irritate your bladder.

- Soda contains carbon dioxide and artificial sweeteners, which are both irritants.

- Surprisingly, milk can also reduce bladder control.

Yogurt — a triple threat against urinary woes

You may not like to talk about what happens "down there," but what's going on below the belt can have serious consequences for the rest of your body. An overgrowth of "bad" bacteria can lead to urinary tract infections and even bladder cancer. But filling your system with good bacteria, called probiotics, may help you avoid those harmful conditions.

Yogurt balances bacteria in your urinary tract. If you've experienced a urinary tract infection (UTI), you're probably all too familiar with the feelings of urgency, burning, and pressure. Believe it or not, eating a cup of yogurt every day could help you avoid these painful symptoms.

A recent research review published in *Urologic Nursing* examined the role probiotics play in fighting off UTIs. Researchers found that *Lactobacillus* probiotics, in particular, may help stop these symptoms from returning.

Antibiotics are the usual treatment for urinary tract infections, but you can't stay on them forever. Although probiotics are not quite as effective in battling recurrent UTIs, researchers consider them a safe alternative because they don't cause antibiotic resistance.

Antibiotics kill all bacteria, both good and bad, so experts often recommend taking probiotics at the same time to replenish the good ones. To get your daily dose of helpful probiotics, look for yogurt with the "Live and Active Cultures" seal, or check the ingredients for *L. bulgaricus* and other *Lactobacillus* strains, *Bifidobacterium* strains, and *S. thermophilus*.

Lactic acid destroys harmful cancer cells. What if eating more yogurt on a regular basis could drop your chances of developing bladder cancer as well? According to research, it can.

In a large Swedish study, people who ate two or more servings of cultured milk products lowered their risk of bladder cancer by 38 percent compared to those who ate none. Probiotics – including lactic acid bacteria – appear to suppress the growth of harmful bacteria that can damage cells and produce cancer-causing substances.

Probiotics reduce kidney-stone-causing compounds. Oxalate is a compound your body absorbs from foods like spinach, beets, rhubarb, and nuts. It gets excreted in your urine, and if too much builds up, you could be at risk for kidney stones. Probiotics may help by reducing the amount of oxalate your body absorbs.

MAKE IT

Easy ways to pep up plain yogurt

Plain yogurt is healthier than pre-sweetened varieties. But if your taste buds yearn for something a little less tart, try these tasty tips.

- Blend plain yogurt into a fruit smoothie.

- Mix bananas, strawberries, blueberries, or other fresh fruit into Greek yogurt.

- Sprinkle on healthy toppings like granola, nuts, or dark chocolate.

- Use plain Greek yogurt instead of sour cream in your favorite dip.

The truth about cranberry juice for UTIs

Half of all women will have a urinary tract infection (UTI) during their lifetime, so it's no surprise that natural remedies are in high demand. But with big demands come big promises. Cranberry juice – often recommended for UTIs – has been splashed across health articles for years. But can it really help you say goodbye to the UTI?

Scientists give cranberry juice the green light. Cranberry juice may help prevent UTIs by coating your urinary tract and keeping harmful bacteria from sticking, so they can't grow and cause infection.

Although many experts give cranberry juice a thumbs up, it may not work the same for you, your cousin, and that guy who lives down the street. (Yes, men get urinary tract infections, too!)

Research shows that younger people, women, and those with recurrent UTIs are more likely to benefit from cranberry juice.

The real deal is better than supplements. In some cases, supplements are more potent than food. This isn't the case for cranberries. In fact, juice may have more benefits than other forms such as capsules or tablets. Scientists are not sure whether this is a result of the extra fluid, which washes out bacteria, or the interaction of ingredients in the juice that supplements can't duplicate.

Pure cranberry juice is extremely acidic, so most studies use a mixture of 25-percent pure juice. Cranberry juice cocktail is an acceptable alternative.

Will a glass a day keep UTIs away? Scientists still haven't determined the best dosage for reducing the risk of UTIs. What works for some may not work for others.

A recent study of Finnish children showed that drinking 5 milliliters (ml) of cranberry juice per kilogram of body weight, up to 300 ml, reduced the number of UTIs by 43 percent. For an adult, that maximum amount would translate to 1.3 cups a day. Other research suggests a cup of cranberry juice cocktail daily can reduce bacteria in your urine and prevent 50 percent of UTI recurrences.

Dried cranberries are a top-notch substitute. If you're not a fan of juice, it's good to know that sweetened dried cranberries may also help prevent UTIs. In one study, women with recurring UTIs ate one serving of cranberries each day for two weeks. More than half the women were infection-free for six months after eating the dried fruit.

When you need to nix the cranberries. Talk to your doctor before regularly drinking cranberry juice or eating dried cranberries if you:

- are taking the blood-thinning medication warfarin (Coumadin). It could increase your risk of bleeding.

- are allergic to aspirin. Cranberries contain salicylic acid, the active ingredient in aspirin.

- have a history of kidney stones. Cranberry juice also has a lot of oxalate, which may raise your risk of kidney stones.

- are taking medicine that is broken down by the liver, such as Valium, Celebrex, or ibuprofen. Cranberries may slow down the time it takes for your liver to break down some medications, which could increase side effects.

3 reasons to drink more water this summer

For some people, summer means long walks on the beach and refreshing dips in the ocean. For others, summer is not quite so much fun. The number one reason – dehydration. If you're prone to urinary problems, hot, dry weather and inadequate fluids add up to a recipe for urinary disaster. Make sure you drink enough water to stave off summer's most irritating complaints.

Wash away UTIs with nature's remedy. Water has been the go-to remedy for centuries – after all, it didn't get the nickname "Adam's ale" for nothing. Water dilutes your urine, which helps flush bacteria from your urinary tract before an infection can begin.

When you're not drinking enough liquids, you don't answer the call of nature as often. That can delay healing if you have an infection as well as encourage the infection to spread.

Water is key to combatting kidney stones. When you have less-concentrated urine and visit the bathroom frequently, stone-causing minerals have fewer opportunities to settle and bind in your urinary tract.

"Kidney stones cause significant discomfort and cost, along with a potential to contribute to the development of kidney disease," says Kerry Willis, chief scientific officer at the National Kidney Foundation. "Drinking water is an effective way to cut one's risk for developing kidney stones in half."

If you've had a kidney stone in the past, focus on getting eight to 10 glasses of water every day. The American College of Physicians says you need that much liquid to produce two liters of urine daily, which will help prevent more stones from developing.

A simple way to flush out bladder cancer. Drink just a little bit more, and you may head off bladder cancer as well. Men who drank between 10 and 11 cups of water every day were 24 percent less likely to develop bladder cancer compared to those who drank less than 5.5 cups, researchers found during a 22-year study. Scientists think water clears out cancer-causing substances, limiting their contact with the lining of your urinary tract.

The surprising scoop on calcium and kidney stones

The solution seems obvious – the best way to prevent calcium stones is to eat less dairy. That's what doctors used to recommend, but recent research shows that eating less calcium isn't the best plan.

Calcium-oxalate stones – the most common type of kidney stones – form when calcium binds with oxalate in your urinary tract. Research shows that having abnormally high levels of calcium and oxalate in your urine puts you at a higher risk of developing these types of stones.

But that doesn't mean you have to limit the amount of calcium-rich foods you eat. Your calcium levels determine how much oxalate your body absorbs. The more oxalate you absorb during digestion, the less that will end up in your urine where it can form painful stones.

A Women's Health Initiative study of more than 78,000 women showed that higher dietary calcium decreased the risk of kidney stones up to 28 percent. Other studies have also found that people with a high calcium intake had a significantly lower risk of kidney stones.

Experts say your best bet is to get the recommended dietary allowance (RDA) of 1,000 to 1,200 milligrams (mg) of calcium daily. A five-year study showed that men prone to kidney stones who ate only 400 mg of calcium a day were 51 percent more likely to have a recurrence compared to men getting 1,200 mg.

So go ahead and enjoy dairy foods like yogurt, cheddar cheese, and milk. You'll get a third of your daily calcium simply by snacking on a cup of low-fat, plain yogurt. If you can't tolerate dairy, eat more white beans, oranges, kale, pinto beans, and broccoli.

Got stones? Better check your bones

People who get kidney stones often have lower bone mineral density. It's not surprising then that they also have a higher risk for bone fractures. One way people combat weakened bones is by taking calcium and vitamin D supplements. But supplements may not be the way to go.

Studies show that calcium and vitamin D supplements can hike up the amounts of calcium in your urine, raising your risk of kidney stones. When it comes to kidney stones, the best way to get calcium is through your diet. It's also the best way to shore up your bones.

2 sweet solutions to kidney stones

Kidney stones can be yellow, brown, black, gold, jagged, round, the size of a pebble, or the girth of a golf ball. But once you pass one, you don't care what it looks like – you just want to make sure you never get one again. Don't wait until you feel a painful stone moving through your urinary tract to get a move on things. You can help prevent certain types of kidney stones with a quick trip to the grocery store.

One risk factor for kidney stones is low levels of citrate in your urine. Citrate reduces kidney stones by combining with free calcium, so your body has less calcium to make stones. Luckily, citrate – also referred to as citric acid – is easy to come by.

When life gives you kidney stones, make lemonade. Fresh-squeezed lemonade may be the staple of sidewalk sales, but this crowd favorite also has a history of preventing kidney stones, particularly in people with low levels of citrate. In one study, volunteers drank just under 3 ounces of lemon juice every day for three months. Urinary citrate levels more than doubled.

Make your own homemade lemonade by squeezing a half cup of lemon juice into 8 cups of water. Avoid sweetening it with sugar – you don't want to undo all the health benefits by piling on the calories. Keep in mind, you're not limited to lemon juice. You can also try fruits like oranges and limes.

Munch on melons for a neutral alternative. If you have stomach issues, highly acidic citrus fruits may sound just as torturous as kidney stones. Melons – including honeydew, cantaloupe, and watermelon – are a perfect non-citrus substitute.

According to a study published in the *Journal of Endourology*, melon is a high source of citrate and can help if you have low amounts in your urine. Scientists measured citrate levels before and after people drank 13 ounces of either orange, melon, or lime juice. Melon juice worked just as well as orange and lime juice at raising citrate levels.

Vision loss

Keep your eyesight crystal clear

2 greens you're not eating — but should be

When you were growing up, you were told to eat your carrots so you would have strong eyes. But eye health isn't just about carrots anymore. In fact, scientists have discovered a new way to avoid vision loss. Introducing the new eye-care superfood – leafy greens.

Like carrots, dark leafy greens contain carotenoids. But greens have specific carotenoids – lutein and zeaxanthin – that can't be found in carrots. These nutrients can help protect your eyes against vision problems like cataracts and age-related macular degeneration (AMD). That's because they are the only carotenoids found in your retina and lens. They act as antioxidants by protecting healthy cells in your eyes and filter harmful lightwaves that can cause oxidative damage.

Combat cloudy eyes with kale. A cataract is a clouding of the eye lens that develops when lens proteins get damaged. You can get cataracts at any age, but they are more likely to develop when you're older.

In a study of over 1,600 elderly people in Finland, scientists learned lutein and zeaxanthin may reduce your chances of developing nuclear cataracts, which affect the center of the lens. Subjects with the highest blood levels of these carotenoids were up to 42 percent less likely to develop nuclear cataracts than those with the lowest amounts.

Your body can't make the lutein and zeaxanthin it needs, so you have to get these nutrients through your diet. According to the National Institutes of Health, kale can protect against cataracts along with sun damage and macular degeneration.

One cup of this leafy green contains around 21 to 27 milligrams of lutein and zeaxanthin. But that's not all. Kale also has 134 percent of your daily value of vitamin C, an antioxidant known for helping eyes stay strong.

COOK IT

Savory slow-cooked collards

Fixing collards in a slow cooker can turn them from just another green to something you'll want to take to every holiday get-together. They're simple, tasty, and easy to cook.

Ingredients

- 1 bag of collards, chopped
- 2 tablespoons ham base
- 1/4 cup apple cider vinegar
- 3/4 cup brown sugar, packed
- water

Pour one to two inches of water into the slow cooker to keep leaves from scorching. Add vinegar, then stir in ham base until it dissolves. Mix in brown sugar and collards, stripping out the thick central stems if desired. Cover with a lid, and cook for 8 to 10 hours on low heat. Stir occasionally to circulate the greens.

Collards: antioxidant support for your retinas. Age-related macular degeneration is the leading cause of vision loss in older adults, affecting more than 7 million Americans.

Studies of more than 3,000 individuals show AMD risk drops among people who get a lot of lutein and zeaxanthin in their diets. These nutrients help sharpen your vision and increase macular pigment, your body's "internal sunglasses" that help protect your macula from harmful blue light.

You may not have ever tried collards, but they can actually help fight macular degeneration. Dig into a cup of collards and you'll get about 15 milligrams of lutein and zeaxanthin. These greens also boast 308 percent of your daily value of vitamin A – an important vitamin for eye health. In addition, collards are high in vitamin C as well as folate, which have been studied for the prevention of eye diseases like cataracts and glaucoma.

Feast your eyes on an eye-healthy meal

You've got a million and one things to do. Between appointments and all the other things on your to-do list, it's easy for your eye health to slip between the cracks. A simple way to make sure your eyes get some attention is to make one vision-boosting meal each week. Try a delicious meal of salmon, sweet potatoes, and broccoli. It's a feast for your eyes – in more ways than one.

The seafood that prevents eye damage. Salmon is a great centerpiece for your meal because it contains lots of omega-3 fatty acids. Your eyes contain high amounts of omega-3, which may help regulate cell survival and inflammation. In one study, people who took around 1 gram of omega-3 each day had a 42-percent lower risk of cataracts in the center of the lens. One 3-ounce serving of salmon packs 1,921 milligrams (mg) of omega-3, or 1.9 grams.

Omega-3 provides protection and prevention for more than just cataracts. The Blue Mountains Eye study showed eating fish three times per week can contribute to a lower risk of advanced age-related macular degeneration (AMD). And research has found omega-3 especially benefits people who suffer from, or are at risk for, heart disease. The American Heart Association recommends two servings of fish per week.

Many fish contain omega-3, but eating too much of certain types can lead to mercury poisoning, so don't go overboard. For more information on mercury and fish, see *Fish that heal and fish that flop* in the *Heart disease* chapter.

Potatoes — one sweet way to get your A. A side of sweet potatoes is the perfect complement for salmon. Sweet potatoes contain beta carotene, an antioxidant that protects your body from damaging molecules called free radicals.

One way your body gets vitamin A is by converting it from beta carotene in plants. Vitamin A helps process light in your retina and keeps your cornea clear and healthy. All this activity uses up small amounts of vitamin A, so it constantly needs to be replenished. One medium sweet potato has a whopping 1,403 micrograms, which provides 561 percent of your daily needs.

Vitamin A is fat-soluble, and your liver stores any you don't use. Your body can't tolerate more than 3,000 micrograms per day, so if your diet is packed with vitamin A foods, plus you take a multivitamin, you could be in trouble. Remember that all those different amounts add up.

Surprisingly, you'll get 20 times more sulphoraphane glucosinolate from broccoli sprouts than from mature broccoli. These three-day-old plants make a crunchy addition to sandwiches, stir fries, salsa, and dips. See the *Heart disease* chapter for tips on growing your own.

If you're having problems seeing in dim light, that may mean you're not getting enough vitamin A. An early sign of vitamin A deficiency is night blindness. So if you have a hard time seeing after dark or recovering from sudden flashes of bright light, try eating more vitamin A foods.

A green superhero can save your sight. To square off your vision-boosting meal, finish with a serving of broccoli. This cruciferous vegetable contains high amounts of vitamin C, vitamin A, vitamin E, and folate – all of which support healthy eyes. But it also has a secret ingredient – an eye-boosting super-nutrient called sulphoraphane glucosinolate.

Research has found that sulphoraphane protects your eyes from damage caused by ultraviolet light, which helps prevent the development of AMD. Although your body makes antioxidants to help reduce damage to the retina, this process becomes less efficient as you age. Sulphoraphane is like a superhero swooping in to save the day.

Mouthwatering solutions for dry eyes

Dry eyes can make it difficult for you to use your computer or read for long periods of time. But that doesn't mean you're condemned to a lifetime of artificial tears. Add these eye-soothing foods to your diet for natural relief from uncomfortable eyes.

Crunchy walnuts provide double-duty relief. You know omega-3 helps fight cataracts and macular degeneration, but did you know it's also a boon for your dry eyes? Omega-3 prevents inflammation and encourages tear secretion. Not only does it lessen symptoms of dry eyes, but it can also help prevent them.

- A study of over 30,000 women showed that omega-3 fatty acids are linked to fewer instances of dry eye syndrome.

■ In another study, people with a high intake of omega-3 were 20 percent less likely to suffer from dry eye syndrome compared to those with a low intake.

Fatty fish like salmon and herring are known for their high levels of omega-3. But for a quick snack, a handful of walnuts is perfect. Fourteen halves boast 2,565 milligrams of omega-3.

Caffeinated drinks turn on the tears. Your morning coffee or tea may be helping you read your newspaper a little more comfortably. The reason suggested by one study is that caffeine stimulates tear production. Although researchers tested people with normal eyes, they think caffeine may help those with dry eye syndrome as well. Pick your favorite caffeinated beverage, like coffee, tea, soda, or hot chocolate, and see if it helps you.

How cereal for dinner can safeguard your sight

Oysters may be known as the king of zinc, but did you know that fortified cereals are also loaded with this eye-supporting mineral? As long as you stay away from the sugary stuff, you can reap the benefits of a cereal packed with nutrients like zinc and B vitamins to help keep your eyes sharp.

Zinc builds strong eyes. One of zinc's important tasks is to help release vitamin A from your liver so it can help strengthen eye tissue. As you get older, zinc becomes even more important to your aging eyes, and a deficiency can lead to a breakdown of the macula.

In a review of more than a dozen trials, researchers found that supplementing with antioxidants plus 80 milligrams (mg) of zinc for about six years helped people with age-related macular degeneration (AMD) reduce their vision loss and delay their progression to advanced AMD. The upper recommended limit for adults is 40 mg, so don't take high amounts of zinc without talking to your doctor first.

A good cry is good for your eyes

You may have been embarrassed last time you were caught bawling at the movies, but those tears are actually doing you some good.

Made by the lacrimal gland, tears are necessary for over-all eye health and clear vision. They wash away dust and debris and bathe the surface of the eye, keeping it moist. In addition, tears have an enzyme called lysozyme that fights bacteria, protecting your eyes from infection.

So next time you go through a breakup, go ahead and let the tears fall. It's good for your eyes.

Evade eye disease with folate. B vitamins, like B6, B12, and folate, are important for keeping your body energized and running smoothly. Scientists say daily supplementation with B vitamins may also lower your risk for eye disease.

- B vitamins lower levels of homocysteine, an amino acid that causes inflammation and can lead to macular degeneration. In lengthy studies, taking a daily B-vitamin supplement made people less likely to develop AMD after two years.

- Folate is associated with a reduced risk of exfoliation glaucoma, the most common type of secondary glaucoma. Researchers came to that conclusion after reviewing 20 years of data from the Nurses' Health Study and the Health Professionals Follow-up Study. Of the more than 120,000 participants, those who took in the most folate were 25 percent less likely to develop glaucoma than those who took in the least.

Fortified cereals contain over 100 percent daily value of some nutrients. For example, Kellogg's Multi-Grain Cheerios has almost 16 mg of zinc – 103 percent of the daily value. It also boasts 103 percent of B6, B12, and folate.

If you eat a lot of cereal, you should watch your zinc intake from other sources. Too much zinc can be toxic and will show up as abdominal pain, diarrhea, nausea, and vomiting. This is a special concern for children, who only need about 5 mg of zinc a day.

On the other hand, adults over age 50 may have problems absorbing zinc and are more likely to develop a mild deficiency. If you're in that category, a daily helping of your favorite cereal may be just what the doctor ordered.

The junk food that can save your vision

According to a Domino's survey, 67 percent of pizza eaters prefer meat and cheese toppings over vegetables and cheese. But while meaty toppings may be delicious, you might want to switch it up for the health of your eyes. With the right ingredients, this party favorite can provide all-out eye support.

A Swedish study published in *JAMA Ophthalmology* showed that combining certain foods like vegetables and whole grains may enhance their antioxidant power.

Scientists monitored more than 30,000 women for eight years to determine if antioxidants had any effects on age-related cataracts. Women who ate greater amounts of antioxidants through food combinations had an almost 13 percent lower risk of developing cataracts than women with a low-antioxidant diet.

Though pizza is not known for being particularly healthy, you can add your own nutrient-rich toppings to whole-wheat crust to make a superb pizza for super sight.

Super ingredient 1: antioxidant-abundant wheat crust. Whole grains have antioxidants that help protect your eyes. And the way you prepare your whole-wheat pizza dough may make a huge difference in the amount of antioxidants you absorb.

Studies show that allowing wheat dough to ferment up to 48 hours doubles the amount of antioxidants. Raising your oven temperature from 400 to 550 degrees boosts grain antioxidants as much as 82 percent. And extending cooking time to 14 minutes will give you 60 percent more antioxidants.

What's the secret? Researchers say these methods pump up the antioxidant level of the wheat by releasing more nutrients from its bran coating. And it's something you can easily do at home to make your pizza more healthy.

Super ingredient 2: vitamin-rich veggies. You can choose from a wide variety of veggies to top your pizza – and even some fruits. Antioxidants like beta carotene, vitamin C, vitamin E, and selenium are abundant in fruits and vegetables, and studies show that antioxidant-rich foods can help prevent cataracts.

Spinach is a good choice because it's filled with antioxidants such as lutein, zeaxanthin, and vitamin A, which are critical to eye health. Peppers and onions are also excellent choices because both are high in vitamin C and several B vitamins.

> Do you tear up every time you chop onions? Try chilling your onion in the fridge for 30 minutes before chopping. Remember, the root end has the most sulfuric compounds, so cut that end last.

Super ingredient 3: mineral-filled mozzarella cheese. Traditionally, mozzarella cheese was made from the milk of water buffaloes. While the mozzarella you buy today will most likely come from a cow, it still has amazing benefits for your eyes. It contains selenium, which acts as an antioxidant, and also has eye-boosting zinc and vitamin A.

Riboflavin is another nutrient found in mozzarella cheese that is important for keeping your eyes healthy. Some studies have linked a deficiency of this B vitamin to the development of cataracts over time.

You may want to go easy on the cheese to keep the fat and calories down, but feel free to pile on the veggies to reap the benefits of their super nutrients.

4 natural fixes for under-eye bags

Tired of looking like you're always tired? You can put a stop to puffy eyes and make dark circles disappear with one of these quick home remedies.

- Hold cold caffeinated tea bags under your eyes to reduce swelling. The caffeine will constrict blood flow to minimize the appearance of bags.

- Wash your face with milk to get rid of puffy eyes. The fatty acids and lactic acid in milk help reduce swelling. Don't use skim milk because it has no fat.

- Dot castor oil under each eye two times a day to make dark circles disappear. The fatty acids help keep in moisture, so the bluish vessels are less visible.

- Cut thick slices of raw potatoes, and place them over your eyes for 20 minutes. The cool slices tighten blood vessels, while alpha-lipoic acid and enzymes lighten skin.

True blue protection for your 'baby blues'

Oxidation and inflammation are a pair of bad guys that play a serious role in all aspects of aging, and eye health is no exception. Though these two may have you seeing double, nature has provided a brilliant berry duo to help fight the cell damage they cause.

Squash inflammation with a tasty blue fruit. A bilberry may sound like a delicious treat made in Willy Wonka's factory, but it's actually a dark blue fruit related to the blueberry.

Bilberries have been used in European medicine for nearly 1,000 years, but you're more likely to come across them in jams and desserts. They're high in vitamin C and powerful chemicals called anthocyanosides that give berries their dark, rich color and help build strong blood vessels and improve circulation.

Researchers think bilberries may help your vision by protecting your retina and boosting the production of rhodopsin, a pigment that helps your eyes adjust to light changes. In fact, British World War II fighter pilots claimed their night vision improved after eating bilberry jam. Some studies have suggested bilberries may also help protect against macular degeneration, cataracts, and glaucoma.

Bilberry extract contains more anthocyanosides than dried berries or leaves. If you suffer from retinal problems due to diabetes or high blood pressure, you may want to see if bilberry extract will help you. But check with your doctor first as it could interact with diabetes medication as well as blood thinners.

You can also make bilberry tea using dried berries or leaves. Steep one to two teaspoons in a cup of hot water for five to 10 minutes.

Fight cell damage with a super-antioxidant berry. Like bilberries, blueberries contain both anthocyanosides and resveratrol and are a good source of the antioxidant vitamin C. Resveratrol is a powerful compound also found in grapes, red wine, purple grape juice, and other berries.

Scientists studying animals have found that resveratrol protects the eyes in many ways. One exciting discovery is that it keeps abnormal blood vessels from developing in the retina, which could help prevent eye diseases such as diabetic retinopathy and macular degeneration.

Researchers had good results when they tested a resveratrol-based nutritional supplement on 80-year-olds with macular degeneration. They found it greatly improved the structure and function of the retina, making them hopeful that even treatment-resistant patients may benefit.

The downside to long lashes

Long, luxurious eyelashes bat at you from every fashion magazine. Although this beauty icon may be alluring, you should think twice before you join the long-lash craze.

Your lashes do more than just look pretty. They have an important job as sensors, sunshades, and now — scientists have recently learned — air filters. Eyelashes redirect airflow, keeping dust out of your eyes and reducing tear evaporation up to 50 percent.

According to research, the ideal eyelash is one-third the width of your eye. Lashes that are too short or too long increase the current of air around your eye, stirring up dust and causing dryness.

While long lashes may be associated with celebrities and elegance, there is nothing glamorous about dry, irritated eyes and rapid blinking.

Diabetes? Fight vision loss with fish

Diabetes can affect your entire body – particularly your heart, feet, skin, kidneys, and nerves. It can also change how you view the world. Literally. The longer you have diabetes, the greater chance you have of developing problems with your eyesight. Vision loss can be a scary thing, but certain nutrients can help cut back your chances of eye troubles.

Diabetic retinopathy is the most common diabetic eye disease. It's caused by damage to the blood vessels in the retina. People with both type 1 and type 2 diabetes are at risk, and between 40 to 45 percent of Americans with diabetes have some stage of the condition. You may not notice symptoms at first. But over time, changes in blood cells located in the retina can begin to interfere with your vision.

One of the best ways to prevent diabetic retinopathy is to eat nutritious foods that help control your blood sugar, while providing your body with eye-supporting nutrients. The Diabetes Control and Complications Trial demonstrated that managing blood sugar levels slows the onset and progression of retinopathy. Other research shows that certain vitamins, minerals, and fatty acids may help protect your eyes as well.

Fortunately, you don't have to look any further than your local fish market to find these eye-protecting nutrients. Herring, catfish, halibut, trout, and salmon are all excellent sources of four nutrients you need.

■ Zinc protects the retina by preventing the loss of the antioxidant glutathione due to diabetes.

■ Selenium can decrease the amount of a protein called vascular endothelial growth factor (VEGF) that stimulates new blood vessels to grow. Studies show that too much VEGF is linked to vascular disease in the retina.

■ Vitamin D may help fight diabetic retinopathy because of its role in battling inflammation. Researchers have found that vitamin D cuts back the production of inflammatory cytokines and other damaging cells. Plus it positively affects glycemic control and high blood pressure, two significant risk factors for retinopathy. A study out of Emory University showed that individuals with type 2 diabetes, particularly those with retinopathy, had lower vitamin D levels than those without diabetes, and were more likely to lack this critical vitamin.

■ Omega-3 fatty acids help prevent abnormal blood vessel growth in the retina, according to studies on mice. Researchers hope these fatty acids may eventually be used as an alternate treatment for diabetic retinopathy.

To learn more about how to eat for diabetes, check out the chapter *Blood sugar control: Nutritional solutions that defeat diabetes.*

Weight control

Dieting do's & dont's

10 foods that help you lose belly fat faster

Choose the right foods and drinks, and you can trick your body into helping you lose fat from your waistline. See how it's done and why it works.

Shed more belly fat when you drink this amazing juice.
Fortifying juice with vitamins and minerals may have surprising effects. A study of overweight people found that those who drank fortified orange juice lost three times as much belly fat as those who drank regular orange juice – and they did it in just four months.

The juice that made the difference was Minute Maid orange juice fortified with calcium and vitamin D. Each 8-ounce (oz.) glass boasted 350 milligrams (mg) of calcium and 100 international units (IU) of vitamin D. So drinking three glasses daily boosted calcium intake by 1,050 mg and vitamin D by 300 IU.

Why would this make a difference in your waistline? Studies have found that getting more calcium means less body weight. Experts say calcium may reduce the buildup of fat in your body because it helps burn more fat and even kills off fat cells. On the other hand, a calcium shortage may encourage your body to store more fat.

Similarly, low blood levels of vitamin D are linked to high body fat, while people with higher levels of D show a lower percentage of body fat.

What's more, a calcium-rich diet can help cut down on hunger, and calcium plus vitamin D has been shown to make people eat less and go longer between meals.

Slim down with 10 belly-busting foods. Fortified orange juice isn't your only option for getting more of these important nutrients. Here are more good choices that will help you add vitamin D and calcium to your diet – and subtract belly fat.

- 3.5-oz. serving of canned salmon

- 3-oz. serving of canned Pacific sardines packed in tomato sauce

- 8-oz. serving of nonfat soy milk fortified with calcium and vitamins A and D

- 1/4 cup of nonfat dry milk with added vitamin A and D

- 3/4 cup of Whole-grain Total cereal

- 8-oz. serving of nonfat milk with added vitamins A and D

- 1 cup of sweetened vanilla almond milk

- 1 cup of Total Raisin Bran

- 8-oz. serving of low-fat 1-percent milk with added vitamins A and D

- 8 oz. of nonfat strawberry Greek yogurt

The surprising appetite blocker that really works

Would you rather use nature's appetite suppressant or some pill created in a lab? Studies suggest one food-based hunger blocker – fiber – may help fortify your body against disease and be a better appetite killer than you expect.

In a recent study of 240 obese people, half the participants followed a complicated diet for a year. The other half were given just one rule – eat at least 30 grams of fiber from plant foods every day. By the study's end, fiber eaters had lost almost as many pounds as people on the complex diet. In fact, the diet group lost only an average of 1 1/3 pounds more. Research suggests three reasons why fiber works so well.

Fiber makes you feel fuller faster. A small Australian study found that people who ate a high-fiber breakfast felt more full than people who ate other breakfasts with the same number of calories – and this lasted for nearly half the day. Fiber eaters also ate fewer calories during the morning and at lunch.

Another small study tested three breakfasts – fiber-rich oatmeal, sugared corn flakes, and 1 1/2 cups of water. Study participants were just as hungry three hours after eating sugary corn flakes as they were after drinking the water breakfast. But people who had oatmeal for breakfast ate fewer calories at lunch, stayed fuller longer, and had less hunger. Their stomachs also took longer to empty.

Studies like these show that fiber adds bulk to your diet to help you feel more full. In other words, fiber helps you fill up instead of filling out.

Fermentable fiber shuts down your appetite. Feeling full is good, but what if you could also reduce your appetite right from the start? Fermentable fiber found in some fruits and vegetables may trigger a chain reaction that shuts down your appetite. Fermentable fiber can't be broken down in your intestines, so bacteria ferment this fiber, creating short-chain fatty acids like propionate, butyrate, and acetate.

In a recent animal study, London researchers tracked acetate produced in the colon. They discovered that 3 percent of it travels into the brain's hypothalamus region, the part of the brain that controls hunger. When it arrives, acetate triggers a chain reaction that causes hunger-squelching neurons to fire.

This may be why previous animal studies suggest that eating foods rich in fermentable fiber leads to taking in fewer calories. To eat more fermentable fiber, enjoy cabbage, beans, onions, garlic, asparagus, chicory, beets, and sweet fruits.

High-fiber foods block hunger spikes. Foods with more fiber usually have a lower glycemic index (GI). That's good news because foods with a high glycemic index may make you even hungrier within a few hours.

The glycemic index (GI) measures a food's ability to raise your blood sugar. Different carbohydrates break down into glucose – or sugar – at different rates. High-GI foods break down quickly, releasing a flood of sugar into your bloodstream. Low-GI foods take longer to digest, giving you a slower, steadier supply of sugar.

Several factors affect a food's GI rating, including fat and fiber content and amount of processing. Good examples of foods with a high GI include low-fiber white bread and other processed, starchy foods as well as sugary foods and drinks.

> Scientists say this easy trick multiplies the amount of resistant starch in rice — and subtracts more than half the calories. Just add a teaspoon of coconut oil to boiling water before adding your rice and simmering it. Then cool the rice for 12 hours before eating.

One small study found that men who ate a high-GI meal were hungrier for four hours afterward compared to men who ate a low-GI meal with the same amount of calories. High-GI foods can make your blood sugar plummet to very low levels after a few hours. This leads you to crave more high-GI foods because they restore your blood sugar to normal levels more quickly.

On top of that, high-GI foods were recently shown to affect the centers of your brain that influence cravings, addiction, and reward-seeking. But eating more fiber-rich foods can help even out your blood sugar and control your hunger, experts say. It can also help you avoid high-GI foods that may tempt you to eat more.

Good sources of fiber include apples, beans, berries, figs, carrots, spinach, pumpkin, broccoli, popcorn, brown rice, and oatmeal. Just remember to increase the amount of fiber in your diet gradually, so you won't experience bloating, diarrhea, and other digestive side effects.

Amazing oil trims fat and adds muscle

Add a little safflower oil to your daily diet, and you could lose pounds of belly fat and add lean muscle. This even works for women over 50!

After menopause, women tend to gain belly fat and lose muscle. But a study of obese, postmenopausal women with diabetes found that those who took 1 2/3 teaspoons of safflower oil daily lost up to 4 pounds of belly fat and gained up to 3 pounds of lean muscle mass in just four months.

The researchers aren't sure why safflower oil works, but they suspect its polyunsaturated oils may help you burn more fat. If you'd like to try this, mix safflower oil into salad dressings or low-heat sauces.

Just remember, most Americans already get too many omega-6 fatty acids, and safflower oil is rich in these fats. So reduce the omega-6 fats in your diet before you start using safflower oil.

The kitchen spice that fires up your fat burners

Researchers say a pungent spice from your supermarket may help you lose more pounds than you can shed by just cutting calories.

Scientists asked two groups of overweight women to cut 500 calories from their daily diets. One group also ate one-half teaspoon of cumin with lunch and dinner every day. Cumin is an aromatic, mildly hot spice common in curry powder, Indian dishes, and Tex-Mex cuisine.

After three months, cumin eaters had lost more weight and more inches from their waistlines than women who hadn't eaten cumin. They also lowered their body mass index (BMI) and fat mass. Some suggest this happens because cumin temporarily speeds up your metabolism, which promotes weight loss.

To see what cumin can do for you, experiment with these ideas.

- Add cumin to make chili, soups, stews, or sauces spicier.

- Mix it into rice, or add it to your favorite Tex-Mex dishes.

- Add a dash of cumin to spice up guacamole, hummus, barbecue sauce, or mayo.

The 5-minute trick that helps you eat less all day

What you ate last night and this morning could be the reason you were hungry so often today. But you don't need to add more food and calories. The secret is to change your protein pattern. Eat more with your first meal of the day instead of at night, and your body will reap huge benefits.

Fight hunger by beefing up your morning protein. Most people get plenty of protein at dinner, but that may not be the best time to eat it if you want to lose weight. Try shifting your dinner proteins to breakfast, says Heather Leidy, a University of Missouri professor who studies protein and weight loss.

"Eating a protein-rich breakfast impacts the drive to eat later in the day, when people are more likely to consume high-fat or high-sugar snacks," she says.

That virtuous feeling you get from shopping with reusable bags could backfire when it comes to your waistline. Harvard researchers found that those who felt good about helping the environment also felt they were worthy of a treat and were more likely to buy junk food like candy, snacks, or chips.

Leidy's research shows that eating the protein part of your supper at breakfast can have amazing effects, even if you eat the same number of breakfast calories as usual. She conducted a small study of overweight young women that compared skipping breakfast to eating either a regular breakfast or a high-protein breakfast.

- Both the regular and high-protein breakfasts reduced hunger and increased fullness more than skipping breakfast. But the regular breakfast only boosted fullness until lunch, while the high-protein breakfast lasted all day.

- The high-protein breakfast cut after-dinner snacking, especially of high-fat foods.

- Brain scans linked the high-protein breakfast to positive changes in how the brain responds to food near suppertime, when Americans are more likely to overeat.

■ Best of all, people who ate the high-protein breakfast totaled fewer calories for the day than people who ate the normal-protein breakfast. This confirms earlier studies, which found that people who ate a high-protein breakfast also chose to eat fewer calories at lunch.

Make the protein switch easy with a little planning. Eating more protein at breakfast doesn't mean you have to boost your calorie count for the day. In the study, the regular breakfast and the high-protein breakfast were both 350 calories, but the high-protein breakfast packed 35 grams of protein into those calories.

All it takes to reach that amount is a little planning. Here are a few tips and tricks to help you get started.

■ Having pork for dinner? Leidy suggests combining it with eggs to make a breakfast casserole you can eat in the morning – or include the chopped pork in a breakfast burrito, omelet, or breakfast pizza.

■ Switch your morning glass of orange juice for a glass of milk.

■ Add some chopped, scrambled egg to a bowl of cooked rice. Mix in chopped tomato or chunky salsa, and chop up the cooked pork or chicken originally intended for dinner. Mix well, and you'll have a delicious breakfast rice bowl packed with protein.

■ Enjoy steak and eggs like you would at a restaurant.

■ Eat morning-friendly proteins like peanut butter on whole grain toast and a cup of nonfat yogurt on the side. Other good options include a breakfast smoothie made with milk or yogurt, or boiled or scrambled eggs topped with low-fat cheese.

■ Emphasize high-protein foods such as quinoa, chia seeds, nut butters, nut milks, and nuts, especially if you're a vegan or vegetarian.

Should you jump on the gluten-free bandwagon?

Everyone you know — and their mother — is going gluten-free. But doctors say only a tiny fraction of Americans need to avoid gluten. So what's all the fuss about?

Gluten is a protein found in oat, rye, wheat, and barley. The Food and Drug Administration began regulating food labels with gluten-free claims back in 2007. That's when packages with gluten-free seals started parading across grocery store shelves. And many people jumped on the bandwagon simply because they thought it was healthy.

But doctors say only people with celiac disease — a severe gluten allergy — need to drop gluten from their diets. That's a meager 1 percent of Americans.

Many people avoid gluten because they say it helps them with all sorts of health conditions as well as weight loss. Critics say there's no proof. And when you give up gluten, you cut out certain B vitamins and fiber found in grains.

So before going gluten-free, check with your doctor. You don't want to give up essential nutrients if you don't need to.

Experts weigh in on top diet choices

Every diet claims to be the best plan to help you lose weight and keep it off, but Weight Watchers has a title to prove it. *US News and World Report* named it the Best Weight-Loss Diet for 2015 in its annual list of top diet plans.

Each year, the magazine convenes a panel of experts in nutrition, weight loss, diet, and health to determine which diets are best. Out of 41 diets, Weight Watchers not only won the Best Weight-Loss Diet category but was also named the Easiest Diet to Follow and Best Commercial Plan. The Health Management Resources (HMR) diet took second place for weight loss, and Jenny Craig took third.

Want scientific proof that these are the best? *Annals of Internal Medicine* recently published a review of the research done on 11 popular weight-loss diets. It found that the Weight Watchers and Jenny Craig programs have the most proven record of helping people lose weight and keep it off for at least a year.

Surprise! You can eat chocolate daily and still lose weight

You don't have to abandon chocolate forever to shed pounds. Discover how you can have your chocolate and lose weight, too.

The best time to enjoy chocolate without encouraging cravings. People who regularly ate chocolate two hours after a meal – when they were hungry – tended to crave chocolate even more, a

British study found. But people who regularly ate their chocolate just 15 to 30 minutes after a meal were more likely to see their chocolate cravings drop. If you must have chocolate, eat it shortly after a meal.

What's good and bad about chocolate. Both milk chocolate and dark chocolate come from the cocoa bean. Cocoa contains more than 300 compounds, including powerful antioxidants like flavanols and flavanoids. But when other ingredients, like sugar and milk, are added to cocoa, the resulting milk chocolate can be bad for your health.

Dark chocolate – especially with a high cocoa content – is more likely to be good for your health. But don't go overboard. One study found that postmenopausal women who ate more of any kind of chocolate raised their risk of gaining weight over time. Another found that even "healthy" dark chocolate can add extra weight.

But don't give up on this delightful treat just yet. Chocolate can still cheer you up and help with weight loss if you know when to stop.

A three-week German study put two groups of participants on a low-carbohydrate diet, but the second group was also told to eat 42 grams (1.5 oz.) of dark chocolate every day. That's roughly the amount of seven Dove dark chocolate pieces.

At first, the chocolate group gained weight. But by the study's end, they had lost slightly more weight than the low-carb-diet group – and kept right on losing pounds while the low-carb group regained some. The chocolate group also felt better and experienced less fatigue than the low-carb group.

Keep in mind the chocolate used in this study was not only dark but also contained a whopping 81-percent cocoa. Although the researchers aren't sure why the dark chocolate helped with weight loss, some experts suggest cocoa nutrients can help suppress your appetite as well as improve your mood.

How to get the best results with chocolate. Chocolate's sugar, fat, and calories are a big no-no if you're trying to lose weight, even though its cocoa may help. So eat only a limited amount of chocolate – preferably after a meal – and make sure it replaces something else in your diet rather than adding to your calorie count for the day.

Choose either dark chocolate or cocoa powder, and aim for a cocoa content of at least 70 percent. Not sure what to do with cocoa powder, besides baking with it? Try sprinkling it on naturally sweet fruit like banana or orange slices. Eat the cocoa-dusted fruit as a snack, or mix it into yogurt or oatmeal. Cocoa powder is also a great low-calorie addition to smoothies.

Overnight success: Burn more calories while you sleep

Looking for a before-bed snack? Try creamy and delicious Greek yogurt. A natural ingredient in this tempting treat will keep your metabolism going all night.

Greek yogurt is rich in the dairy protein casein. Other foods high in casein include cheeses, cottage cheese, and milk.

Dutch researchers discovered that a diet higher in casein and lower in fat increases the number of calories you use for the day — mostly because it boosts the calories you burn while sleeping. They think the extra casein may make your body burn more fat for hours after you finish eating.

But don't sabotage your weight-loss progress. If you add Greek yogurt as your new bedtime snack, subtract calories from elsewhere in your diet. That first delicious bite — and sleeping off extra calories — will make it all worthwhile.

3 tasty snacks for a trimmer waistline

Need a pick-me-up to help get you through the afternoon slump?
Ounce for ounce, these sweet, healthy snacks cost half as much as
cookies or chips and are less likely to pile on the pounds, yet they
still taste fabulous.

Re-energize with oranges.

Oranges not only taste sweet and
smell fabulous, but they're also
more filling than cookies and less
prone to cause a sugar crash. For
around 60 calories, a medium
orange is a good source of
sustained, satisfying energy.
Add extra flavor by sprinkling
on a little ginger.

Keep your oranges fresh
and juicy longer by wrap-
ping each whole fruit in
wax paper. Then store in a
cool, dry place or in the
refrigerator. Whole
oranges should keep for
two — even four —
weeks. Toss as soon as you
see mold start to grow.

Try this a-peeling twist on bananas. A popular brand of packaged chocolate chip cookies lists its serving size as three cookies.
But if you eat those three cookies, you instantly rack up 160 calories to add to your waistline. Satisfy your sweet tooth and save 55
calories by eating a banana instead. For added pizzazz, sprinkle it
with a little cinnamon and nutmeg.

When you absolutely must have a cookie, mix a very ripe
mashed banana with one-half cup of old-fashioned rolled oats and
a pinch of cinnamon. Place cookie-sized dollops of the mixture on
a greased baking sheet, and bake for 10 to 15 minutes at 350
degrees. You've got yummy warm bites that taste like banana
bread for only about 30 calories each.

Cut calories and hunger with watermelon. Get two weight-loss
tricks for the price of one. Experts say eating foods with a high
water content help fill you up and reduce how many calories you
eat during the day. That makes juicy watermelon a much better
choice than dry potato chips.

What's more, a wedge of watermelon has around half as many calories as a serving of 15 potato chips, but the watermelon still tastes like a treat. Amp up the wow factor by splashing your wedge with lime juice and chili powder, a combination one nutritionist claims will help burn fat.

Want to burn fat? Add some hot sauce!

If you can take the heat, get in the kitchen and start spicing up your recipes. Why? Because these three smokin'-hot, fat-burning foods can help your extra pounds go up in flames.

Cayenne powder burns more than your mouth — burn up fat and calories, too. People who ate spicy foods less than once a month got a big surprise when they added half a teaspoon of cayenne powder to tomato soup. After the peppery dish, they burned more calories and weren't as hungry as people who ate a blander soup.

Purdue University researchers also suggest cayenne pepper helps destroy fat and could tone down those cravings for salty, sugary, and high-fat foods. Don't bother with cayenne powder capsules, though. They didn't work nearly as well as mixing the seasoning into food. Raid your spice rack and liven up stews, soups, sauces, dips, and even cornbread.

> The wildly popular sriracha sauce may seem like the perfect choice to spice up your life, but you can do better. Unlike the original Tabasco sauce, sriracha contains sugar. It also has more calories than Tabasco and more than twice as much sodium. Stick with Tabasco, it's a healthier choice.

Want another hot tip? Add a pinch of cayenne powder to a glass of tomato juice and guzzle it down about 30 minutes before a meal. In a Dutch study, people who tried this ate fewer calories and less fat, yet felt more satisfied.

Splash on some awesome sauce to beat hunger pangs. Chili peppers, containing the powerful compound capsaicin, are in practically every hot sauce recipe known to man. Experts say this fiery ingredient will not only make you sweat, but may help you feel full, keep you from overeating, and even reduce that urge to eat after dinner. Get more heat in your diet by adding hot sauce to every meal. From breakfast to dessert, and every snack in between, there's an easy way to kick it up.

A peppery punch fights fat. Hot sauce and cayenne powder are convenient, but you can also go straight to the original source of capsaicin – chili peppers. In animals, capsaicin from these peppers triggered production of a special protein that fights weight gain from a high-fat diet.

So chop up chili peppers to throw on sandwiches, burgers, or add to stir-fries. They're also good in Asian dishes and sauces as well as Cajun, Mexican, and Southwestern cuisine.

A final word of warning. Talk to your doctor before adding cayenne powder, chili powder, hot sauce, or chili peppers to your diet if:

- you have heartburn or ulcers.

- you take medications like ACE inhibitors for high blood pressure, theophylline for asthma, acid-reducing drugs, aspirin, blood-thinning medications like warfarin, or medications that lower blood sugar.

- you are allergic to latex, avocados, kiwi, or bananas. You may also be allergic to anything that contains red chili peppers.

Wear gloves or wash your hands very thoroughly after handling fresh peppers. The capsaicin in them can burn your skin, lips, and eyes.

Is stevia safe?

Stevia is an intensely sweet, low-calorie sugar substitute made from the stevia shrub. The Food and Drug Administration (FDA) won't approve whole-leaf stevia or crude stevia extracts as food ingredients because of concerns about possible effects on kidney function, sperm counts, blood sugar, and the heart and blood vessels.

But recently, the FDA allowed Generally Recognized as Safe status for special, highly purified extracts of the stevia compound. These extracts are in products like Truvia and PureVia.

Although several studies say the extracts don't increase your risk of cancer or fertility problems, a few studies suggest stevia-related compounds may cause DNA changes that could lead to cancer.

The CSPI considers highly purified stevia extracts safe, but they want the FDA to conduct studies to confirm the extracts won't raise your cancer risk.

Fun fermented foods are good for your waistline

Tired of boring diet foods? Take a tip from Hilary White, owner and executive chef at The Hil restaurant near Atlanta. She regularly whips up fermented foods in her restaurant kitchen – and you can, too. These flavorful, low-calorie treats can dress up even the dullest dishes, plus you'll benefit from the health-boosting bacteria, called probiotics, they produce.

Use homemade fermented vegetables in sandwiches, salads, and more. You won't need much to add a lot of flavor. For instance, a quarter-cup of commercial sauerkraut – enough to generously top a hot dog – is less than 7 calories. Just show a little restraint or you may end up eating an unhealthy amount of salt.

You can ferment many types of vegetables, but for safety's sake, only choose vegetables you'd eat raw after washing. And you'll want to keep the pH level of your ferments below 4.6 to prevent botulism. You can do this with simple supplies you order online.

Radishes, broccoli, cauliflower, and all sorts of sweet and hot peppers ferment well. But Sandor Katz, author of the New York Times bestseller *The Art of Fermentation*, recommends you start with sauerkraut. Here's his recipe.

Ingredients

- A little over 2 pounds of vegetables per quart. Use any cabbage variety alone, or combine at least half a cabbage with radishes, turnips, carrots, beets, kohlrabi, Jerusalem artichokes, onions, shallots, leeks, garlic, greens, seaweed, peppers, or other vegetables.

- Approximately 1 tablespoon salt, any variety. Start with a little less if you use a coarse grind.

- Other seasonings as desired, such as caraway seeds, juniper berries, dill, hot peppers, ginger, turmeric, or whatever you can imagine.

Directions

1. Chop or grate vegetables into a bowl to expose surface area and draw liquid out. You will need these juices to submerge your vegetables.

2. Salt vegetables lightly and add seasonings as you chop. Sauerkraut does not require heavy salting.

3. Squeeze salted vegetables with your hands for a few moments or pound with a blunt tool. This bruises the vegetables, breaking down cell walls and enabling them to give up their juices. Keep doing this until you can squeeze a handful and see juice release as from a wet sponge.

4. Pack salted and squeezed vegetables into a wide-mouth jar or crock at least 1-liter in size. Press vegetables down with force so the juice rises up and over them. Fill the jar almost all the way to the top, leaving a little space for expansion. Screw on the lid. Be aware that fermentation produces carbon dioxide, so pressure will build up in the jar and need to be released daily, especially the first few days when activity is most vigorous.

5. Wait. Be sure to loosen the lid to relieve pressure each day for the first few days. Rate of fermentation will be faster in a warm environment, slower in a cool one. Some people prefer their krauts lightly fermented for just a few days; others prefer a stronger, more acidic flavor that develops over a longer time. Taste after just a few days, then a few days later, and at regular intervals to discover what you prefer. In a cool environment, kraut can continue fermenting slowly for months.

6. The most common problem people encounter in fermenting vegetables is surface growth of yeast and/or molds, facilitated by oxygen. If you encounter surface growth, simply scrape off the top layer and discard. The fermented vegetables beneath will look, smell, and taste fine.

7. Enjoy your kraut! And don't forget to start a new batch before this one runs out.

Raw vegan diets: the good, the bad, and the ugly

Eating a raw vegan diet means eating only plant-based foods that are raw, fermented, or dehydrated. This diet includes delicious fruit and vegetable juices, and "green smoothies" made with leafy greens. But is this a healthy, practical diet?

A recent German study found that a raw vegan diet lowers cholesterol and triglycerides. However, the study also suggests this diet can lower "good" HDL cholesterol, raise harmful homocysteine levels, and increase your risk of vitamin B12 deficiency — as well as deficiencies in selenium, zinc, iron, vitamin D, and omega-3 fatty acids.

What's more, the lack of energy-generating foods in this diet may tempt you to overeat high-calorie nuts and fruits. You may also miss out on nutrients normally released by cooking.

Beware the sweetener that saps willpower

Once upon a time, fructose was just a natural sugar found in fruits, vegetables, honey, and table sugar. Then in the 1980s, it became a key ingredient in high fructose corn syrup (HFCS), a sugar replacement added to sodas, junk foods, and many other packaged products.

Today, HFCS is so widely and heavily used that the average American gets roughly 10 percent of their daily calories from fructose alone. Some get as much as 23 percent, quadruple the amount of added sugar the American Heart Association recommends for most people.

A diet this high in fructose means you'll gain more weight and body fat, even if you don't eat extra calories. Animal studies hint you could become up to 11 percent heavier in just a few months. That would mean an extra 16 pounds for a 150-pound person in less than a year. You might think all sugars would cause equal amounts of weight gain, but that's not true.

Fructose overload changes your brain. Compare fructose to another natural sugar, glucose, also found in table sugar. They both provide energy, but fructose can affect your brain in ways you don't expect.

A small study from the University of Southern California had volunteers drink either a high-glucose or high-fructose beverage. Then the researchers showed both groups pictures of high-calorie foods.

MRI scans revealed that the fructose-drinkers showed spiked activity in their brain's reward-processing centers upon seeing the food pictures. When given a choice, most opted to immediately receive the high-calorie food they'd just seen rather than take a cash reward that would arrive in a few weeks.

Experts say this alarming reaction is because fructose and glucose cause different effects in your body. Glucose triggers an insulin response that, like magic, sends a "fullness" signal to your brain so you'll know to stop eating. Fructose, on the other hand, does not trigger this response.

Should you stop eating fruit? Absolutely not, say the California researchers. Fruit has a lot less fructose than canned sodas and packaged foods, so you should definitely keep it on the menu. But if you're trying to lose weight, check the ingredient lists of your foods and drinks for high fructose corn syrup. Eliminating this sweetener could turn off those mysterious – and fattening – cravings.

Overeat and lose weight? New diet says yes!

Imagine a diet where you lose a few pounds even though you eat until you're full. That's what happened in a recent Danish study. Obese people who followed the New Nordic Diet for six months lost several more pounds than obese people who ate a normal diet. The New Nordic Diet also helped lower blood pressure.

Designed by food professionals from five Nordic countries, the New Nordic Diet is similar to the Mediterranean diet, but emphasizes foods from colder climates. These include apples, root vegetables, pears, whole grains, fish, wild game, berries, cabbage, and other cruciferous vegetables.

To mimic this diet, eat at least six servings of produce a day, especially foods that are in season. Cut saturated fat; reduce red meat by one-third; and add more whole grains, fish, and unsaturated oils like olive oil.

Lose 4 inches in just 6 months

What could your weight problem and a skin rash from your jewelry possibly have in common? It's strange, but true – a nickel allergy could be making you fat.

Less than 13 percent of all women are allergic to nickel, a metal most often found in jewelry, watchbands, belt buckles, and the like. Yet, a small Italian study found that nearly 60 percent of the overweight women participating in their research had this sensitivity.

Nickel allergies usually show up as a rash within a couple of days of touching the metal. But nickel is also present in certain foods and just might trigger weight gain, if you're allergic. Experts believe it may cause an insulin overload, increase levels of inflammation in your body, or shift the balance of microbes in your intestines.

To help figure things out, overweight, allergic women ate a low-nickel diet for six months, but did not cut calories. Instead, they completely avoided high-nickel foods like beans, soy, and whole grains. They also restricted other foods with some nickel content, including tomatoes, lettuce, spinach, carrots, onions, and cauliflower. The women lost more than four inches off their waistlines and lowered their BMI by four points in just six months.

If you have symptoms of nickel allergy, talk to your doctor. She can test you and determine whether you can safely try a low-nickel diet. Medical professionals can also help you get the details needed to follow this diet correctly, and provide information about possible side effects like constipation. Although doctors say they're not sure how long people can safely stay on a low-nickel plan, even a few months may help you lose stubborn inches from your waistline.

Got belly fat? Fix the one mistake you're making every day

You won't believe what a recent study found out about diet sodas. Here's what you should know right away.

Can a daily drink widen your waistline? To find out, University of Texas researchers followed more than 400 seniors for nine years. Those who drank diet sodas every day added a button-popping three inches to their middles. That was more than four times the belly bulge experienced by people who avoided sodas.

Even the occasional drinker had to let their belts out by a couple of inches. All in all, especially alarming statistics since this growing portion of the population already carries a higher risk of serious medical conditions linked to belly fat.

The researchers suggest older adults – and everyone else, for that matter – may benefit from drinking fewer sweetened beverages like diet soda.

6 ways to ditch diet drinks and prevent belly fat. If you suspect your waistline would be better off without diet sodas, try these tips to ease them out of your life.

- Count how many sodas you drink each week or each day, and cut back by just one at first. Subtract one more drink each week.

- Start drinking your soda with ice, or dilute it with a few tablespoons of soda water. Add more water to the drink with each passing week.

- Need that jolt of caffeine? Try a substitute such as unsweetened coffee or green or black tea. Add a splash of lemon or orange juice to your tea to amp up its flavor.

- Make homegrown soda with seltzer water, a drop of vanilla extract, and some fruit juice. Start off with at least three times as much seltzer water as fruit juice. Gradually reduce the amount of juice until your drink has no more calories than your diet soda did.

- When your soda supply runs out at home or work, don't buy more. Removing the temptation of readily available soda makes switching easier.

- Experiment with different low-calorie, healthy drinks. For example, try a variety pack of herbal or flavored tea bags. Most don't contain calories, but check the label to be sure.

Or experiment with options like fruit or herb water you can make at home. Start with a pitcher of water, then drop in cucumber slices, a few berries, lemon or lime wedges, or mint leaves. Allow time for the flavor to spread, then enjoy.

Diet war winner: Mediterranean trumps low-fat

Want a yummy diet that can help you lose more weight? Surprise – it's not low-fat. The Mediterranean diet, which allows a modest amount of fat from foods like nuts and olive oil, is a great way to get a slimmer body or even keep from gaining weight in the first place. Celebrity Maria Menounos, who lost 40 pounds on this delicious eating plan, agrees. And by the way, she's kept that weight off for 15 years.

Greek island eating beats a low-fat diet. Here's another incredible success story. An Israeli study found that overweight men on a Mediterranean diet dropped more pounds than those on a low-fat diet even though their calorie counts were equal. The Mediterranean dieters also:

■ lost more weight up front.

■ kept more weight off after two years.

■ lost more inches from their waistlines.

■ reduced their BMI more.

Their Mediterranean-inspired meals were packed with vegetables, while the main sources of fat were five to seven nuts a day and about three tablespoons of olive oil. They also ate small amounts of chicken and fish in place of beef and lamb. But that really doesn't describe just how tasty this diet can be.

On the Greek island of Ikaria, a place famed for the extraordinary longevity of its residents, popular foods include fresh-picked leafy greens, garbanzo beans, lentils, potatoes, herb teas, yogurt, and seasonal vegetables. Traditional Mediterranean fare also means plenty of fruits and whole grains, a little red wine with meals, and limited sweets, cheese, and processed meats. Since this diet is full of delicious foods you probably already eat, you may find it easier to follow than other eating plans.

GROW IT

The perfect spot for an herb pot

Think you can't have fresh herbs or tomatoes because you have no space for a garden? Grow oregano, mint, and parsley indoors next to a south-, west- or east-facing window. Tuck them in deep pots close to the glass, and check regularly to see if they need watering — keeping mint more moist than the other herbs.

A large hanging basket is ideal for a trailing cherry tomato plant, which can produce hundreds of fruits. After the last frost, position it outdoors where it will get at least six hours of sun. Water it daily, and give it regular feedings once tomatoes start forming.

2 ways you may be sabotaging your weight loss. Hundreds of firefighters were studied by Harvard researchers, and they discovered those who really stuck to the Mediterranean diet had the greatest weight loss success. But those who cheated a little and drank sweetened or low-nutrition beverages with meals and ate fast food frequently were more likely to be obese.

These two habits make it particularly hard to follow some of the Mediterranean diet rules – like avoiding fried or processed foods, red meat, and high-fat dairy. The bottom line? Kick these bad habits to the curb.

While it's terrific that the Mediterranean diet will help you lose weight and look good, it may also help prevent illness, misery, and disability for decades to come. Studies suggest people who eat a Mediterranean diet are rewarded with lower cholesterol and blood pressure, stable blood sugar, and even reduced risk of cancer and Alzheimer's. In fact, doctors were prescribing this diet for heart-related health problems long before anyone realized it could also be a delicious way to slim down.

Tips and tricks to make the switch. If you'd like to leave your low-fat diet behind and try eating the Mediterranean way, keep in mind you should still limit your calories – but also try delicious ideas like these.

- Drink water regularly, but enjoy herbal teas, coffee, and the occasional glass of wine, as well. Just don't add calories from sugar and sweeteners.

- Pile a spinach salad high with vegetables and beans, add in some feta cheese or chopped nuts, and top it with a dressing made with olive oil.

- Try hummus with whole-grain bread.

- Mix fruit and oats into yogurt.

- Toss vegetables like tomatoes, sliced zucchini, mushrooms, onions, roasted red peppers, and olives in balsamic vinaigrette. Layer between slices of whole-grain bread along with spinach and feta.

- Enjoy a small serving of salmon brushed with olive oil and spices.

- On a cold day, eat spicy lentil-vegetable soup to warm up.

- To add flavor without many calories, use one or more of these Mediterranean ingredients: garlic, lemon juice, oregano, paprika, rosemary, basil, bay leaf, parsley, sage, or balsamic vinegar.

Healthy way to renovate your dinner plate

You probably remember the Food Guide Pyramid from years past – that popular icon of nutritional information created by the United States Department of Agriculture (USDA) to help Americans balance their diets. In 2011, the USDA launched a new icon, MyPlate. The following illustration is adapted from the USDA's image and is intended to help senior adults build healthy eating habits.

MyPlate for Adults Over 60

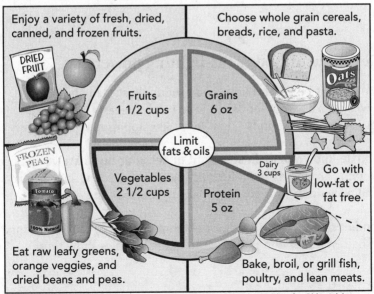

Enjoy a variety of fresh, dried, canned, and frozen fruits.

Choose whole grain cereals, breads, rice, and pasta.

DRIED FRUIT

Oats

Fruits
1 1/2 cups

Grains
6 oz

Limit
fats & oils

FROZEN PEAS

Tomato

100% Natural

Dairy
3 cups

Go with
low-fat or
fat free.

Vegetables
2 1/2 cups

Protein
5 oz

Eat raw leafy greens, orange veggies, and dried beans and peas.

Bake, broil, or grill fish, poultry, and lean meats.

Adapted from the USDA's MyPlate and the University of Florida's MyPlate for Older Adults.

Food amounts based on a daily diet of 1,800 calories.

A fat substitute that should never cross your lips

Olestra, also known as Olean, is a fat substitute found in some fat-free and low-fat foods. It preserves the food's taste and texture, while reducing fat and calories — but it isn't a healthy choice.

Even when Olestra doesn't cause digestive symptoms, it can slash your body's ability to absorb fat-soluble nutrients like lycopene, beta carotene, and vitamins A, D, E, and K. Olestra-laden snacks also replace more nutritious foods your body needs.

Check for Olestra or Olean in the ingredient lists of your favorite fat-free and low-fat foods. Limit or avoid foods that contain this unhealthy fat substitute, and enjoy delicious, nutrient-rich whole foods instead.

Rev up your body's fat-fighting powers

Wouldn't it be great if your body suddenly started absorbing fewer calories from foods? New research suggests that's not as far-fetched as it sounds – and foods like apples may be the key.

A little-known belly buster right under your nose. We've all been carrying around extra fat-fighting potential for years, scientists say. The bacteria in your gut may make a difference in your weight.

Studies of gut bacteria suggest obese people have a different mix of bacteria than thin people. And animal studies show those microbes may help you absorb more calories as well as accumulate and store fat. Researchers believe these gut bacteria studies may lead to new ways to help fight obesity.

"What determines the balance of bacteria in our colon is the food we consume," says Washington State University scientist Giuliana Noratto. She and her colleagues recently studied seven different varieties of apples to determine which one shows the most promise against obesity.

They were particularly interested in apple compounds your body can't digest because they affect your gut bacteria. These compounds are called prebiotics. They include pectin and other forms of fiber as well as phytochemicals called proanthocyanidins.

Previous research suggests these prebiotics may promote weight loss for two reasons. They've been linked to an increase in bacteria that help prevent weight gain from high-fat diets. They may also help increase the population of bacteria linked to lower BMI. Plus, it could help change the mix of gut bacteria in obese mice to more closely match the mix in lean mice.

So which apple is best? Noratto's team found that the apple with the best effects combined low carbohydrate content with plenty of prebiotics. The researchers tested Braeburn, Fuji, Granny Smith, Gala, Golden Delicious, McIntosh and Red Delicious, but it was the Granny Smith that won.

More research is needed to determine how effective Granny Smith apples can be, but meanwhile you can try eating more of these healthy fruits to see what they can do for you.

Show your creativity with green apples. Granny Smith apples are tart. To make the most of their delicious flavor, try these clever ideas.

- Instead of eating a high-calorie dessert, pour a bit of honey on apple slices and sprinkle with cinnamon.

- Add a chopped Granny Smith apple to chicken salad.

- Mix grated Granny Smith apples into your hamburger patties to replace some of the meat.

- Add chopped or grated "Grannies" to muffins or bread.

- Make your Waldorf salad with two kinds of apples, one sweet and one Granny Smith.

- Mix in one diced apple per pound of beef to tone down the spiciness of chili that's a little too hot.

Index